JOAN CRAWFORD

Bernard Wohl Collection

JOAN CRAWFORD

the essential
biography

LAWRENCE J. QUIRK
and WILLIAM SCHOELL

UNIVERSITY PRESS OF KENTUCKY

Scholarly publisher for the Commonwealth,
serving Bellarmine University, Berea College, Centre
College of Kentucky, Eastern Kentucky University,
The Filson Historical Society, Georgetown College,
Kentucky Historical Society, Kentucky State University,
Morehead State University, Murray State University,
Northern Kentucky University, Transylvania University,
University of Kentucky, University of Louisville,
and Western Kentucky University. All rights reserved.

Editorial and Sales Offices: The University Press of Kentucky
663 South Limestone Street, Lexington, Kentucky 40508-4008
www.kentuckypress.com

Library of Congress Cataloging-in-Publication Data

Quirk, Lawrence J.
Joan Crawford : the essential biography/ Lawrence J. Quirk
and William Schoell.
p. cm.
Includes bibliographical references and index.
ISBN 0-8131-2254-6 (alk. paper)
1. Crawford, Joan, 1908-1977. 2. Motion picture actors
and actresses-United States-Biography. I. Schoell, William. II. Title.
PN2287.C67 Q57 2002
791.43'028'092-dc21

ISBN 978-0-8131-8049-6 (pbk. : alk. paper)

This book is printed on acid-free paper meeting
the requirements of the American National Standard
for Permanence in Paper for Printed Library Materials.
∞

Manufactured in the United States of America.

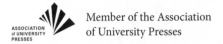

Member of the Association
of University Presses

To the Memory of

Henry Hart
(1903–1990)

and

William Theodore Schoell
(1909–1991)

CONTENTS

Preface   ix

Acknowledgments   xvii

1. Childhood's End   1

2. Pretty Lady   13

3. Window Dressing   25

4. Life at El Jodo   37

5. Two of a Kind   51

6. Skin Tone   67

7. Love on the Run   83

8. Jungle Red   000

9. Scarred   97

10. Mildred   123

11. Possessed   139

12. Victim   153

13. The Bitch is Back   169

14. The Queen of Pepsi-Cola   189

15. Teen Idol   205

16. War of Nerves   219

17. Secret Storms   233

18. End of an Icon   245

19. Serpent's Tooth   253

Afterword   269

Filmography   271

Notes   275

Bibliography   283

Index   285

Photographs follow page 142

PREFACE

I knew Joan Crawford for thirty years.

I first met Joan in 1947, during my first trip to Hollywood, on the set of *Daisy Kenyon*. I was then twenty-three years old and working for Hearst's *Boston Record-American*. I was in Hollywood not only to do stories on stars and movies, but also to interview some friends of my uncle, James R. Quirk of *Photoplay*, because I had gotten the idea to write a biography of him. At our first meeting, Joan asked me how old I was; when I told her, she muttered under her breath, "Cute!" (At the time, this was inexplicable to me). She told me that my uncle had helped her a lot in her career, and she was very helpful in introducing me to people who had known him and could pass on anecdotal material about him, such as William Haines, an actor with whom Joan made several films in the late 1920s. (I also asked these people about Joan, whom I found fascinating.) Many years later, Joan admitted to me that she had been one of the gals Louis B. Mayer had used to "entertain" visiting executives and the like when they were in California. The girls were provided as dates; whatever happened afterward was up to them. It even emerged that my uncle had been one of these men. Joan said that, unlike a lot of the other men, Uncle Jimmy always treated her with kindness.

Joan began corresponding with me on the stationery she always used; her friend Jerry Asher (to whom she also introduced me) called them "Joan's baby blues." Over the years, Joan and I became friends. I met her again in 1952 while I was in the Army and she was appearing at a Broadway theater in connection with her new film *Sudden Fear*. She said then that she hoped that the movie would jump-start her career, which it did. In May 1956, Joan visited New York and I went down to Penn Station to greet her; a Columbia Pictures photographer took a picture of us. When I worked for the *Motion Picture Herald* in the late 1950s, she was so happy with my review of *Autumn Leaves* that she and her husband Alfred Steele invited me to '21' in 1957. At that meeting,

Alfred said that it wasn't Joan's fault that her adopted son Christopher was behaving like a juvenile delinquent, and she went on a long disquisition of why Katherine Albert, a onetime writer for Uncle Jimmy, stopped speaking to her after Joan sponsored the wedding of Albert's daughter Joan (who was named after Crawford) to a man, Kirby Weatherly, of whom her mother did not approve. She and Albert had been very close friends until that time. Over the following years I dined with Joan frequently and often visited her on film sets for an interview or just to say hello.

Joan was very generous to people she liked and tried to help them. During my tenure with various fan mags, I did my best to build up and enhance the reputation of Joan's *Autumn Leaves* costar Cliff Robertson, showcasing him as best I could despite the fact that many editors did not care for him, for one reason or another. Robertson was having trouble with the studio, as he didn't like the parts Columbia was offering him. Along with other friends of his, such as Wilson Ashley and his wife Roberta, Joan was very concerned for him when I mentioned the situation to her, because she thought he was a promising talent. She made a personal plea to Harry Cohn to give Robertson the right parts.

Joan was very cooperative when I did a major story on her for *Films in Review* and a number of other articles on her for various fan mags (the *People* and *Us* of their day). Joan also made a point of inviting me to parties, not only promotional gatherings in restaurants but soirées at her various apartments in New York. She was extremely helpful and cooperative when I put together my first book, *The Films of Joan Crawford,* even going so far as to do publicity for the tome, although she made not one dollar for doing so. As her film career began to wind down, what had started out in 1947 as interviews with a lofty star had long since become simple conversations with a friend. Not that there was anything simple about Joan.

I liked and admired Joan—still do—but like most movie stars, she could be difficult at times. For her part she always admired the way I— and others—spoke up to her if we thought she was out of line. If she agreed, she would apologize. She had been such a major star for so many years, a woman who went after and got what she wanted, that it was sometimes hard for her to accept that the rest of the world wasn't as interested in her as they had once been or as ready to jump to her tune. This sometimes made her seem "bitchy" to others. In truth, she got annoyed with simpering toadies, and she didn't suffer fools gladly. "I don't expect people to kiss my ass," she said more than once, "but they can be polite. They can be respectful." Often fans and others incurred her wrath because they were blatantly tactless, forgetting that even a movie star has feelings. While her fans often knew more about the details of her career than she did (she used to say that I and other film historians often surprised her with our knowledge), she didn't care for it when people argued with her as if they had been there and she hadn't been. After all, it was *her* career. Again, it was a simple question of tact.

Except for the year or so before her death, when she saw hardly anyone but continued to call her friends on a regular basis, Joan did have spells of heavy drinking, had trouble sleeping, and she would call sympathetic listeners at all hours of the night. I cared about her and felt sorry for her, but after a while I had to tell her to cut it out (nowadays I love late night phone calls, but back then I had to get up early in the mornings) which led to a temporary rift until Joan apologized and started calling at a more reasonable hour.

Joan was not a perfect human being—who is?—but for her hard work alone she deserves better than what she has gotten since the publication of *Mommie Dearest*. Being a movie star was serious business to her, and she worked harder at her career and at her acting than perhaps any other star in Hollywood. She was in no way a freak or a monster, and she does not deserve to be a national joke. My take on *Mommie Dearest* is that it is a wild exaggeration; my co-author feels it has absolutely no credibility at all. Whatever the case, a career like hers deserves to be looked at with objectivity, her abilities analyzed honestly.

When I wrote *The Films of Joan Crawford* thirty-four years ago, I was disappointed that the format did not allow me to analyze her pictures and roles fully. Now that I have the opportunity to do so (and I believe that any biography *should* discuss the performances and pictures of an actor—why else are we interested in their lives in the first place?), I find that I have seen her films so many times over the years that any analysis of mine would not be sufficiently fresh; therefore I have left the analysis of her acting in the capable hands of my co-author (although I do throw my two cents in from time to time). I believe that he delves into Joan's many films and roles, her approach to each, and the relative effectiveness of that approach, with greater insight than has been recorded in any previous book on Joan.

Sprinkled throughout this book are quotes from many of the people who knew and worked with Joan; I collected them from my personal conversations and from my own published and unpublished interviews with these same sources over the years. Along with half a dozen or so of my Hollywood favorites, I had always hoped to do a major biography of

Joan someday and collected a lot of material on her. Of course, most of the best quotes are from Joan herself, from the many interviews and conversations I had with her. Occasionally I used a pithy quote from another source, but generally I let the lady speak for herself, which she was always able to do with great enthusiasm and often with surprising candor.

Lawrence J. Quirk

During college in the 1970s I joined a movie book club in which you could order three books for a dollar and a trial membership. The three books I selected were *Film Fantasy Scrapbook* by Hollywood special-effects wizard Ray Harryhausen (the one I really wanted), *The Films of Marlon Brando* (for reasons that frankly escape me, although I have no doubt it was a good book), and *The Films of Joan Crawford* (because I had always gotten a kick out of *What Ever Happened to Baby Jane?*).

A short while later I was introduced to Lawrence Quirk, the author of *The Films of Joan Crawford*. I told him how much I had enjoyed his book, although at that time I had seen few of the movies it covered. *Baby Jane. Strait-Jacket.* Maybe *Mildred Pierce.* He told me that he had felt constricted by the formula of the "Films of . . ." series of the time. He hadn't been able to analyze Joan's films or her acting the way he'd wanted to. Along with lots of pictures, all the publisher wanted was a synopsis of each film and quotes from one or two sample reviews.

He then surprised me by asking if I'd like to meet Joan Crawford. Perhaps I'd like to interview her? I knew that he was well acquainted with Joan; in his book there was a wonderful picture of him with his impish Irish face standing next to Joan and her poodle, framed in a train doorway. I won't say I jumped at the chance; I was never that impressed by celebrities and there were others I wanted to meet more than Joan Crawford. Still, she was part of Hollywood history. . . . I told Larry to give me a couple of weeks to reread his book and possibly see some more of her movies. This was before the videocassette revolution (a boon to film historians!), so I had to rely on screenings in New York's great re-vival movie houses (Frank Rowley's Regency, for example), or *The Late Show* on TV. I saw *A Woman's Face, The Women, Flamingo Road, The Unknown.* When the day came that Larry and I had our lunch with Joan—he was a frequent visitor at her apartment—I was prepared to ask questions, if she permitted, or just sit and talk. I thought my friends back in college would have found it bizarre that I was actually going to meet the star of *Trog*.

I was in my early twenties, so the woman who greeted us in her small living room was quite an old lady to me. She seemed a little frail and ill but happy to have company. I was introduced as a "big fan," and I hoped that she didn't think I would gush or ask for her autograph, which was not about to happen. The small talk, mostly between Larry and Joan at first, seemed strained for a while, and I sensed that Joan was more anxious to make an impression than I was. Joan couldn't relax at first because although she knew Larry well, I was a perfect stranger. This is not to say that she was "on"—she seemed too tired to give a damn about that.

A woman came in to serve us lunch—salads and such—and Larry asked if I might ask Joan a few questions. "What would you like to know, dear?"

I mentioned something about *Strait-Jacket*. Larry rushed to say, "Bill's a big horror fan, you know," and while Joan didn't exactly glare at me or pop out her eyes, her "Is he, now?" was borderline chilly. Larry hadn't warned me that she didn't really like to talk about her later films, all of which she pretty much hated. I made up for my inadvertent blunder by quickly saying, "I thought you were terrific in that. I know it was weird, and not the kind of thing that made you famous. But it isn't easy playing that kind of shocker and making it real. I honestly think you were the best thing about the movie. You're a very good actress." No movie star's toady, me—that was how I sincerely felt.

Joan smiled at my genuine admiration and seemed much more at ease than she had been before. She told me a few things about the director of *Strait-Jacket*, William Castle—nothing scandalous—and how she felt about the horror genre, and the difference in the way films were made today from the way they were made in the Golden Age of Hollywood. She said in certain aspects *A Woman's Face* had much in common with the horror film. "Did you know I had the same make up man as Lon Chaney?"

We talked about New York—a city we both loved—and she was delighted that I was a native New Yorker, born in Manhattan. "The greatest city in the world!" We clinked classes and drank a toast to the city. She and Larry and I then talked about people and places and things—a normal, intelligent, entertaining conversation—until all the food was gone, and we had had our dessert and coffee.

"What did you think of Joan?" Larry asked once we were out on the sidewalk. "I liked her," I told him. I found her a little self-absorbed (but far from egotistical)—virtually all actors are that way, I was to learn eventually—but then, what was I to expect of a Great Movie Star? She had had seventy years of fascinating experiences behind her. Considering that, I was impressed by the way, once she'd discovered some common ground with me (and *Strait-Jacket* wasn't it), she bothered to ask me questions about my life and experiences, which at that time were no match for hers.

"I thought there was something a little desperate about her," I said. "A little sad. It must be hard to have been so famous and sexy and in the public eye and all that, and to become old and on the sidelines." Larry asked if I wanted to see her again, and I said, "Maybe, but not for a while." Young men generally like to stay away from lonely or emotionally needy people. Plus I sensed that people like Joan could be demanding acquaintances, out of that very need. Larry himself warned me about this factor and eventually had to temporarily sever contact with Joan when it simply became too much. He told me that Joan told him that she had found me too "charming" and ingenuous to be upset by my questions on her least favorite "hack 'em up" period in films.

But I never forgot her. I watched a lot of her old movies, and I wondered what it was like for her to be living that kind of fantasy life in the grand, old, utterly unreal world of Hollywood. She had met everyone and been everywhere, been a top star, had had an incredible sex life, and been married four times.

Often it was hard for me to square that vibrant, so-alive young woman on the screen with the old, ill woman I had met weeks before. I wonder what really happened, I asked myself. What was it like for her during those crazy, exciting, wonderful days?

This book is an attempt to answer that question—and to provide some perspective on her life. As I researched this volume, I realized that virtually all of the books about Joan that have come out since her death seemed to accept *Mommie Dearest* as gospel, incorporating many of Christina Crawford's stories and thereby turning them into "facts." I have never found *Mommie Dearest* a particularly credible document and I see no reason to accept anything in it as the truth. Just as the members of a jury must carefully examine the words and demeanor of a witness to assess his or her credibility, keeping in mind that if the witness exaggerates or lies about one thing then the entire testimony may be a lie, I carefully examined *Mommie Dearest* and found too much suspect about it to take it seriously.

Ever since the publication of *Mommie Dearest* (and the release of the film version), the public has found it impossible to take Joan Crawford seriously. Even if her daughter's allegations are true, Joan's career and achievements deserve to be looked at *separately* and *distinctly*. Not to compare Crawford to Richard Wagner, but since Joan walked into the sea to the strains of Wagner's "Liebestod" in *Humoresque*, it is perhaps fitting to remember that while Wagner may have been a terror in his private life, he was still a magnificent composer. Joan was not the genius that Wagner was, but neither was she a monster. She was a human being with good points and bad, a talented actress whose career deserves to be examined with fairness and impartiality.

Hence this book.

William Schoell

ACKNOWLEDGMENTS

The authors tender their appreciation to Kenneth Cherry, Angelique Galskis, Leila Salisbury, Allison Webster, Wyn Morris, Mack McCormick, and the staff at the University Press of Kentucky.

With special thanks to John Cocchi of J.C. Archives, Inc., and to Bernard Wohl, who lent many beautiful portraits of Joan; Jerry Ohlinger; and Doug McClelland.

And our thanks to the staff of the Film Library at the Museum of Modern Art; the staff of the Billy Rose Theater Collection at the New York Public Library of the Performing Arts at Lincoln Center; the staff of the Margaret Herrick Library of the Academy of Arts and Sciences in Hollywood; the staff of the British Film Institute in London. Also thanks to Seth Joseph Weine; Val Holley; the late Don Koll, a good friend; Bob Dahdah; Arthur Tower; John A. Guzman; Mary Atwood; and Ed MaQuire. Our thanks also to the great many friends, co-workers, and even enemies of Joan's, and other interested parties, who spoke about Joan to the authors over the years, many of whom are mentioned in the text, as well as those who specifically asked not to be mentioned. Special thanks to Caroline Schoell and Carol, Thomas, and Tara Altomare.

Jerry Ohlinger

Chapter One

CHILDHOOD'S END

On March 23, 1904, in San Antonio, Texas, Anna Bell Johnson LeSueur gave birth to a little girl, whom she and her husband, Thomas, named Lucille Fay. Lucille was the couple's third child; another daughter, Daisy, had died in infancy, and Lucille's brother, Hal, had been born the previous year. (Many years later, when little Lucille was the famous woman known to the world as Joan Crawford, the year of her birth would mysteriously change to 1906 or 1908.) Tom LeSueur was of French-Canadian extraction; he worked as a contractor, and his assignments frequently took him out of San Antonio. One day when Lucille was still a small child, he left for a job and never came back.

After her husband's abandonment, Anna became very bitter, but she was determined to do the best she could for herself and her two children. Anna moved Hal and Lucille out of their shabby rented apartment and together they all made their way to Lawton, Oklahoma, where Anna hoped life would be better. It wasn't long before she met the town's most interesting citizen—and most eligible bachelor—Harry Cassin, owner of the local opera house, which put on various forms of entertainment. When the relationship between Harry and Anna became more serious, Anna managed to track down her first husband and get a divorce. Realizing that another man would now care for his wife and pay for his children's needs, LeSueur was eager to agree to Anna's terms. Anna married Thomas out of love, but she married Harry Cassin for security.

Little Lucille—now known as "Billie" Cassin—fell in love with show business; she spent time backstage at the opera house, mingled with the artists, and dreamed of going on the stage herself someday and garnering applause. She was especially interested in dancing, and she observed the fancy footwork of the entertainers very carefully. She mounted her own amateur productions in the big barn where Cassin kept the scenery for his shows. Billie was very much a tomboy and a scrapper. Her mother, whose marriage to Cassin was essentially loveless, found her a trial and always compared her unfavorably to her better-behaved (at least at that time) brother, Hal.

In early interviews and in her autobiography, Joan related an incident that changed the situation entirely. One day, she discovered some gold coins hidden in her home. Apparently the money had been stolen by one of Harry's business associates. Harry had hidden it, but he was afraid to turn it in, because he thought he might be charged as an accessory. The authorities investigated, and Cassin was arrested but eventually acquitted. According to Joan, this incident was the beginning of the end of the family's happy life in Lawton.

Whatever the truth was, it was not money that tore the Cassin clan apart, much less the gold coins. It was only very late in life that Joan was able to reveal the real reason that her mother resented her all her life and that her mother's marriage to Harry Cassin fell apart. Anna discovered that her husband was having sex with her daughter—and had been doing so since Billie was eleven. Joan admitted that her deep attachment to her thirty-four-year-old stepfather caused her, as she put it, to "entice" him into having sexual relations with her. "It wasn't incest. We weren't even related. He was gentle and kind and I led him into it." Decades later, Joan still blamed herself and defended her stepfather, even when confronted with the fact that the man was undeniably a child molester and the sole guilty party in the matter. When Anna discovered the two in a compromising position, her husband was only too willing to pin the blame on Billie as well. While Anna did not quite see it this way—she promptly divorced Cassin and forbade him to see her daughter ever again—part of her did blame her precocious daughter for her part in the situation.

Billie was devastated by the departure of Harry Cassin; she had even wanted to bear his child. Although she claimed to be stunned when she was informed that Cassin was not her real father, she also interpreted this as yet another proof that she and Harry were meant to be together. Her stepfather's sexual abuse of her made her sexually "sophisticated" at an early age; afterwards she saw sex, especially with older male authority figures, as something entirely natural. She was very serious about sex, bestowing it on those she cared about and/or wanted to exert control over; at the same time, she could also see it as something quite casual, nothing more than a quick thrill.

In her revised curriculum vitae, Harry Cassin accompanied Anna and the children to Kansas City. In reality, he was left behind, as the others moved into the rundown hotel that Anna managed for a time; later she managed a laundry. Harry may have followed his wife to Missouri in an attempt to patch up their marriage, and Anna may have continued to call herself Mrs. Harry Cassin, but Harry was gone for good. Billie saw her former stepfather and lover in Kansas City on one occasion by accident but never again after that.

Fully awakened sexually, but her first lover having joined her real father in exile, Billie was restless. As her brother later recalled it to *Photoplay* writer Ruth Waterbury, she "explored my pants and every other kid's." Since her mother was as sexually active as Billie was soon to become, Billie was convinced that Hal was at best her *half*-brother, and might not even be related to her at all. (This is unlikely, as the two had certain features in common.) When Anna found Billie "fooling around," as she put it, with Hal in bed one night, Anna slapped them both, and from then on kept a close watch on them. In no time, Anna kept Hal and Billie busy twelve hours a day by putting them on hot, dirty laundry detail.

At age thirteen, Billie was enrolled in St. Agnes, a parochial school whose students mostly consisted of well-heeled girls who paid for their lessons, except for those, like Billie, who had to work—and work hard—in lieu of tuition. Billie spent hours cleaning rooms, washing toilets, waiting on tables, and doing other menial chores in exchange for a haphazard and unsatisfactory education. Billie hated the way girls from good families looked down on her, and she felt that the nuns took terrible advantage of less fortunate students. "I was a workhorse," Joan remembered. "Not a child, but a workhorse." Yet those hours of scrubbing and cleaning never wore off on Joan, who would revere the spit and polish of a good honest cleaning for the rest of her life, never averse to using a little elbow grease to get things looking just so. The hard work Billie had to do at St. Agnes probably didn't bother her as much as the attitudes and pretty dresses of the wealthy girls and the envy it all engendered in her. What is clear is that her memories of St. Agnes remained negative her entire life. In later years, when she was asked to contribute money to the school, Joan always refused and would tell the administration so in no uncertain terms. "They'll never get one single dollar from me!" she vowed.

Things were even worse at Billie's next school. At fifteen, she transferred from St. Agnes to the Rockingham Academy, a boarding school for "difficult" upper-class children. This move came about because Anna was living with a new man, "Mr. Hough"; whether Anna ever married him is unclear. Once again, Billie was put to work in order to pay for tuition, but this time her duties were far more strenuous. The headmistress of the institution expected Billie to get up at dawn, make all the beds and perform all manner of drudgery with little time out for a rest or even classes. Billie's education was essentially ignored, and the headmistress would slap her if she dared to complain. Later, Joan may have exaggerated her miseries at Rockingham—for example, it's unlikely that she cooked the meals for all of the students—but it was not an easy time for her.

At home, however, things were even worse. In her autobiography, Joan claimed that Mr. Hough made a pass at her, after which she eventually left home for good; later Joan admitted that her mother didn't want her around because of her daughter's sexual precociousness. "She was afraid that I'd seduce the new man in her life, not the other way around. I was older, aware of my sexuality, and so were all the boys. My mother was jealous of me and wanted me out of her life."

Billie may not have received much schooling at either St. Agnes or Rockingham, but the truth is she was more interested in chasing boys than acquiring a decent education. At sixteen, she had the reputation around town as a "boy-crazy easy lay," as Joan later termed it. She dated many of the male students at Rockingham and attended a lot of dances, where she'd kiss the boys out back or indulge in substantially more erotic behavior in the back seat of someone's car. She was very grateful to boys who showed her even minimal kindness. Hal, her brother, was remarkably good-looking and for the most part studiously ignored his sister. He spent most of his time hanging around pool rooms and hustling older homosexuals. "The life was Kansas-style Bohemian for those two, that was for sure," Adela Rogers St. John remembered.

In her pursuit of boys (and, while she was at it, higher learning), Billie next matriculated at Stephens College in Columbia, Missouri. Once again Billie was put to work, this time as a waitress in the dining room. Some at the college sensed something in Billie aside from her remarkable sensuality; they noticed her basic intelligence and her remarkable tenacity and drive. One such person was the president of the college, Dr. James Wood, who became a father figure of sorts for Billie; she always referred to him as "Daddy Wood." But Billie was woefully unprepared for college. Never having acquired a proper high-school education, Billie soon fell so far behind the other students that she felt more isolated than ever. Despite her innate curiosity and her desire to better herself, she found herself questioning the importance of a college education for someone

who wanted to be an entertainer, specifically a dancer. Dancing and boys—
these were her two obsessions. Although Joan was always intelligent and
later cultivated an appreciation of the finer things in life—particularly
literature and classical music—she was never really an intellectual.

Tired of being treated like a second-class citizen, Billie left Stephens
before the first term was over. Her brief tenure at Stephens did have a
substantial impact on her, however. She never forgot her excitement when
she was asked to pledge a popular sorority on campus—or her disappointment when she was then told that girls who had to work were not
permitted to join. She hated the "rich bitches" who made fun of her
cheap dresses, which she tried to trick up with ornamentations of imitation lace and roses. Such slights only hardened her determination to get
ahead. For the rest of her life, if anyone took a condescending tone with
Joan, she would slap him or her down with every bit of force she could
muster—and an angry Joan Crawford could be very forceful indeed.

Billie went home to Kansas City and worked at a number of dull
jobs, because Mr. Hough insisted that she pay her room and board. In
1921, while she was working at a department store—she also wrapped
packages and was a telephone operator—Billie met an intense young
man named Ray Sterling. Joan would later tell interviewers that Ray was
her "first love." Billie was seventeen years old. Sterling took her to dances,
where she wore the wrong clothes and too much makeup and tried—
unsuccessfully—to disregard what others thought of her. Sterling was a
wonderful influence on Billie; later, Joan would recall that, although young
and essentially underprivileged (as she was), Sterling was intelligent and
well-read. He urged Billie to make something of herself—to read more,
to listen to good music, and to take an interest in the opportunities for
growth all around her. It didn't take long for Billie to pin her hopes for a
better future on Sterling, but he felt that, at seventeen, they were too
young to get married. Billie eventually encountered another problem,
realizing—perhaps even before he did—that the sensitive and introverted
Sterling was essentially a homosexual. Although this insight shocked Billie
at first, it also motivated her to try lesbian relationships. Later, Joan
explained of her experimentation, "It made me feel close to Ray."

By this time, Billie had fallen deeply in love with Sterling, and the
knowledge that he could never fulfill her sexual needs—however supportive he might be emotionally—left her deeply disillusioned at life's
rude shocks. Soon she was back to her "easy lays" with whatever attractive boys were at hand. "It broke Ray's heart to see me like that, but
what was I to do?" Joan later remembered.

At the age of seventeen, Billie was blessed with hope and vitality, and kind, gentle, unattainable Sterling had awakened her creative instincts. The spring of 1921 found her looking forward to her dancing career. She began to invest most of her small department-store salary in clothes. As Sterling had helped her sharpen her sense of style, her choices in clothing were by now quite sound. Billie incessantly practiced dancing in front of full-length mirrors and tried out for amateur contests at dance halls. People began to notice her natural grace and terpsichorean expertise. At a hotel in Kansas City, Billie auditioned for a job with Katherine Emerine's traveling revue and was hired, much to her delight. She was one of the chorus girls who backed up the middle-aged entertainer, who specialized in interpreting songs from operettas and Broadway musicals. Billie decided to perform under her original name, Lucille LeSueur. "It sounded more glamorous and naughty," Joan recalled.

Unfortunately, the traveling show never made it past Springfield, Missouri, and her first professional dancing job ended after only a week. It was back to the department store for Billie, who now combined attractive clothes and hairstyle with a polished seductiveness. Not surprisingly, the better-heeled men began paying attention to her. Billie was fed up with her horrible, dull job and disgusted with the situation at home, where her mother watched her like a hawk every time she came near Mr. Hough. It was perfectly clear that the two of them did not want Billie around. "My mother wasn't going to lose her latest boyfriend or husband or whatever the hell he was to her own daughter," Joan remembered. "I had absolutely no interest in Mr. Hough. I was only too happy to get out."

Having won several more dance contests, at the age of nineteen, Lucille, as she was now calling herself, decided to try her luck in Chicago. No one in her family told her that they would miss her or asked when she might be coming back. In spite of this apathy, Joan did her best to help and support her brother and mother after she made it big in Hollywood, but her relationship with them would never become close. The one person who really did miss her was Ray Sterling. Although Joan later wrote that she chose her career over marriage to Sterling, the proposal she might once have hoped for never came about anyway. Instead, Ray gave her support, love, and encouragement, and wished her the best.

In Chicago, Lucille looked up Ernie Young, an agent Katherine Emerine had recommended to her. In her memoirs, Joan mentioned how nice Young's wife was to her when, hungry and scared, she broke down in tears; what she didn't mention was that Emerine had warned her that Young was a "casting-couch cougar." Bitterly wise to the male and his ways, Lucille "jumped on Ernie's couch"—Joan's words—and he got her a $25-a-week job in a Chicago nightspot. She worked hard, proved herself a reliable performer, and was moved to the Oriole Terrace, a club in Detroit. There she did eight routines a night as part of a large group of chorus girls. Many of these girls were competitive and jealous, but a few were kind to Lucille, passing on a number of helpful tips. Her efforts in self-polish stepped up around this time: By now, Lucille's clothes were chic, her makeup relatively subtle, and her speech and manners more polished than before. As sexually ravenous as ever, Lucille had a few brief affairs with other chorus girls and slept with some of the wealthier and more attractive "Stage Door Johnnies"—those from Detroit and elsewhere.

One night at the Oriole, she caught the eye of famous Broadway impresario J.J. Shubert. He could see that Lucille was not the most beautiful of the girls, that she didn't have the best figure, and that she certainly wasn't the most talented dancer. But Shubert spotted a certain something—indefinable but definitely there, a quality that made her stand out among the other girls. After dinner with the nineteen-year-old starlet, Shubert offered her a job in *Innocent Eyes,* his latest revue. Joan remembered being "extra nice to Mr. Shubert. I wanted to make his Detroit stay pleasant—even memorable. And I think it was!"

It must have been memorable, for Lucille LeSueur soon became known in New York City as one of Shubert's "pet babes." By the fall of 1924 Lucille, then twenty years old, was holding down two jobs: one in the chorus of *Innocent Eyes,* the other filling a late-night singing and dancing spot at Harry Richman's nightclub. Soon her name began to creep into the New York gossip columns; for a time she practically had a man a night. Several men a week, each giving her clothes and jewelry, taking her to parties—and afterward? "It depended on my mood and how cute the guy was," Joan said later. But she was never above accommodating married, middle-aged men, who may well have evoked memories of "Daddy" Cassin.

Joan's abundant sexual activities, particularly in her younger days, have sometimes made her a subject of ridicule, but her conduct was by no means all that unusual. First, in her relationship with Harry Cassin she was the victim, regardless of how she might have later characterized it; that episode affected her attitude toward men and sex for the rest of her life. Second, why criticize Joan for sleeping around and having affairs in the '20s and '30s when so many of today's female stars behave in exactly the same manner? No one bats an eye when they hear of Julia Roberts's latest romance, Meg Ryan's affairs with male costars, or Madonna's erotic wanderings, so why think less of Joan because of her behavior? Indeed, in approaching sex just as a man would, Joan was ahead of her time. She saw no reason why sexual adventuring should be the exclusive domain of the male of the species.

Some biographers have suggested that Lucille found New York City a bit overwhelming and "immoral"; others have described her as being anxious to borrow money to go home to Kansas City. As Joan remembered it, the truth was that in New York she felt truly at home for the first time in her life. While her movie career would keep her in California for many decades, she always loved Manhattan and was happy to return there many years later. "New York was the most exciting place I'd ever been," she said, "and still is. There seemed to be so many options, so many opportunities. I spent all the time that I wasn't on the stage or rehearsing walking up the avenues and soaking in all the sights and sounds, the whole atmosphere of the city. I was wide-eyed at first, but got used to it pretty fast. Those of us who are meant for this city just *know* it when we get here. But my future was in Hollywood, not the theater."

In late 1924, MGM producer Harry Rapf came to New York on a talent scouting trip for the studio. The Metro Company had joined up with Samuel Goldwyn's company and Louis B. Mayer to create MGM, which had ambitious plans for top productions. Rapf wined and dined Lucille, who later implied that they slept together as well. When she did well on the screen test he set up for her in New York, he put her on a train for Hollywood with an MGM stock contract. It was now January 1925; she would soon be twenty-one. A stop in Kansas City to see her mother, who berated her for her career choice and lack of morals, only convinced her all the more that she had made the right decision.

During her first year in Hollywood, Lucille did the usual thing: She doubled for top stars, posed for cheesecake pictures and track-running publicity stills, and gradually worked her way into more substantial ingénue roles, thanks to help from Rapf and others—and thanks to her usual party-girl skills, especially well-honed now that she was in the movie capital of the world. It wasn't long before it was known around the studio—and all over Hollywood—that she had become one of the fleet of young MGM contractees that studio honcho Louis B. Mayer kept to "entertain" visiting bigwigs from New York. These services may have been "classed up" by the people and surroundings, but Lucille had mixed feelings about it all. Anxious to get ahead, Lucille was willing to do what was necessary, but she resented always having to make trade-offs: work for education, sex for attention from the Hollywood higher-ups. As mentioned in the preface, one of the men Lucille "entertained" was James R. Quirk, then editor-publisher of *Photoplay* magazine. (Jimmy Quirk was also co-sponsor, along with his close friend *Cosmopolitan* editor Ray Long, of a high-class "house of assignation" on New York's West 58th Street, where friends such as Joe Kennedy joined them in revels with ambitious young actresses and other available ladies, many from good families and on the upwardly mobile path of easy virtue. Lucille, however, was never employed there.)

Enormously vital and energetic, Lucille did late-night exhibition dancing in various Hollywood hot spots. She had become particularly adept at the Charleston and the Black Bottom, two dances that enjoyed bewildering popularity for a time. Her energy and uninhibited charm won her admiration from many men, among them Michael Cudahy, young scion of the Chicago meat-packing clan. Between them, she and Cudahy won many trophies in Charleston tournaments. Besides being handsome, well-endowed, and charming, Michael represented an upwardly mobile catch for Lucille, but the Cudahys, not fond of her free-wheeling past and Bohemian ways, pulled the protesting Michael away from her. In her autobiography, Joan claimed that Cudahy's mother actually liked her and wanted her for a daughter-in-law, but this is highly unlikely. Cudahy's mother may well have gotten a kick out of the girl with the wide eyes and vivid personality, but Lucille LeSueur, the quintessential "flapper," was simply too déclassé at that time to have been considered acceptable wife material for the likes of Michael Cudahy. She would have been dismissed at best as a diversion and at worst as a gold-digger.

Lucille came to see many heterosexual men as users who could, in turn, be used by her. She sought friendships with sympathetic women— among them Dorothy Sebastian, another MGM starlet—and with men who had no interest in her sexually. These included homosexuals such as MGM star William Haines, who became one of Lucille's best friends, and fatherly MGM producer Paul Bern, who took Lucille under his wing in his role as mentor to upcoming MGM personalities. Bern was heterosexual; he committed suicide several years later, only a few months after marrying Jean Harlow. "Paul Bern and Billy [Haines] were such a relief," Joan said later. "No groping into my panties, no pawing and panting!" Another of Lucille's early boosters was cameraman Johnny Arnold, who told her that she had a unique look and a face with a strong bone structure. He took some photos of her emphasizing her strong features; these helped bring Lucille to the attention of the MGM executives.

Lucille LeSueur was on her way.

But first she would have to bury the past.

J.C. Archives, Inc.

Chapter Two

PRETTY LADY

Lucille's first appearance in front of a movie camera—unbilled—was in *Lady of the Night* (1925), in which star Norma Shearer played a dual role. When Shearer was playing one part, Lucille would double for the other one, shot from behind or in profile from a distance. Lucille knew that Shearer was going places—she was dating Irving Thalberg, for one thing—and Shearer was what Lucille wanted to be: a star. So Lucille studied her carefully. For her part, Shearer acted as if Lucille hardly existed, something Lucille wouldn't forget when they worked together many years later.

Billed as Lucille LeSueur for the only time in her career, in 1925 she had a small part in *Pretty Ladies,* the first movie in which she actually acted. *Pretty Ladies* starred Zasu Pitts as Maggie, a plain dancer/comedienne who longs for the kind of love life enjoyed by the more attractive chorus girls. She eventually falls in love with a drummer named Al Cassidy (Tom Moore). When Al strays with a beautiful vamp named Selma (Lilyan Tashman), Maggie forgives him and takes him back. The storyline takes place in a revue similar to the Ziegfeld Follies. Lucille played Bobby, a showgirl. At one point, Bobby dresses up in a big white wig as a lady of the court. Later, in a production number, she hangs on a "human chandelier" with another extra—Myrna Loy. In order to look svelte in her costumes, Lucille lived on practically nothing but black coffee for days.

Norma Shearer had a much larger part in *Pretty Ladies* and had little to do with Lucille. Loy, however, got to know Lucille well, and their friendship would last for years. One day, after filming a production number in which the two played snowflakes, Lucille rushed into Loy's dressing room and started to cry. She told Loy that Harry Rapf had chased her around his desk, hardly for the first—or last—time. "She was having a

terrible time," Loy remembered in her memoirs. "She had such a beautiful body that they were all after her."

It was around this time that MGM supposedly decided that "Lucille
LeSueur" didn't sound right for a developing screen personality and sponsored a contest for a new name. The truth was that Lucille's reputation
had preceded her; while MGM wanted its emerging stars to get into the
gossip columns, there was a limit to how much improper behavior the
public would tolerate from their screen idols. Mayer knew that many of
the men that Lucille had "dated" as part of her unofficial MGM duties
would remember her even with a different name, but why make it easier
for them? Of course, some of them knew who "Joan Crawford" was but
kept quiet because they liked her and saw potential in her—James Quirk,
for instance, became one of her supporters. Her name was still Lucille
LeSueur when some of her early films were being shot, but the new
name was used in every picture but her first. Moviegoers the world
over would come to know Lucille as "Joan Crawford"—a name she
initially hated.

There has been some confusion over which picture Joan did next,
The Circle or *The Only Thing* (both 1925). The correct answer: both.
Only comparatively recently has Joan been spotted in stills of *The Circle*,
but there have always been several stills of her from *The Only Thing*,
including some close-ups. The confusion may have resulted because both
films were period pieces starring Eleanor Boardman. Joan almost certainly had the small role of Young Lady Catherine in the prologue of *The
Circle*, which was based on the play by W. Somerset Maugham. She
leaves her husband and runs off with her lover. In the rest of the film, the
same character—now older and wiser—is played by Eugenie Besserer.
Frank Borzage, director of *The Circle*, would work with Joan in later
films.

In *The Only Thing*, an Elinor Glyn story about star-crossed lovers
during a revolution in the nation of "Chekia," Joan's bit part is as a lady-
in-waiting. It was undoubtedly released just before *The Circle*. Joan later
confided that director Jack Conway probably put her in *The Only Thing*
just to get her to stop pestering him for roles. There is no documentation
to prove conclusively that she was also in *Proud Flesh*, another 1925
Eleanor Boardman vehicle.

Joan's next silent film—a considerable leap forward from *Pretty
Ladies* and the others in terms of her screen time—was *Old Clothes*
(1925), in which she appeared with child star Jackie Coogan. Coogan
and Max Davidson play Tim Kelly and Max Ginsburg, partners in a

business that deals in second-hand clothing and other junk. They take in a destitute boarder named Mary Riley (Joan) and help her get a job and win the man of her dreams, a Wall Street financier named Nathan Burke (Allan Forrest), whose snooty mother disapproves of Mary. It all ends happily and improbably, with Tim and Max just happening to have a lot of the very stock that Burke needs to save his business.

Joan recalled that 150 girls tried out for the part of Mary in *Old Clothes*. "They had us in a big lineup. I wanted that part so bad I could taste it," she said. "The director and I, Eddie Cline—a sweetheart, always had a cigar in his mouth—laughed about it later, about how determined and intense I was, but that little part meant the world to me back then. Jackie Coogan was hot stuff, a big name in the business, and it didn't hurt to be in one of his movies. His father was very nice to me, and thought I'd go places. Little Jackie was adorable." In a later conversation, Joan admitted that Coogan's father had a casting couch of his own, and that he didn't put Joan in his son's movie until they had a "hot" session together in his office bungalow. "He was a dirty pig!" was her more candid view on Coogan's father. About forty years after the release of *Old Clothes,* Jackie Coogan Jr. played bald-headed Uncle Fester on TV's *The Addams Family.* Watching an episode of the show, Joan commented, "You know, I wouldn't have recognized him, except he's still got that certain look on his face. The big, wide eyes, the same expression. It's old and wrinkled but it's the same face." Joan got some nice notices for *Old Clothes,* but she still had a long way to go.

Joan's final 1925 release, *Sally, Irene and Mary,* won her even more attention. Joan worked with her friend William Haines for the first time, although he was paired with Sally O'Neil, who was playing Mary, and not Joan, cast in the tragic role of Irene. Constance Bennett, at the time the biggest name of the three women, rounded out the trio as Sally. In part because her character comes to a frightful end, Joan's approach to the character was deadly earnest, in marked contrast to Haines's more frivolous performance.

Although Joan suffered some in *Old Clothes* before the happy ending, *Sally, Irene and Mary* was the film that first presented Crawford as a tragic heroine—albeit in a minor key. The movie is about three chorus girls looking for men, money, success, and romance. Sally latches onto a wealthy older man named Marcus (Henry Kolker), who wants to be her "sugar daddy"; Mary tries to land him herself but eventually settles for an adoring plumber named Jimmy (Haines); Irene is torn between a handsome lothario named Glen (Douglas Gilmore) and a nice, if less exciting, guy called Charles (Ray Howard). When Irene refuses to put out for Glen, with whom she's fallen in love, he tells her he is only interested in a physical relationship; disillusioned, she goes back to Charles. A morbid finish has Irene and Charles killed when an oncoming train smashes their elopement car. In a bizarre finish perhaps meant to take the chill off her grisly demise, Irene shows up as a ghost jitterbugging on the stage with the rest of the (living) lovelies.

Bennett, who got the lion's share of the notices, did not mingle much with Joan during the filming. Joan got nice reviews for the picture, with some critics commenting on her "polish." By 1925, there were already many movies about chorus girls, but the ever-admiring James Quirk wrote in *Photoplay* that *Sally, Irene and Mary* for once showed "the tinseled creatures as they really are—hard-working, ambitious youngsters who go home to corned beef and cabbage, usually, instead of to nightclubs and broiled lobster." He also had nice things to say about Joan, of course.

Years later, Joan singled out *Sally, Irene and Mary* as the movie that first made her think that she might have some staying power in the motion-picture industry. Much of the credit for that goes to director Edmund Goulding and cameraman Johnny Arnold. For instance, Goulding taught her how to move in relation to the camera. Goulding also got Joan to tone down some of her mannerisms, focusing especially on tempering her intensity when the scene didn't call for it. She might be playing a dancer, he reminded her, but she didn't have to "dance" her way through the entire picture. For his part, Arnold gave Joan acting suggestions as well as tips for looking good on film. Apparently Joan felt she had overacted badly in *Old Clothes*, and she eagerly soaked in this helpful advice. Joan was also forever improving her makeup and carriage. Some ideas came from studying the leading ladies of her early films; some came from advice from friendly starlets on the lot; some were entirely her own. There was a makeup department at MGM, but it was only for the stars; all of the other actors had to fend for themselves.

Joan's first 1926 release for MGM, *The Boob*, wasn't exactly calculated to advance her film career. She played a badly conceived supporting role in this George K. Arthur movie. Arthur was one of the wistful, floundering, well-intentioned young heroes of the silent screen who for a time held strong appeal to audiences, especially in smaller towns and rural areas. Gertrude Olmstead played May, the love-interest, opposite Arthur, as Peter, a dreamy farm boy who wishes that he lived in the Middle Ages rescuing damsels in distress. May rejects Peter for Harry, a city slicker played by Antonio D'Algy (in later credits he went by the name Tony D'Algy). Determined to win the lady's respect, Peter uncovers Harry's rum-running activities, and, his poetry writing and colorful cowboy suits having failed to impress his object of desire, he joins prohibition agent Jane (Joan). Peter and Jane catch Harry digging up a casket full of booze. All ends in triumph for Peter: May admires her hero at last and requites his love.

As the prohibition agent, Joan was stuck with a thoroughly throwaway role. She has one playful scene, in which Jane flirts with Peter, but it is strictly a supporting part, and she always regarded *The Boob* as a waste of time. Nor was much attention paid to her makeup and hair styling. Years later, she said, "I was just an MGM contract player and had to take whatever was thrown at me. I was earning a weekly salary and ways had to be found to keep me busy, no matter how unsuitable and carelessly conceived the part. It was a period in which I was not getting an active buildup and not that much attention was being paid me." She also felt that Olmstead, one of the beauties of the '20s then getting leads (although she would soon be utterly forgotten), was jealous of her. Joan overheard Olmstead asking director Bill Wellman (yes, the famous William A. Wellman) why such a "pretty girl should be shoved into a picture that has no real need of her," adding, "Why, they could have given the part to any unattractive character actress!" Joan recalled that veteran actors Charlie Murray and Hank Mann were kind to her; she remembered Murray encouraging her by explaining that young contract players had to make do with whatever parts came along and that "it all amounts to experience, doesn't it!"

Of director William Wellman, Crawford had darker memories:

> This was, of course, before either Bill or me had made our major marks, but he was totally oblivious of me as a person or as an actress, though he did pinch my bottom and grab one of my breasts on a few occasions. Bill developed in the '30s a reputation as a major director and was widely admired by various stars, but during *The Boob* he was just a horny wiseguy with, I felt, little respect for women. He had to cater somewhat to Gert Olmstead, who had the leading female part, but even she got his "just another broad" leers from time to time.

Joan remembered an incident about fifteen years later in which she, by then a famed star, and he, a highly respected director, met at a party, and "damned if he didn't give me a pinch on my behind, chuckling 'for old times' sake!'" A man's man, Wellman once said of the Joan he knew in the '20s, "She used to get so affronted when you kidded her, but she did have a reputation in those early days as quite a wild slut. So what did she expect?"

The critics were not kind to *The Boob*. *Film Daily* wrote of it, "The development is of such an episodic nature that the initial idea is eventually lost in a variety of comedy gags, slapstick and otherwise." Worse was to come on the other coast. The film critic of *The Baltimore Sun* dismissed *The Boob*: "A piece of junk. . . . The company has simply covered itself with water and become soaking wet, for this tale of a half-dumb boy who turned prohibition agent to convince his girl he had nerve is as wishy washy as any pail of dishwater." Joan resolved to make the best of the experience. She said later, "*The Boob* strengthened my ambitions. . . . That was a *rut,* and I became rut-allergic with a vengeance after I made it! I was never cut out for slapstick anyway, and the script for that one was just awful, which made it worse."

On loan to First National in early 1926, Joan appeared in *Tramp Tramp Tramp,* in which she served as romantic foil to Harry Langdon. In the '20s, Langdon's career as a comedian was thriving, thanks in part to his partnership with Frank Capra (before he became Hollywood's most sought-after director), who wrote stories that highlighted Langdon's distinctive comic gifts. Harry Edwards directed *Tramp Tramp Tramp* for the Harry Langdon Corporation. Langdon's wistful, befuddled persona enjoyed quite a vogue during that period, until an oversized ego, quarrels with helpful associates such as Capra, and bad judgment in his financial and personal relationships combined to bring him down.

At 62 minutes, *Tramp Tramp Tramp* was Langdon's first feature-length comedy, and he was very anxious that it go well. Capra felt that Langdon was more at ease in shorter works, because he could put across his turns in sharper, more focused form, whereas in a feature-length film he was forced to be more inventive. "He liked to economize," Capra said. "He didn't like to spread his comic turns too thin; that was the basis of Harry's fear of lengthier films."

The Capra-conceived story of *Tramp Tramp Tramp* had Langdon playing a character named Harry, a poor sap who needs to make money fast to keep himself and his father Amos (Alec B. Francis) from being evicted when the mortgage comes due. Harry is in love with the Burton Shoes poster girl, Betty Burton (Joan), who is also the daughter of shoe manufacturer John Burton (Edwards Davis). Harry decides to make his fortune by entering a cross-country hiking contest sponsored by Burton Shoes that will pay $25,000 to the winner. During the cross-country "tramp," Harry gets into the embarrassing and unpredictable straits and mishaps to be found in any Langdon film (with Capra's inventive story turns and situations)—but he pushes on, determined to win the money.

Among Harry's adventures: a flock of sheep forces him to a fence; when he escapes from them over the fence, he finds himself at the edge of a steep precipice. At another point, he gets arrested for stealing fruit and lands on a prison rock pile; then he can't get free himself from the ball and chain in which he has gotten entangled. Next comes a cyclone he barely survives, and many other adventures—but he perseveres. In the end, the prize winnings pay his father's mortgage, he lands the girl, and as a young husband and father he ends the picture looking fondly down on a baby in a crib—a baby with his own features! (Many of these ideas would be endlessly recycled, for instance in pictures starring Hope and Crosby, or Martin and Lewis.)

Variety dismissed Joan as "a nice leading lady with little to do." She later recalled that she was "playing not second fiddle, not third fiddle, but more like *fifth* fiddle to Harry's comic stunts!" Cameramen Elgin Lessley and George Spear seemed quite taken by Harry's feminine foil, however, and she was photographed very flatteringly. Ironically, the First National cosmeticians made her look better than she had in movies made at MGM. "When I got back to MGM I had picked up some makeup tricks that I clued in the MGM people on," she recalled. "I was made up better for the camera from then on, I feel."

Harry Langdon's wistful and confused lost-baby persona captivated audiences—for the moment. Joan's own memories of Langdon were mixed. "I never thought he was a very happy person," she told Quirk during one of their frequent conversations. "There seemed to be some deep dark hole in him, a hole he could never seem to climb out of." She remembered that working with him was a "very remote, detached experience. He put on the required gestures and expressions, but as soon as the camera stopped rolling, he retreated into his own private self," Joan remembered. "He was self-destructive, got too big a head, thought he knew it all." She recalled Capra later saying of Langdon that he "could have had a much longer career if he had had more self-awareness, had had a more objective awareness of his weaknesses and his strengths." For his part, Capra felt that whenever the leading lady was particularly charming and beautiful, Langdon would feel threatened and overdo his comic shticks accordingly.

Variety's verdict on Langdon in *Tramp Tramp Tramp* was apt: "[He] does some remarkable work ... aside from all the expert handling of the gags assigned him, he does several long scenes in which facial expression is the only acting." Langdon is indeed excellent in the movie. Joan was cast primarily as window-dressing—she looks pretty, emotes well, but has little to do. She does come off as very sweet and sympathetic, however, and her gestures and expressions are natural and unaffected. *Tramp Tramp Tramp* remains a classic comedy of Hollywood's silent period. The precipice scene, in which Harry pulls nails out of the fence to secure his sweater to it so he won't fall—oblivious to the fact that his actions are making the fence fall apart—is outstanding, as is his descent down a steep slope on a section of wood. The cyclone scene, shot in a special "shaking" room constructed for the movie, and the scenes of whole buildings falling apart or sailing into the air are still impressive. And Langdon cavorting in his giant crib as a baby is hilarious.

In her memoirs, Joan recalled how claustrophobic she felt during the cyclone scene when Langdon has to push her into a manhole—alas, that sequence is not in the final print. Then again, Joan recalled co-writer Capra as the director; it was actually Edwards who helmed the film, although Capra was certainly on the set.

Joan found herself again under the direction of Edmund Goulding in *Paris*. The story, written by Goulding (with help from Joseph Farnham), involved Joan as an Apache dancer in Paris with a possessive, demanding, sometimes brutal lover, also an Apache, played by Douglas Gilmore, in a role somewhat out of his usual métier. The lead was Charles Ray. At that moment he was trying to revive his once-flourishing career (he had won his original fame as a wistful boy-next-door type). He had lost a fortune on an ill-advised production of *The Courtship of Myles Standish,* and found himself in 1927 at MGM trying to revive his once-major career. *Paris* was not a film designed to help him accomplish that goal.

In *Paris*, Ray plays Jerry, a young American millionaire living it up in Paris, where the night life and exotic scenes keep him titillated and excited. He meets "The Girl" (Joan) in an Apache den, incurs the jealous anger of "The Cat" (Gilmore), and gets knifed for his pains. The Girl nurses Jerry back to health in her room while the Cat goes to prison for attacking him. Jerry tries to improve her life, offers her money and clothing, and—in time—proposes marriage. But all she feels for him is friendship and concern, and she informs him that money cannot buy her love. When the Cat gets out of prison, thinking that the Girl has taken up with Jerry, he tries to choke her to death. Jerry defends the Girl and begins to throttle the Cat, when she saddens and shocks Jerry by declaring that she is really in love with the Cat. Realizing that her heart belongs to the man with whom she shares a common background, Jerry leaves dejectedly while the Girl and the Cat unite in a reconciling embrace.

Goulding worked hard with Joan on *Paris*. At age twenty-three, she is lively, flirtatious, vital, and flatteringly photographed by her old friend Johnny Arnold. At 67 minutes, the picture is not long, but Goulding managed to recreate the Parisian atmosphere effectively, and in scene after scene he showcases Joan to maximum advantage. The only prints of the silent film available are not in good condition and, of course, they do not include the piano accompaniment that moviegoers of the day would have heard, but it is clear that *Paris* would have lent itself well to the piano scorings of the period. Joan and Gilmore make a lively pair—in what little we see of them on the dance floor, they mesh gracefully and with a mutual rhythm that indicates some degree of offscreen chemistry between them. Their love scenes are convincing as well. Years later, Joan said of Gilmore, "He was a handsome lug, and a good actor, and he deserved a longer career than fate gave him."

Charles Ray is affecting and convincing, even though he was more mature in this movie than the boyish hero that had worked so well for him earlier. To be sure, Gilmore and Joan had much better chemistry than did Ray and Joan; they were obviously not each other's types, but they performed well enough together. Of Ray, Joan confided, "He was slipping badly at that time, knew he was on the way out, and I felt an awful sadness about him in our scenes together. He made me want to help, somehow, some way, but I didn't know how." Of Goulding, she said, "As always, he was supportive, helpful, and highlighted me effectively in scenes I might, on my own, have thrown away."

In *Photoplay*, James Quirk called *Paris* "an absorbing tale of love"— at least until the final reel. Joan played the girl "exquisitely" and Ray was "amusing and believable." The magazine deplored, however, the Girl's ultimate choice of the Cat over Jerry. "Good," *Photoplay* pronounced, "but not to the last shot," urging patrons to leave before the final reel. While not made up to her best advantage (although well shot by Arnold), Joan won generally fine reviews for *Paris*. In later years, she wouldn't think much of her performance: "I was overacting all over the place in that one."

But Louis B. Mayer was taking note of his new acquisition, this "Joan Crawford," and more and more he liked what he saw. It was rare for any of the girls Mayer used to entertain visiting out-of-towners to graduate to major—or even minor—screen careers, but Mayer had always seen something special in Joan. She knew how to handle men—and not just by sleeping with them. Mayer gave her a new contract of $250 a week, in those days a veritable fortune. Throughout her life, Joan would always speak well of Mayer, to whom she was always grateful. "I was free to go to [Mayer] for advice of any kind, any time," she remembered. "He was patient with people, had great judgment, and didn't play games. Mr. Mayer always had a magic sense of star material, of personality. He knew how to build and protect his 'properties' and he had a genuine love for them as people." Years later, after Mayer's death, his reputation came under attack from the Hollywood community; he was called a tyrant, among other things. Along with Robert Taylor and a few others, Joan loyally defended him after his death, claiming that negative reports of him had been exaggerated and distorted.

Flush with new success, Joan rented a bungalow, bought a car, and prepared herself for the great things to come that so many people had predicted for her.

And then Hal and mother came to town.

Bernard Wohl Collection

Chapter Three

WINDOW DRESSING

Joan had kept in touch with her mother and brother, if for no other reason than to let them know that despite their dire predictions, she had amounted to something after all. To say that she was not thrilled to see them in Hollywood, though, would be a supreme understatement. Nevertheless, they were her closest relatives and she couldn't bring herself to turn her back on them. In later years, she would wish that she had done just that.

Brash Hal showed up first—out of the blue, insisting that if little Lucille could make it in the movies, then so could he. For one thing, he was much better-looking, he told her. Hal *was* exceedingly handsome, and he knew it. But whereas Joan had begun to make her mark in Hollywood by dint of hard work, persistence, a willingness to listen and learn, and "special contacts," Hal was willing to apply himself in only one direction, developing his own "special contacts." Joan's goal in life was to become a highly successful movie star, but her brother was more interested in the trappings—above all the dough. It didn't matter to him which of them earned the money, as long as he could spend it. Joan did her best to get him work as an extra, but Hal proved too unreliable. He stayed out all night when he had an early call the next morning, more than once wrecked her automobile, drank too much, and continually got into trouble. Worse, he expected Joan—as "the woman"—to wait on him all the time, even though she was the breadwinner. Hal had plenty of dates, mostly with hopeful actresses, but he continued his practice of hustling older gay men for extra spending money. He also dropped Joan's name whenever he thought it might do him some good, net him some extra loot, or get him into bed with some tootsie whom he promised to introduce to "big sister Joan." (Hal also pretended to be younger than his sister.) "Hal wanted to live it up on my dollar," Joan remembered. "He simply did not want to work."

Joan sent for her mother, to whom she had been sending money, more because she wanted her to look after Hal than because she missed her; she also figured it would be cheaper to have her in California. In this she was quickly proven wrong, as both Hal and Anna went on a spending spree behind Joan's back. "No matter what I gave those two," Joan recalled, still bitter after all those years, "it was never enough." Mother Anna and Brother Hal would also invite people Joan had never met over to her house without telling her. Trying to get some sleep for an early call, Joan would frequently be awakened by the sound of loud, drunken parties in the next room. When she could finally afford it, she moved into her own place, but Anna and Hal remained on the dole—Joan's dole—for years. Joan would cut them off, feel sorry for them and send more money, then cut them off again, only to give in again—all because of the familial connection Hal and Anna both exploited. It didn't take long for Joan to become thoroughly disillusioned and disgusted with the both of them.

Eventually, Joan would cut off all ties to her mother and brother. This has been mentioned time and again as proof of her cruel, ruthless nature, but Joan had done everything in her power to get Anna and Hal on their own feet. When the checks stopped coming, both mother and brother would threaten to sell nasty "inside" stories about Joan to newspapers; Hal was particularly notorious for the deals he tried to make with many different (generally appalled) writers. It was Hal who spread the untrue rumor that Joan had appeared in porn films, among many others.

In some ways, Christina Crawford proved to be more her uncle's child than her mother's.

In *The Taxi Dancer* (1927), Joan was again paired with Douglas Gilmore. Joan played Joslyn Poe, a Southern gal who comes to New York City to make it as a dancer. The best job she can land is at a ten-cents-a-dance emporium. She falls in with Jim (Gilmore) and his fast-paced partying crowd; meanwhile, Lee (Owen Moore), a neighbor from her home state of Virginia, falls in love with her. When Jim kills someone in a fight, and Joslyn exchanges her body for Jim's freedom, she finally becomes disenchanted with her life in New York and runs home to Virginia with faithful Lee. *Photoplay* remarked that Joan had at least as much "It" as Clara Bow and applauded her ability to overcome mediocre material, but noted—oddly—that she still needed "good direction." This did not sit well with Joan, as her personality had not blended well with that of director Harry Millarde, and as she insisted she had essentially directed herself. "Everyone thought I was better than the material," she recalled. "*I* thought I was better than the material. But they said I 'needed direction.' It seemed such a contradiction. As far as needing direction, Eddie Goulding's direction, yes—but sometimes I knew better than other, lesser directors did what was required in a scene."

The "understanding heart" of Joan's 1927 feature of that name belongs to Bob (Rockliffe Fellowes), a wrongly accused fugitive who hides out in the woods where he soon falls in love with a forest ranger named Monica Dale (Joan). Once the flames of the obligatory forest fire are quenched and Bob's innocence is established, he obligingly steps aside so that Joan can remain with her true love, Tony Garland (Francis X. Bushman Jr). The plot of the film was contrived to fit footage the studio had acquired of an actual woodland conflagration. Joan got some of her best early reviews for this picture. In some interviews, she gave the credit to Bushman, of whom she always spoke highly. But she was being self-deprecating when she suggested that Bushman simply let her walk off with the picture; she already knew quite a bit about acting and how to get herself across on camera. She didn't need anyone to defer to her. Bushman had hoped to follow in his father's footsteps (Bushman Sr. had appeared in the 1925 version of *Ben-Hur,* among other notable films), but he didn't have his father's talent or ambition, and he faded quickly. Joan found Fellowes attractive but too reserved for her tastes.

Winners of the Wilderness (1927) was a forgettable bit of trivia about a colonel named O'Hara (Tim McCoy) who falls in love with a general's daughter named Renée Contrecoeur (Joan) during the French and Indian War of the eighteenth century. Joan acquitted herself nicely throughout the plot contrivances, which included Renée getting kidnapped by Pontiac (Chief John Big Tree), leader of the Indian contingent. After a number of improbable episodes (all crammed into a scant 68 minutes), Colonel O'Hara and Renée live happily ever after.

Winners of the Wilderness was the first time Joan worked with director Woody Van Dyke, popularly known as "One-Take Woody" because he was so efficient in his direction. He was fast and workmanlike, but he was for the most part an uninspired director. Joan always thought Van Dyke was a character. He would arrive early in the morning and immediately begin swigging from a container filled with Orange Blossoms, a mixture of gin and orange juice. "At the end of the day, he was pretty much sloshed," Joan remembered. "It made for some interesting final scenes." She also recalled that "Woody was as good-looking as most of the leading men in his movies, maybe better looking. If he hadn't been such a big drinker, who knows?" The one interesting aspect of the production is that the Cherokee Indians were played by real Cherokees, putting *Winners of the Wilderness* ahead of its time in its casting practices, if nothing else. Joan thought that McCoy was a very naturalistic actor and that he walked off with the picture. "It was more his thing than mine," she said later. The pants McCoy wore were so tight that he had to climb up a ladder and be helped onto his horse. Meanwhile, Joan discovered that she was not made for horse operas. "The minute I met my first horse I knew I was not destined to be a female Buck Jones," she recalled in her memoirs. "[The film] almost sent me back to Kansas City."

She did one more film with McCoy, *The Law of the Range* the following year (although there were a number of features in between). In *The Law of the Range,* McCoy plays Jim Lockhart, a ranger unaware that his archenemy, a bandit called The Solitaire Kid (Rex Lease), is actually his brother. Joan plays Lockhart's girlfriend Betty, who encounters the Solitaire Kid when he holds up her stagecoach; naturally, The Solitaire Kid falls in love with her, too. Lockhart shoots his brother in a gunfight, but the Solitaire Kid manages to be reunited with his mother before he expires. William Nigh directed the picture. Of *The Law of the Range,* Joan recalled, "I galloped through it, dreaming of Douglas [Fairbanks Jr.]."

Joan regarded her appearance with the great Lon Chaney in *The Unknown* in 1927 as one of the highlights of her early MGM years. In this story, directed and written by Tod Browning based on Waldemar Young's scenario, Joan played an assistant to armless wonder Alonzo (Chaney), who headlines a Madrid circus. Making his feet do the work of his missing arms, Alonzo stars in a sensational knife-throwing act in which he throws knives at Nanon (Joan), all of which expertly miss her body. Nanon has a deep fear of men's hands and arms, both of which she associates with sexual encroachment and domination. In actuality, Alonzo has two perfectly serviceable arms, which he keeps tightly strapped to his sides, and two thumbs on one hand, facts only his dwarf assistant Cojo (John George) knows. Later, Alonzo kills Joan's father Antonio (Nick de Ruiz) because of his attempt to assault Alonzo. Believing Alonzo to be armless, the police dismiss him from suspicion. Meanwhile, Nanon forms an attachment to Alonzo, because she too believes that he has no arms, hence no threat to her deep fear of male sexuality. However, the circus strongman, Malabar the Mighty (Antonio Moreno), is able to quell her fear of men's arms and win her love. Unfortunately, by this time Alonzo has had his arms surgically removed. Deeply in love with Nanon and horrified at the grisly sacrifice he made for her, Alonzo tries to tear out his rival's arms by sabotaging the treadmill on which Malabar has placed two horses he is holding, which move in opposite directions. Nanon saves Malabar by quieting the horses; Alonzo slips and is trampled to death by them.

The plot may seem extraordinarily strange and contrived, but the movie explains at the outset that it is essentially a fairy tale and therefore does not need to conform to everyday reality. If it did, one might wonder why Alonzo doesn't simply have his extra thumb cut off instead of both of his arms. After all, he tells Cojo of his belief that should Nanon marry him, she will forgive him on their wedding night when she inevitably learns that he has arms. Cojo, however, reminds him that Nanon knows that her father's murderer has two thumbs on one hand (she had seen the attack from a trailer window but Chaney's back is to her); it is this observation that prompts the dismemberment. Chaney is so effective that he manages to make an unpleasant, stupid character seem sympathetic at times, and Joan is also very good. Looking sexy and haughty in some scenes, sweet and pitying in others, she indulges in broad, stereotypical "silent film" gestures only on occasion.

Tod Browning's direction of *The Unknown* is pedestrian—as flat and dull as it would be in later years in *Dracula* and the overrated *Freaks*. The picture really only comes to life during the superb and grotesque climax involving the treadmill and the horses. Although Malabar's arms are not torn off and Alonzo's trampling is not graphic, the sequence still packs a gruesome punch and is extremely suspenseful. Antonio Moreno played Joan's love interest, but she later dismissed him as "just another handsome rascal in love with his own appeal." Of Chaney, however, she spoke with awed, admiring respect—a respect as fresh in her mind some thirty years later as it was in 1927. "[With him] I became aware for the first time of the difference between standing in front of a camera and acting. Until then I had been conscious only of myself. Lon Chaney was my introduction to acting. The concentration, the complete absorption he gave to his characterization filled me with such awe I could scarcely speak to him. He demanded a lot of me. A lot of times I was afraid I wasn't giving him what he wanted to play off, but I guess he thought I was okay." Of his performance in *The Unknown*, she wrote, "He was giving one of his absolutely unique characterizations in this. His arms were strapped to his sides (in his role of an armless circus performer). He learned to act without hands, even to hold a cigarette between his toes. He never slipped out of character. Watching him gave me the desire to be a real actress."

By 1927, Chaney was famous for his formidable performances in movies like *The Hunchback of Notre Dame* and *The Phantom of the Opera*. He went to extreme lengths to make his horribly deformed characters convincing, often jeopardizing his own physical well-being in order to achieve verisimilitude. The contortions he put himself through are believed to have contributed to his relatively early death in 1930, after only one talkie. Joan remembered that when he died, studio operations were temporarily shut down and everyone was in tears. "An era went with him," she said years later, "an era of creative, daring, larger-than-life strivings," adding, "I have never, never forgotten him and the inspiration he provided."

She did agree with several actresses who said that Chaney was great as a friend, an advisor, and a film associate—but romantically? Not at all. Norma Shearer, who had worked with Chaney on *He Who Gets Slapped* and *The Tower of Lies*, had warned Joan that "there's something strange about the man. He makes you glad he's self-involved, as he usually is, because it would be goose-pimply to be the direct object of that man's attention or interest." Joan said it as well as anyone when she once remarked that being the object of Chaney's romantic or sexual advances would have been "the scariest of experiences," adding "I'm glad it didn't happen to me." Obviously not all women agreed, for Chaney did marry. He had a look-alike son who later became the respected character actor Lon Chaney Jr. Chaney's son played the same kind of roles as his father did but less successfully, although he could be moving in certain roles, such as the retarded Lennie in *Of Mice and Men*. "When I told Lon Jr. what his father had meant to me creatively, he burst into tears," Joan later recalled.

It was in *The Unknown* that Joan got her first serious attention from the critics. Langdon W. Post of *The New York World* wrote, "When Lon Chaney is in a picture, one can rest assured that that picture is worth seeing. When Joan Crawford and Norman Kerry are also present to help Mr. Chaney put it over, its value is that much enhanced. Not only is Mr. Chaney a very remarkable actor, but he almost invariably chooses a good story with which to display his talents, a practice all to seldom indulged in, in the case of other stars of his prominence," adding, "Joan Crawford is one of the screen's acknowledged artists and each picture seems to merely justify this characterization. Certainly her performance in this picture is a most impressive one." Joan said years later, "*The Unknown* was my first 'horror' film, if you want to call it that, and probably my best, because of Chaney." It would be forty years before she would return to the circus milieu and gruesome murders in *Berserk*.

Mayer and company then decided that, at long last, Joan was ready for a stellar pairing with the legendary matinee idol John Gilbert, known for his "burning glances" and hypererotic lovemaking style. In 1927, Gilbert's love scenes with Greta Garbo in *Anna Karenina* had scorched the screens all over the country. At the time, Mayer said, "Jack Gilbert will give Joan the ultimate cachet—and the chemistry will be right, too!" Released in mid-1927, their first picture together was *Twelve Miles Out*. Joan played a society girl and Gilbert a hell-for-leather rumrunner. Of Gilbert, Joan later said:

> He was so in love with Garbo at the time—Garbo was living in his house—that he seemed completely distracted most of the time. Oh, he could work himself into the mood when that mood was called for—but as soon as the director called "Cut!" he switched off so abruptly it made my head spin. He was always rushing to call Garbo. Once, I recall, she came to see him from a nearby set and he was as excited, showoff-y and nervous as any high school boy. What that lady did to that man was a caution indeed!

Despite these disadvantages—if such they were—Gilbert and Joan played very well together, and, as Mayer predicted, the chemistry was just right. No romance was ever to develop between them, but they did do another picture together a year later. Joan explained:

> Our chemistry on-screen may have been pretty hot—let's face it, as a couple we were pure sex, I think the first time that ever really came across with one of my leading men—but there was nothing face-to-face, person-to-person, when the scene was over. To be honest about it, Jack seemed too flibbertigibbety intense for my taste. I don't mean he was in any way effemi-nate—indeed, he was "all man." But he never stayed put, so to speak, you never felt he was giving you his entire attention. Oh, he was in love with Garbo, yes, at the time, but it was something else, too. I think it was narcissism. He seemed to be mostly in love with *himself,* with the effect he was producing. I used to feel sorry for him because he didn't have a mirror—a big one—handy to catch his every mood and look. I for one

wanted a man who gave me his complete attention. Maybe Greta got that—I certainly didn't!

Twelve Miles Out was directed by the efficient, no-nonsense Jack Conway, with whom Joan liked working. It ran for 85 minutes—a lengthy film for the time. In the film, Gilbert plays Jerry Fay, a hell-raiser who is looking for easy money and easy women "from Singapore to Buenos Aires," as the ads had it. Jerry becomes a rum-runner, with his pal (and sometime rival) Red McCue (Ernest Torrence). Jerry takes over the coastal home belonging to Jane (Joan) for his rum-running activities. Naturally they fall in love, there are more rivalries and fights—one fade-out has Jerry dying in Jane's arms after an epic gunfight. Fans didn't like the ending during a preview and wanted the Gilbert-Crawford combo to live happily ever after. Another ending was shot, but the original ending won out, tears seeming more appropriate than cheers. Joan got some good reviews for *Twelve Miles Out*. Robert E. Sherwood in *Life* called the picture "amusing and exciting," and praised Joan's acting. The *Chicago Tribune* felt she played "with charm, force, and restraint."

Joan appeared again with Gilbert in *Four Walls* the following year (although there were a few films in between). Since Gilbert's cultured, Ronald Colman–like voice—which, contrary to rumor, was not high and squeaky, and did not ruin his career in talkies—had not yet been heard by the public, he was accepted in the role of a gangster, albeit one who reforms after he's let out of prison. Joan played his moll, Frieda, her first "bad girl" role, many decades before movies like *The Damned Don't Cry* and *This Woman is Dangerous*. In *Four Walls*, Benny (Gilbert) tries to resist Frieda and asks a nicer and plainer woman, Bertha (Carmel Myers), to marry him. But when Bertha refuses his proposal, he finds that he can't get sizzling Frieda off his mind. The movie ends in melodrama, with a shoot-out at a party and Benny again accused of murder. This time, he's cleared of the charge and he and Frieda are reunited. Some critics thought that Joan stole the movie from Gilbert.

During the shooting, Gilbert was also working on *A Woman of Affairs* with Garbo and Douglas Fairbanks Jr. in an adjacent studio. By now things between Gilbert and Garbo had cooled down a bit, but even if Gilbert had had his eye on Joan, she was otherwise preoccupied; Joan had met Fairbanks between the Gilbert films, and they spent every minute off-camera meeting and cooing in neutral territory. Joan found the less-lovestruck Gilbert much more vital and animated than before. "I learned from him to always maintain your energy and vitality in front of a camera," she recalled.

Spring Fever (1927) was Joan's second feature with William Haines, and the first in which they were teamed romantically. After that they were immediately reteamed in *West Point* (1928). In *Spring Fever,* Joan and Haines both played characters who pretend that they are rich. Haines plays Jack Kelly, a cocky shipping clerk whom the boss falsely introduces as his nephew at an exclusive country club (the boss is looking to get some golf tips from him). Allie (Joan) marries Jack, but she leaves him once she discovers his true position in life. Jack manages to win her back by winning $10,000 in a golf tournament, whereupon Allie reveals that she never had any money either. In *West Point,* Haines's character, Brice Wayne, is genuinely rich and even cockier—indeed, spoiled and obnoxious—earning the enmity of his fellow cadets at West Point and the contempt of his girlfriend Betty (Joan). Brice resigns from the academy, but has a change of heart just before the big game, in which he naturally plays a crucial role in the victory. He also has a change of attitude, which earns him Betty's love again.

Much of *West Point* was filmed on location at the actual military academy, where Joan nearly caused a scandal because she wore no stockings, and was "furious" because she had to wear a bra. Joan dallied with more than one cadet during the shoot, and one young man was rumored to have been expelled because he played hooky to pursue assignations with her. Joan enjoyed working with her friend Haines, but she knew that she was only window-dressing in his movies: "He had great naturalness and charm and an overwhelming sense of humor. He would take you in his arms in a love scene, joking so you had to brace yourself not to laugh, but his mood for a sad scene of *yours* was immediately responsive. I was strictly secondary in both these pictures." Both films did very well at the box office, garnering Joan a lot of welcome attention.

Once, at a party at Haines's Hollywood home, one of the guests made a rude comment to Joan, and Haines ordered him to leave. The guest didn't take kindly to this request, and the two men got into an argument, which turned into a fistfight as soon as both of them were outside of the house. The rude guest got the brunt of the attack, losing a couple of teeth. When the dust settled, Haines insisted that he would pay for necessary dental work, and then asked Joan to pay for half. Joan was astonished: "I didn't ask you to fight him. I could have handled him myself." Years later, Joan couldn't remember what the guest had said, but she didn't think it was anything that required fisticuffs on Haines's part. "Still, it was rather sweet of him," she remembered. She and Haines remained lifelong friends. When Joan told Haines how much she hated her new name of Crawford, Haines told her that they could have called her "Cranberry," which would have been a lot worse, considering the word's connection to "turkey," something no actor wants to appear in. He mischievously decided to call Joan "Cranberry," a nickname that stuck for years.

"Cranberry" and Haines made a third film together two years later, *The Duke Steps Out* (1929). By that time, Joan had made her mark in *Our Dancing Daughters* and she regarded playing the romantic interest in a William Haines comedy as a professional comedown, despite her fondness for Haines himself. In *The Duke Steps Out*, she played Susie, a college girl courted by a mysterious classmate who is actually a famous boxer (Haines) enrolled under a fictitious name. It turns out that the boxer, Duke, has decided to pursue higher learning simply to pursue the pretty coed. After a series of misunderstandings (Susie thinks that Duke is already engaged) and humiliations (Duke is knocked out by the school champion, a mere amateur), Susie finally realizes that Duke is the man for her. Like Joan's other films with Haines, the film was a very big hit. It was also her last silent picture.

William Haines's career was eventually ended by a blacklist brought about by the production code, which sent most of Hollywood's more or less open gays back into the closet; to do otherwise would mean career suicide. Haines pursued a highly successful career as an interior decorator, and his clients came to include major movie stars and other famous people like Walter Annenberg, Nancy Reagan, and many others. Joan not only encouraged Haines and was one of his biggest clients, but also recommended him to many of her friends and associates.

In her most important early film, *Our Dancing Daughters*, Joan would finally have the role that would send her spiraling into the dizzying heights of stardom for decades to come.

She was also to find mad love and man trouble in equal measure.

J.C. Archives, Inc.

Chapter Four
LIFE AT EL JODO

Just before starting work on *Rose-Marie,* Joan went with Paul Bern to see *Young Woodley* at the Vine Street Playhouse. The star of the play was Douglas Fairbanks Jr., the son of the macho silent action star, Douglas Fairbanks by his first wife, Beth Sully. Young Doug was trying to carve out a career of his own without slavishly imitating his father, with whom he had an essentially sterile relationship. Joan had met Doug Jr. briefly at the studio, and found him stuffy, but she so admired his sensitive performance in *Young Woodley* that she sent him a congratulatory telegram. That was the beginning of their relationship. "I thought his performance was wonderful," Joan remembered years later, "but I also had set my cap for him. Not so much marriage, at first. I just thought he was delectable and wanted to get to know him better, if you know what I mean. At the studio he was cool and distant, and that made me angry. I wanted him to notice me. What better way to an actor's heart than through a telegram telling him he's wonderful? It did the trick."

While generally well-liked in youth (as he would be later in life), Doug Fairbanks Jr. was also considered a bit of a snob and a pantywaist, a pretty boy trading on his father's name. He wore an air of entitlement, and acted decidedly "superior"—at least until he got to know someone. He was a product of impeccable breeding, however, and usually was well-mannered enough not to make his contempt obvious. But Joan, sensitive to slights and condescension, had noticed his somewhat haughty demeanor at the studio and was determined to thaw the iceberg. No one could stick up his nose at her and get away with it.

Doug was "thawed" by Joan's telegram, and by her obvious sex appeal. Joan was also shrewd enough to play up to the actor's vanity. Doug may have been more cultured and better-educated than she was, but Joan was no dummy. She let him patronize her—up to a point—

letting him feel that he was the big, strong man giving the little girl the advantage of his masculine counsel and advice. But at all times it was the more sophisticated Joan who was really pulling the strings.

After a while, Doug Jr. became more than just a catch, but someone Joan liked, was attracted to—and then fell in love with. Underneath his snobbery, he was boyishly sincere and unsure of himself sexually. "For all his good looks," Joan recalled, "Doug was not that sexually experienced. I think I taught him plenty of new tricks and from then on he was putty in my hands." Joan didn't need Doug's money—she had plenty of her own—but it was part of her upwardly mobile nature to seek a mate with an impressive pedigree, and in that regard he was the right stuff. Both Doug's father and his stepmother, Mary Pickford, were Hollywood royalty. Invitations to their estate, Pickfair, were highly coveted. Joan would definitely be marrying up, if she could just keep him as starry-eyed as he had been since their first encounter involving the big telegram.

But Joan had two obstacles to contend with: Doug's mother Beth did not want her little boy to get married, especially not to a "fast" girl like Joan; his father thought that Joan was just a fling, certainly not the kind of woman who should marry the "Scion of Pickfair." Not as influential as far as Doug Jr. was concerned, but definitely part of the equation, was Mary Pickford herself, who looked down on Joan as just another sluttish chorus girl. There would be no invitations to Pickfair for Joan from that quarter. As Doug and Joan continued to see each other and fall deeper in love, they both continued making movies, first at separate studios, and then both at MGM. Joan continued to be sexually active with other men (and sometimes women) during the period that her friendship with Doug Jr. blossomed into a full-fledged love affair. Rumors of her activities undoubtedly got back to his parents—and Pickford—which made them doubt Joan's suitability as a bride all the more.

Illogical as it may seem to us today, it was common during the silent era to make straight dramatic film adaptations of famous operas and operettas; the pianist or orchestra might play some themes from the score but there were no individual arias or song numbers. (Actually, it was not so strange to adapt musical works, as many silent films had already borrowed their basic plots from them, without credit.) Even stranger, Joan found herself in two of these productions, *Rose-Marie* and *Dream of Love*, both released in 1928. The former was based on the famous operetta by Rudolf Friml, Otto A. Harbach and Oscar Hammerstein II; the latter was not so much based on Francesco Cilea's Italian opera *Adriana Lecouvreur* as it was on the French play *Adrienne*

Lecouvreur by Eugène Scribe and Ernest Legouvé that Cilea had used as his source material, although for the most part the story stayed the same. In *Rose-Marie,* Joan received fine reviews in the title role of a French-Canadian mountain gal who bewitches men at a trading post. A soldier of fortune named Jim Kenyon (James Murray, who also starred in King Vidor's masterpiece *The Crowd* that same year) comes along and the two fall in love, but Kenyon is falsely accused of murder and has to flee. Rose-Marie goes so far as to promise her hand to another man in the hopes that he will use his influence to save Kenyon from a posse. The real murderer is revealed, the lovers are reunited, and all is well in the French-Canadian Rockies once again. Joan thought the picture worked better than it had any right to. She recalled that the highlight of making the picture was when Doug Fairbanks Jr. came to Yosemite to visit her during filming.

In *Dream of Love,* Joan played Adrienne Lecouvreur, a gypsy girl who dallies with a handsome prince (Nils Asther) and doesn't meet up with him again until she has become a famous actress. By this time, the prince has earned the enmity of the duke he's cuckolded as well as of the duchess, who learns of his affair with Adrienne and is hell-bent on revenge. The prince finds himself in front of a firing squad, but he is saved by a revolution at the last second. According to most contemporary reviewers, the melodramatic goings-on were poorly served by James McKay's editing and Fred Niblo's direction, not to mention by "ludicrous" title cards. Joan was generally found to be "charming," although she came to see the picture as "a load of romantic slush." Joan said of Asther, who later appeared with Joan in *Letty Lynton,* that he was a "sensitive, self-destructive type. Considering his accent, I'm surprised he lasted as long as he did in talkies." As with Haines, she knew that Asther was gay. She also recalled that while director Fred Niblo redid scenes as often as he felt necessary (unlike "One-Take" Woody Van Dyke), the results were less felicitous.

Between *Rose-Marie* and *Dream of Love,* Joan appeared in the aforementioned *Law of the Range* and *Four Walls,* and also did a third film for director William Nigh, *Across to Singapore* (1928). It was the only film that she did with the great silent star Ramon Novarro, who like Haines and Asther was also gay. While perhaps not as upfront as Haines, Novarro was more accepting of his orientation than his friend, the conflicted Rudolph Valentino. Like most people, Joan liked the charming and attractive Novarro, and was horrified in 1968 when she heard of his death at the hands of two sadistic male hustlers. "He was much too nice a man to deserve to die like *that*," she said. She was also reunited with her friend from *Twelve Miles Out,* Ernest Torrence. "He was nothing like his bad-tempered, horrible screen image," she recalled. "He was a very sweet, good-natured man, generous, loving, and helpful. He helped me make it through the three or so pictures I did with him." In her autobiography, she referred to Torrence as "the lamb of the world."

The convoluted plot of *Across to Singapore* involved two seafaring brothers, Joel and Mark Shore (Novarro and Torrence) who are both in love with Priscilla Crowninshield (Joan). Mark has the gall to announce his engagement to Priscilla without bothering to ask her to marry him. The two brothers set sail for Singapore, where too much drink and the machinations of an evil shipmate lead to Mark being deserted on shore and Joel winding up in irons. After several trips back and forth across the Pacific Ocean, some fistfights, a mutiny, and an encounter in a dope den, Joel and Priscilla are finally reunited, after Mark is killed coming to the aid of his brother. Most critics found the film outlandish and the two stars grossly miscast; Joan herself thought little of the picture and of her own work in it. Several years later, when Joan met the great theatrical husband-and-wife team Alfred Lunt and Lynn Fontanne, the latter told her how much she admired her work in films. When Joan asked her which of her pictures she might have seen—*Possessed,* perhaps, or *Grand Hotel?*—she would always remember her mortification upon hearing *"Across to Singapore"* instead. A far happier memory of filming *Across to Singapore* was the day that Douglas Fairbanks Jr. proposed marriage, in Long Beach on New Year's Eve. Joan agreed without hesitation.

Our Dancing Daughters (1928) has always been considered the film that made Joan Crawford a superstar of the silent era and beyond. In it, she plays Diana Medford, a jazz-era flapper who puts up a wild front but underneath has her head on straight. Her friend Anne (Anita Page), conversely, seems childlike and innocent on the surface but is actually immoral and irresponsible. Both women pursue a handsome rich man, Ben Blaine (Johnny Mack Brown). Turned off by Diana's outward manner, Blaine marries the seemingly demure Anne instead—but deep down he still pines for Diana. Unfaithful Anne unfairly accuses Diana and Ben of carrying on behind her back; a drunken tumble down a flight of stairs eliminates her for good, and Ben and Diana end up together.

As soon as she read the script, Joan fought hard for the part. On the set, she loved working on the film. She liked the way the director, Harry Beaumont, allowed the cast the free range of expressions and emotions.

"I think it helped that Harry Beaumont let us be uninhibited because deep down he wanted to be uninhibited like us, too, but couldn't," she recalled. "Another director might have held us back, constricted us, and compromised the picture. I remember at the time thinking that I had never been in anything like it. The characters may seem like stereotypes now but back then they were fresher and more novel than they would be seen as today."

Many critics compared Joan in *Our Dancing Daughters* to Clara Bow, predicting that her career would overtake and outlast Bow's, which it eventually did. The movie caused a sensation, especially with the Jazz-Age youth, who ate up its apparent message of free love and fun but also understood that Joan was playing a woman who was essentially kind and decent. Suddenly, thousands of female fans wanted to dress, dance, and in all ways be like Joan, who received more fan mail for this film than for any other before it. Although Joan was not the star of the film on the title cards—no one was—the reaction to her was so positive that theater owners began highlighting her name on their marquees. Joan had really arrived: she bought a big Hollywood home with ten rooms.

Around the time of the shooting of *Our Dancing Daughters,* rumors of Joan's bisexuality began to surface, in spite of (or perhaps because of) her highly publicized relationship with pretty-boy Fairbanks. Part of it was her intense desire to become friends with costar Anita Page, which some thought indicated that she had a crush on Page. For her part, Page later told writer William Mann that "it may have been true in the beginning, that she wanted to know me for that reason." Her friend and confidant Jerry Asher was certain that Joan had lusted for Page, revealing that she had more than once admitted as much. Asher also related that Joan got farther with Dorothy Sebastian, cast as Beatrice in *Our Dancing Daughters,* and with Gwen Lee, who would appear with Joan in *Untamed* and *Paid.* He felt certain that Joan and early roommate Mae Clarke had been on and off lovers for a time. In later years, Joan would become very close to her Hollywood neighbor Barbara Stanwyck. Asher confirmed that Joan had admitted to him that the two had had a sexual relationship. "Missy [Stanwyck] and Joan were very alike, interested in men and women alike," said Asher. "They had adjoining properties in Brentwood. When Barbara was mistreated, beaten, by her first husband, Frank Fay, Barbara would escape from his drunken rantings by fleeing to Joan's house, where Joan would console her. Eventually one thing led to another." Helen Ferguson, a bisexual former actress who was Stanwyck's press agent for many years, confirmed this.

"There is no doubt in my mind," said Ferguson, "that Joan and Barbara were intimate on more than one occasion."

Joan also was sexually curious about Bette Davis, but, according to Asher, more than anything else it had to do with Joan's amusement over Davis's crush on her then-husband Franchot Tone:

> Joan would laugh about it. "Franchot isn't interested in Bette, but I wouldn't mind giving her a poke if I was in the right mood. Wouldn't that be funny?" I was never certain if she was serious or not—Bette wasn't the kind of beauty these other women were—but I do think Joan was attracted to Bette's vitality and energy. Mostly she wanted to be Bette's friend because she admired her ability and sensed some similarities between them. Bette was always convinced, due to her ego, that Joan had the hots for her and that's one reason why she was always so antagonistic and called her a phony.

Asher added that by the time of *What Ever Happened to Baby Jane?*, Joan had no sexual interest whatsoever in the overweight, slatternly Davis, "but I'm sure when Joan sent her gifts Bette was convinced she was still trying to get into her pants."

Late in life, Martha Raye claimed that she had had an affair with Joan when both were working for the USO during World War II. Most of the women Joan was attracted to were highly pulchritudinous or at least very sensual (for example, Davis in her youth), neither of which Raye was, at least on-screen. But not all of the men Joan had affairs with were so handsome. In some cases, it was the masculine aura that attracted her; in other cases, Joan was using her body to garner favors. But what favor could she have wanted from Raye? Was Joan responsive to Raye's lust due to her own narcissism? As intriguing as it is, it's more likely that this story was an example of a former star thinking they could get away with saying nearly anything about Joan's behavior.

Joan met Jerry Asher at MGM, where he was a gofer and office boy. He was obviously gay, and he brought out Joan's maternal instincts. She was instrumental in getting Howard Strickling, head of MGM's publicity department, to hire Asher as a press agent. Joan frequently invited Asher to her home, and the two became extremely close. Joan was perhaps more indiscreet with him than with any other person in those days. When Asher, who died in 1967, told these stories about Joan, he wasn't trying to be nasty, he simply saw nothing wrong in Joan's involvements,

homosexual or otherwise. Rather, he found her various sexual entanglements too fascinating to withhold from people he knew were sophisticated enough to deal with them. Also, this was during the '20s and '30s,
before the production code inflicted a more conservative morality on
Hollywood. Knowing of Asher's own orientation, Joan introduced him
to William Haines, and she felt safe in talking about her occasional indiscretions with her own sex, which she never took very seriously. "Joan's
main interest was *men*," Jerry often remarked. If one were to try to place
Joan on Kinsey's Heterosexual-Homosexual Rating Scale (where 0 is
exclusively heterosexual and 6 is exclusively homosexual), she would
probably rate about a 2 ("predominantly heterosexual, but more than
incidentally homosexual"). At this time, lesbian experimentation was
sometimes seen as just a way of expressing freedom and lack of inhibi-
tion. "At least you can't get pregnant," Joan joked many years later,
when the subject of lesbianism somehow came up at a luncheon.

Joan's primary sexual interest *was* in the male of the species. She
may have thought Anita Page of *Our Dancing Daughters* was luscious,
but her heart really pounded for the male lead, Johnny Mack Brown,
who was a former football hero. "He was as handsome as all get-out,"
she remembered, "but much too reserved and a little *too* gentlemanly for
my taste." He did not light Joan's fire as much as Clark Gable would;
apparently Joan did not interest Brown either. "I think he liked Anita,"
Joan remembered.

Asher's opinion was that Joan was a virtual nymphomaniac and
gave all of her leading men, and many of the male supporting players,
the once-over to assess their potential bedmanship. These hurried encounters were strictly for quick thrills (and, occasionally, control) and
had nothing to do with Joan's romantic feelings for, or engagement to,
Douglas Fairbanks Jr. during this period. Joan was like a man (at least
how we see some men) in that she could be in love with someone and see
nothing wrong in having "meaningless sex" with others. "Joan did not
like to be rejected, but who does?" Asher said. "She once told me about
the guys who rejected her: 'If they're gay they're forgiven, but if they're
straight—never!'" A lot of Joan's forgiveness had to do with the manner
in which the rejection came. It did not necessarily impress her if a man
was married or engaged, because she knew how many men cheated on
their wives and fiancées and basically assumed that everybody cheated at
one time or another, as she did. But if she sensed that a man sincerely
didn't want to cheat, then she would let it pass, especially if it was someone she wasn't that interested in. "She wouldn't necessarily blackball a

guy because he wouldn't sleep with her," Asher said, "it's more that she'd rather make a picture with a compatibly randy fellow—Clark Gable, for instance—than a less pliable Johnny Mack Brown. However, she never objected very strenuously to being cast with a male player when she knew the on-screen chemistry would be good for the picture," for instance her films with Robert Montgomery.

Our Modern Maidens (1929) was Joan's last silent picture at MGM. There was some concern at the studio that the movie wouldn't seem very contemporary without sound, so it was eventually released with background scoring, some spoken narration, and sound effects, making it a "semi-silent." This fooled no one, as the dialogue was still revealed in title cards, and Joan's voice was never heard. In spite of this, the picture did extremely well at the box office because of the public's fascination with the very public love affair between Joan and Douglas Fairbanks Jr., not to mention the success of *Our Dancing Daughters*. Although not a sequel to *Our Dancing Daughters*, *Our Modern Maidens* also concerns young "jazz babies"—"moderns" who have up-to-date ideas about sex—and their love troubles. *Our Modern Maidens* is a far superior film to *Our Dancing Daughters*. (*Dream of Love* and *The Duke Steps Out* came between these two "Our" films.)

Billie (Joan) wants her boyfriend Gil (Fairbanks) to keep their engagement secret until he makes his way in life. To that end, she begins a fake romance with a wealthy older man named Glenn (Rod La Rocque), hoping he can use his connections to get Gil an appointment for diplomatic service, assuring Glenn that Gil is "just a friend." Glenn does as he is told, Gil is sent off to Paris, and news of his engagement to Billie hits the papers. This understandably devastates Glenn, who had thought that Billie was really in love with *him*. There is another victim to Billie's manipulations as well: "Kentucky" Strafford (Anita Page), a friend of hers who begins a romance with Gil while Billie was spending all of her time with Glenn. Lifelong sweethearts Billie and Gil get married, but after the ceremony Billie discovers that Kentucky is pregnant—of course, by Gil. "Couldn't you have told me an hour ago?" she asks a distraught Kentucky. Billie has the marriage annulled so that Gil can marry the woman he—apparently—truly loves. Recognizing that she was the original architect of this unhappiness, Billie allows her father and her friends to think that Gil is pulling out of the marriage because of *her* indiscretions. But who should show up in Paris, where Billie has fled, but a forgiving Glenn wanting her back. Realizing that she really loves Glenn, Billie takes him into her arms. Fade to black.

Some fans were disappointed that Joan didn't walk off into the sunset with her real-life fiancé Douglas Fairbanks Jr. However, Rod La Rocque was on the payroll at MGM and Doug was not. In addition, the conclusion of *Our Modern Maidens* is more dramatic and less predictable the way it is.

Despite the lack of trenchant dialogue and in-depth characterization, *Our Modern Maidens* remains an effective movie over seventy years after its initial release. The basic premise of a woman keeping company with one man in order to help another is borrowed from Lillian Gish's silent film version of *La Boheme*, although the results are quite different. *Our Modern Maidens* could be dismissed as a hackneyed romance were it not for the suspense it creates as the wedding approaches and the audience wonders what new disaster will ensue. Moreover, the resolution, with Billie and Glenn reunited, is a surprising tearjerker. What also makes it work is the performances.

Joan is at the top of her form in every scene: alone with La Rocque after he learns of her deception, she registers compassion, anxiety, and then relief (Glenn locks her in a room, ostensibly to have his way with her, but then he can't go through with it). Billie's expression at the end when she sees Glenn at the door in Paris is priceless. So is the look on her face when she discovers that Kentucky is pregnant by her husband. Joan does not play a "bitch" in the movie: her Billie does what she does out of love for Gil, and in some ways she seems more upset by the result of her actions than Glenn or Kentucky is. It's true that at this stage of her life Joan was by no means a raving beauty—short hair was rarely if ever becoming on her, for one thing—but she is still quite attractive. In any case, she arouses interest more because of her personality than her looks—Anita Page was prettier.

In an early scene, Billie performs a kind of mock ballet at a party for the benefit of Glenn—no one would have mistaken Joan for a prima ballerina. Joan was endlessly curious about the effects she was making; she would watch the rushes every day and talk to the editor to see if improvements could be made. "We all bounced, danced, skipped and hippety-hopped . . . but we also exhibited a rather touching sincerity," she remembered about the film—and she was right about the way it plays on-screen. She also thought that *Our Modern Maidens* was the first time the wardrobe department really had a chance to go all-out on her costumes.

The other performers match Joan in intensity. None of the players in the movie ever exhibit those dreadful hammy mannerisms that so often plagued silent film actors; on the contrary, for the period they are very natural. Director Jack Conway kept things moving, and the production had all the gloss and extravagance MGM could muster. It did better for the studio than expected. It was the only movie Joan and Doug ever made together.

After the picture wrapped, the couple then flew to New York to be married. By this time Joan had managed to win Doug's mother Beth over, but his father and stepmother were nowhere in evidence as they tied the knot on June 3, 1929, at St. Malachy's Roman Catholic Church. Doug was only twenty-one; Joan took four years off her age, becoming twenty-one again. They spent their honeymoon at the Algonquin Hotel, never venturing from their room. "I saved up some 'tricks' for the wedding night," Joan remembered, "but Doug made up for what he didn't know with plenty of enthusiasm."

The fans were thrilled (and some a little disappointed), but not everyone in Hollywood was impressed. There were no parties at Pickfair, at least none to celebrate the nuptials. Many thought that Doug Jr. had married beneath himself, and would be cuckolded by Joan before the week was out. Even Joan's supporters figured she had an angle, no matter how much in love she may have been with Doug. Adela Rogers St. Johns, famed chronicler of the stars for *Photoplay,* summed it up when she observed, "Though it was a love match, Joan was anxious to better herself." Helen Ferguson, Stanwyck's press agent, was later to remember the unkind gossip surrounding the alliance, such as, "She started off tramping for middle-aged big shots—now she's a cradle robber!" On the other hand, while Doug Jr. helped Joan gain polish and social poise, she reaffirmed his belief in his acting abilities—as Fairbanks himself recalled in later years—encouraging him to strike out on his own, and to trust his own judgment. Thanks in part to Joan's efforts, Doug Fairbanks Jr. was no longer Mama's Little Boy, and he was no longer in his Father's Long Shadow either. For this, among other things, Fairbanks Jr. would remain grateful; in later years, he rarely said anything negative about his former wife. It was largely the same for Joan. She was certainly exaggerating when she wrote in her memoirs that Doug taught her how to laugh— she'd had plenty of laughs working, partying, and dancing with William Haines and others—but it was her first warm and sustained relationship with a man who was in love with her and with whom she was in love.

Not long after they got married, on September 14, 1929, Joan and Doug visited Grauman's Chinese Theatre in order to put their footprints

in cement in the forecourt outside. As Fairbanks Jr. related it in his autobiography, *The Salad Days*:

> One of the supposed guerdons of film fame was planting
> one's hands, feet, and signature in wet cement in the forecourt
> of Grauman's Chinese Theatre. . . . When it was MGM's turn
> to plug its newest star, Joan Crawford, she and I were both
> sent downtown to a big . . . event in front of the theater. The
> report that we both left our marks for posterity was only half
> true. The film and the star were MGM properties and I was a
> corporate foreigner from First National. Hence, no provision
> was made for my recorded hands and feet at all.

Joan and Doug moved into Joan's large house after they were married. Playfully mimicking the name of "Pickfair," they combined their
names and christened their love nest "El Jodo." Since they weren't invited to Pickfair's soirées for quite some time, they held their own parties
instead. Joan remembers this period as a rather blissful one, and no doubt
it was. They were young and in love; they were good-looking; they had
successful careers, plenty of money, and fans all over the country. By all
rights their existence should have been perfect. Perhaps it was a little too
perfect, a little too calculated, a model home with matching Ken and
Barbie dolls merely playing at being a normal wife and husband—when
that was hardly what they were. When not spending quiet hours together, enjoying sex, or carousing with assorted guests, they reported to
the studio. Married life was not about to deter Joan Crawford from her
career.

A plotless revue staged for the cameras, *Hollywood Revue of 1929*
(1929) was Joan's first sound film, featuring Hollywood stars undertak-
ing activities, both appropriate and otherwise, in front of an unseen audience. Jack Benny (appropriate) and Conrad Nagel (inappropriate) were
the masters of ceremonies. Norma Shearer and John Gilbert performed
the balcony scene from *Romeo and Juliet*. Laurel and Hardy did a comedy spot. Marie Dressler and Polly Moran clowned around. Joan sang
"I've Got a Feeling for You" (she puts the number over but proves herself no great song stylist) and danced—none too impressively. It seems
more like faux dancing than anything else, but she did kick up her legs
with great vigor. Not well-served by the makeup department, Joan looks
rather plain—too scrubbed, virtually lacking in sex appeal. Her pal William Haines also got to do a bit.

Her next film, *Untamed* (1929) was Joan's first real talkie. This was the first time she worked with Broadway star Robert Montgomery (with whom she would costar several more times), and the third time with her chum and admirer Ernest Torrence; Jack Conway was back as director. In the movie, Joan plays "Bingo," who inherits millions of dollars after her oilman father is killed. Transplanted from South America to New York, she finds that she lacks the polish and social graces that people expect of a woman of means. (Perhaps Joan's exclusion from Pickfair made her relate to the script.) Bingo falls for Andy (Montgomery), a man she has met on the boat ride to New York, but he is intimidated by her wealth and goes off with Marjory (Gwen Lee). Having already scandalized most of Manhattan, Bingo shoots Andy in the arm, which somehow makes him see the error of his ways and agree to marry her.

Reviewers found Joan's speaking voice "alluring," and her career in sound films was therefore assured. The reviews of her performance were mixed: some critics thought she was convincing in both the South America and Manhattan scenes, while others found her completely "ill-at-ease" throughout. All in all, the material took the brunt of the negative criticism. For the most part, Joan made a good impression and great things continued to be predicted for her. Joan had two song numbers in *Untamed*. On "Chant of the Jungle," her voice is simply too deep and bassoony to be sexy. Montgomery joins her for "That Wonderful Something is Love," in the process proving that he wasn't much of a singer, either.

Joan and Montgomery worked well together over the years, but in terms of temperament, they were oil and water. There were no major blow-ups, and certainly no romance, but after a while Montgomery got tired of what he perceived as Joan's grand manner and her single-mindedness about her career, a quality that many male actors found unattractive in women. It didn't help that Montgomery played mostly supporting roles under Joan until he became a star in his own right. Even then, he never quite came up to the level of—or had the staying power of—a superstar like Joan, even though, with his theater background, he was convinced that he had more talent than Joan. (A lot of Joan's male costars felt that way.) They often had fun working together, depending on how they felt about the rest of the cast, but they would never have a warm relationship. Jerome Cowan, who worked with Montgomery in the Bette Davis vehicle *June Bride* many years later, said, "Bob had a kind of feline, feminine talent for getting under a lady costar's skin. I heard that Joan Crawford had cordially hated him during their films together at MGM and I could see why." Later on, Joan was more blunt: "He was a big bitch!" (Note: such references to "bitch" or being "feminine" in no way reflect any opinion about his sexuality—they were both merely saying that Montgomery was displaying characteristics perceived as feminine.)

By her next film, *Montana Moon* (1930), Joan had managed to raise her singing voice an octave or so, but she still doesn't sound that great warbling the interesting number "Montana Call." Joan dismissed the picture as an attempt to do something for the career of Johnny Mack Brown, although it ended up doing little for anybody's career. In this bit of froufrou, Joan plays "Montana" Prescott, daughter of a wealthy rancher who meets a cowpoke named Larry Kerrigan (Brown) and decides to marry him. At the wedding reception, Montana outrages Larry by doing a torrid number with a sexy fellow named Jeff Pelham (Ricardo Cortez), which ends in a steamy kiss. Infuriated by what she feels is her husband's overreaction, Montana takes the train to New York, but "bandits"—Larry and his pals in disguise—pretend to hold up the train and Montana is carried off by Larry to hearth and happiness. Technical problems of the new sound process did not distract reviewers from noticing that *Montana Moon* was a pretty silly, flimsy concoction. About all Joan got out of it were pleasant memories of several "dates" (and then some) with the handsome Cortez, who would have a respectable Hollywood career as a character actor.

It seems Joan was already finding life with Doug at "El Jodo" rather boring. And Joan Crawford could not tolerate boredom.

She would have to take steps to find outside stimulation.

Bernard Wohl Collection

Chapter Five

TWO OF A KIND

It was a year after Joan and Doug Jr. were married that they were finally invited to Pickfair. "I was so desperate to go," Joan remembered. "But by the time we finally got the summons I felt like telling them what they could do with it." Spending frequent days at Pickfair, Joan watched as Doug and his father grew closer than they had ever been before. Unfortunately, she never became close to Doug's stepmother. During the remaining years of her marriage to Doug Jr., Mary Pickford hardly ever deigned to speak to Joan, and when she did it was always in the context of a group conversation. Joan never felt welcome, felt no warmth—at least from Mary. Doug Sr. was a different story, which may have contributed to Pickford's chilliness toward Joan. Doug's father got to know and like Joan, and the two became close. Still, Joan bristled at Pickford's attitude, the way she was always made to feel like a gauche outsider at Pickfair. In numerous film roles over the years (*Queen Bee, Flamingo Road,* for example), she would call on her memories of her treatment at Pickfair to fuel portrayals of characters who had finally been let into certain vaunted settings, only to discover that they would never be truly accepted. It was only after Joan divorced Doug Jr. in 1933 that Pickford exhibited any friendliness or warmth toward Joan—perhaps it helped that Mary divorced Doug Sr. some years later. During the years that Joan and Doug Jr. were married, Pickford was still acting, and she couldn't help but regard Joan as a younger, more attractive rival. She also couldn't help but notice that her husband, Doug Sr., was as "charmed" by Joan as most men. She may have feared that her husband was a little bit smitten with Joan, or at least attracted to her. In any case, Pickford married Buddy Rogers in 1937, only six months after divorcing Doug Sr., who died in 1939. Her future meetings with Joan would always be cordial.

Home at "El Jodo," Joan and Doug continued to make a show of marriage. It bothered Doug that Joan seemed so focused on her career, while she fretted over his inconsistent commitment toward his career. Joan was clearly the more ambitious and determined of the two. After a while, Joan began to realize that it was mostly sexual attraction that had held them together for so long. By this time, Joan was bored with Doug's lack of imagination and grinning boyishness and wanted to sample something different. In addition, when not in the bedroom or in company, they simply didn't have much to say to each other, something that their belated honeymoon only seemed to emphasize. Joan threw herself into her work, hoping that the problems at home would sort themselves out and that she'd somehow become excited again.

Our Blushing Brides (1930) had a different screenwriter than *Our Dancing Daughters*, but once again the director was Harry Beaumont. It was a grim story about three gals trying—what else?—to land husbands while they share an apartment and work in a department store. Together again, Joan, Anita Page, and Dorothy Sebastian were all excellent as the roommates Gerry, Connie, and Franky, respectively. Connie winds up committing suicide after being dumped, Franky falls in with a crook and nearly gets thrown into jail. Gerry falls in love with Tony Jardine (Robert Montgomery), the department-store boss seeking a dalliance with her. But Gerry isn't satisfied to be an idle fling for Tony, no matter how attractive she finds him. After seventy or so minutes of depressing incidents, the movie ends—rather improbably—with rich Tony settling down with Gerry. The plot is haphazardly constructed, and the ending is completely out of sync with the rest of the movie.

Joan got good reviews for *Our Blushing Brides*—"she plays the part of a mannequin with enough assurance for a marchess and enough virtue for a regiment," went one—but many were double-edged. Many critics found it completely inappropriate for Joan to exude Park Avenue sophistication when she was playing a mere shopgirl. Joan might have countered that it is not only society gals who have manners. While the critics may have had a point that she was a bit too classy for this and similar parts, they were also being a tad snobbish. If Joan could polish and reinvent herself, why couldn't the characters she played do the same? Why couldn't a gal from a poor family develop poise and sophistication? In any case, *Photoplay* singled hers out as "performance of the month." By this time, however, she felt that the shopgirl characterization was wearing thin. She would later say that the film was a "dud," commenting that "Poor Bob Montgomery didn't stand a chance." During this period, she also felt that she was being used to help build up her male costars' careers, as she was already considered a name. Unfortunately, in her opinion, the parts tended to be throwaways.

Joan's next film was supposed to be a film adaptation of a musical called *Great Day* with Johnny Mack Brown as her leading man, but she was uncomfortable with the part. Joan had played likable, sweet women in earlier films, but they always had a dash of spice, a soupçon of sexiness—it was integral to her persona. Knowing that she was all wrong for the girl in *Great Day*, she begged Mayer to take her off the film and put her in something that could take advantage of her talents. When Mayer looked at the footage that had already been shot for *Great Day*, he decided that she was right. Not only that, he decided that *Great Day* was shaping up as a Grade-A stinker. He scrapped the movie and gave her a script, *Within the Law*, that had been earmarked for Norma Shearer, who was then pregnant and couldn't do the film. The title of the movie was changed to *Paid*.

Paid (1930) showcased one of Joan's strongest performances as ex-con Mary Turner, unjustly imprisoned and looking to exact revenge on her accuser, Edward Gilder (Purnell Pratt), by marrying his son Bob. (The actor playing Bob was listed as Kent Douglass, whose real name was, coincidentally, Robert Montgomery; for most of his career he used his middle name and was billed as Douglass Montgomery.) The interesting storyline was somewhat undermined by a subplot in which Joe Garson (Robert Armstrong), a crook Mary meets after leaving prison, is entrapped by the police, who plant the story that the *Mona Lisa* is being kept with Mary and her husband. Predictably, Garson snatches the copy of the painting, and a lengthy scene (one that does absolutely nothing to advance the main plot) has him captured and interrogated by the police who had set him up. As for Mary? All's well that end's well—apparently she will forget vengeance and find contentment as the daughter-in-law of her hated accuser.

Backed by a strong supporting cast, including Armstrong, Marie Prevost, William Bakewell, and Gwen Lee, Joan got mostly excellent notices and *Paid* did very well at the box office. The movie turned Joan into a top box-office attraction, and it also turned her into a more viable candidate for the more dramatic MGM pictures. She always saw the film as her first really meaty role and her first opportunity to show what she could do, and she would seek out opportunities to do so in the future. However, despite the debacle of *Great Day* and the complete lack of song numbers involving Joan in *Paid*, she would not completely shed her song-and-dance jazz-baby image for quite some time. True, the title of the next picture, *Dance, Fools, Dance*, didn't even refer to musical theater (rather, it was a clumsy attempt at irony), but *Dancing Lady* and *Ice Follies of 1939* were also in her future, as well as other films that had her singing and dancing.

Dance, Fools, Dance (1931) was a minor but interesting B-style melodrama bolstered by a colorful cast. William Bakewell and Joan played "Roddy" and "Bonnie" Jordan, a brother and sister who have to make their way in the world after their father goes bankrupt in the stock-market crash and dies of a heart attack. Bonnie goes to work as a reporter, and Roddy becomes a "society bootlegger" working for gangster Jake Luva (Clark Gable). Roddy unknowingly drives a car used during the St. Valentine's Day Massacre and is forced to murder a sneaky reporter, while Bonnie is improbably assigned to infiltrate Luva's gang to find out who killed her friend and associate. These and other illogical developments mar the picture's entertainment value, and it's all a bit too quick while, conversely, being rather slow-moving.

Joan hated *Dance, Fools, Dance* and thought she was lousy in it, but making the picture had one unexpected bonus: Clark Gable! Joan and Gable really click in this movie, even though her character is intended to be repulsed by his. They clicked offscreen as well, to put it mildly. Mayer was so excited by the on-screen chemistry of Joan and Gable that he fired Johnny Mack Brown from *Laughing Sinners* (then titled *Complete Surrender*), scrapped his considerable footage (including his scenes with Joan, all of which were reshot), and replaced him with Gable. For his part, Brown was not amused. A mediocre actor, Brown would undoubtedly have seen his career peter out whether he'd appeared in *Laughing Sinners* or not. Still, Mayer's decision seemed harsh. Considering his willingness to scrap so much of *Complete Surrender* and *Great Day*, the incident reinforced the idea that Mayer was willing to spend a great deal to protect his special investment named Joan Crawford.

Unfortunately, Joan's desire for strong dramatic parts did not exactly include *Laughing Sinners*. However shoddy his acting, Brown would have been more appropriate for the role of Carl Loomis, a Salvation Army officer, than Gable; neither was Joan well-used as "Bunny" Stevens, the cafe entertainer who comes under his evangelistic spell. Loomis saves Bunny's life after she throws herself off a bridge because her boyfriend "Howdy" (Neil Hamilton) has deserted her. Bunny joins the Salvation Army and starts hanging around street corners with Loomis, but by chance she runs into Howdy and threatens to start up with him again—until Loomis intervenes. Then it's back to the street corners and tambourines and a lasting love—presumably—with Loomis. The slapdash, creaky, frequently laughable *Laughing Sinners* was no *Rain,* which Joan would make the following year, although oddly enough Joan got better reviews for *Sinners* than she would for the superior Maugham adaptation. In *Laughing Sinners,* Joan again had dancing scenes and even a torch number ("What Can I Do? I Love That Man") that she performed with her characteristic aplomb, even if her voice was as ordinary as ever.

Neil Hamilton, who had started out as a prominent D.W. Griffith player, became a character actor after the Griffith projects evaporated— he eventually played Commissioner Gordon on the *Batman* TV show. He said that he cultivated a great respect for Joan during his two screen appearances with her. "I have never known anyone who works so hard on a performance to bring it up to its highest level," he remembered, "or who was more conscientious about her acting. It wasn't just about stardom with Joan; she wanted to be good, she wanted the picture to be good, and she wanted you to be good, too. She invested everyone else in the picture with that same sense of responsibility, to make a film that was as good as it possibly could be, regardless of the script." Like a lot of other Hollywood stars, Joan thought it might be fun to appear as a guest villainess on *Batman,* but it never worked out. "Neil's still a handsome guy," she noted; she recalled him as being a hard worker as well.

With Hamilton again as her leading man, Joan offered another snappy, well-acted portrayal in the entertaining, if minor, *This Modern Age* (1931). She played Val Winters, a young woman who comes to live with her mother, whom she has never met, and who she doesn't realize is the mistress of the man who owns the house in which they live. Hamilton played Bob, a more upstanding fellow than the crowd with which Val and her mom normally run. Bob falls for Val but is dismayed by the truth about her mother. The picture is marred by a somewhat sanctimonious approach to a subject that had been elsewhere handled more frothily (and honestly), but in its way the film was an accurate depiction of the attitudes of the day. Joan looks very gorgeous as a blonde—she wore her hair that color because the actress who was originally to play the part of the mother, Marjorie Rambeau (who'd played her mother in *Laughing Sinners*) was a blonde. When Rambeau became ill, the part was recast with a brunette actress, Pauline Frederick, whom Joan greatly admired. Joan's scenes had already been shot, and the difference in hair color was not reason enough to reshoot them. Besides, there was no reason why a brunette mother couldn't have a blond-haired daughter—or maybe she was just into peroxide. Joan remembered *This Modern Age* as being "hopelessly artificial," but she was gratified when it went on to make quite a bit of money.

One of Joan's best films—and performances—of the early '30s was her next feature, *Possessed* (1931), in which she was again teamed with Clark Gable. It was during the filming of *Possessed* that Joan fell passionately in love with Gable. Although Joan was cautious in her autobiography and in other public statements, frequent indiscreet remarks made privately indicate that she had an intimate, romantic and long-lasting affair with Clark Gable that probably began with the first film they made together, *Dance, Fools, Dance*. Their relationship became such common knowledge that Joan began talking about it openly after a while, in TV interviews and the like. The raw, physical part of the relationship had existed for quite some time before it bloomed into a full-fledged love affair during the shooting of *Possessed*, although Joan was undoubtedly more in love than Gable was. For months, unbeknownst to their respective spouses, the two had passionate trysts at a secret beach house, where they spent as much time with each other as possible. This was one of a few occasions where Joan urged a lover to leave his wife and marry her (while remaining good friends with the wife, if possible). It wasn't until many years later that Joan would be able to understand the wife's viewpoint, if she ever did. Joan's affair with Gable lasted throughout her marriage to Fairbanks and into her marriage to Franchot Tone.

What ended the affair? Not only did Gable not want to divorce his second wife, Ria Langham, an older woman who held much influence over him—although Gable on several occasions told Joan that he was going to do it. Deep down, Joan knew that her wild fling with Gable would lose its raw, tempestuous quality if they were to get married. Marriage had seemed to dampen her feelings for Douglas, and she was afraid that it would happen again if she were to marry Gable. Years later, Joan remarked that she suspected that Gable took his women for granted and hankered after ones he didn't have; she was certain that he would not have remained faithful. It did not at first occur to Joan that she might as well have been talking about herself. In many ways, Joan and Gable were alike—too alike: both ambitious, both hustlers, both comfortable with using sex to get ahead. When he was still an unknown, Gable had even been "serviced" by gay men (William Haines among them) he thought could advance his career. It wasn't until Gable met Carole Lombard that he was able to shed his previous dependency on older women (his first wife, Josephine Dillon, was an acting coach 17 years older than Gable, and Ria was quite wealthy). Joan and Gable remained friends throughout their lives, and Joan never fell entirely out of love with him. Years later, when Joan told Adela Rogers St. John that her fourth husband Al Steele was the only man she ever really loved, Adela reminded her that she had said the same thing about Fairbanks Jr., Gable, and others. Joan broke down and told her the only man she ever really loved. "It wasn't the Pepsi Vice President," St. John noted in her book, *The Honeycomb*. It was, of course, Clark Gable, a fact that Joan confirmed on more than one occasion. "Lovemaking never felt with anyone like what it did with Clark," she remembered some years after Gable's death.

In *Possessed*, Joan plays Marian, who leaves her dull factory town and manages to latch onto millionaire attorney Mark Whitney (Gable, charismatic but not as good as Joan), then winds up branded a tramp because Whitney is afraid to remarry another woman after his first wife's bitter betrayal. This well-paced picture is nothing deep, but it manages to avoid a few clichés. For instance, that nice hometown boy who comes to the city and still loves Marian turns out to be a louse. Marian makes a sacrifice for Whitney's political career (unlikely, but typical for the genre), but eventually wins him back in a moving wind-up. An especially nice sequence has Marian identifying with and befriending a "woman of loose morals" that one of Whitney's male friends brings to a party. *Possessed* offers very nice work from a resplendent-looking Joan. Joan always liked the movie and liked her work in it; she credited director Clarence Brown for making both her and the movie turn out as well as they did.

Joan's real feelings for Gable are very clear in the party scene, when she sits at the piano and begins to sing some songs in foreign languages. Gable asks her for the English version of the last song, and one guest remarks that there can be no English verse because "English is not the language of love." Joan proves him wrong by launching into a very effective interpretation of "How Long Will It Last?" (referring to the length of a love affair) staring at Gable, singing to him and to him only, as he leans against the piano in rapt attention. (As Joan was the bigger star at the time, Gable gets no reaction shots.) This wasn't just good acting—Joan, desperately in love with Gable, was herself wondering how long it would last. Joan wasn't a great singer, but she could certainly put a song over when she really felt it, and she felt it then. She was also a good enough actress always to sing with the requisite expressiveness; this moment in *Possessed* is proof positive of that. The same year *Possessed* was released, Joan made a recording of "How Long Will It Last?" with the piano replaced by Gus Arnheim's orchestra and the tempo sped up. Joan's voice sounds better and is more effective in the film than on the record, which may explain why the recording was never released to the public.

In *Grand Hotel* (1932), Joan found herself in an all-star major motion picture, one that would become a true classic. Based on the novel and subsequent play by Vicki Baum, the story takes place in a major old-style European hotel where the lives of several guests intermingle in dramatic fashion. The theme of a need for money runs through the picture and links the separate vignettes. Baron Felix von Geigern (John Barrymore) needs $5000 to pay off a debt; the severely ill Otto Kringelein (Lionel Barrymore) needs his life savings to have a final fling before his death; industrial magnate Preysing (Wallace Beery) needs the influx of cash that will accompany a merger with another firm; and struggling stenographer Flaemmchen (Joan) needs a man with money to give her the kind of life she desires.

Flaemmchen is an underwritten part, but Joan makes the most of it, exhibiting a lot of charm and personality, the very magnetism that made her a famous woman indeed. She first shows up looking pert and pretty in basic black, keeping an appointment with Preysing, who needs a temporary secretary. Flaemmchen manages to keep the industrialist (who repulses her) on his toes, but when he suggests she accompany him on a trip to London for more than merely business purposes, she reluctantly agrees. Some might feel that Joan could have done more to get across her character's ambivalence over what could not have been an easy decision, but one senses that Flaemmchen had long since made up her mind that should such an opportunity present itself, she would seize it—much like Joan herself. In these scenes, wise Joan didn't let the great Wallace Beery intimidate her, any more than Flaemmchen did Preysing. Beery was not impressed by Joan—or at least he pretended not to be. He barely spoke to her when the cameras stopped rolling, and spent most of his time studying his lines in his dressing room, studiously avoiding her. Joan admired his talent, but not the man himself—so she couldn't have cared less if he wanted to be alone (à la Garbo).

Joan also did not let herself be intimidated by the Great Barrymore Brothers, John and Lionel, but she was thrilled to be working with them. The boys have their first scenes with Joan outside Preysing's hotel room. When she first encounters the impoverished baron, who makes a date with her, she's half flirtatious and half pert with him—Joan and John are marvelous together—and she's also a little wary of the elderly Kringelein, who innocently invites her to share some caviar with him. At the end of the picture, Joan plays very affectingly with Lionel when Kringelein asks her to go away with *him*, after Preysing is arrested for killing the baron. Flaemmchen realizes that, unlike the industrialist, this man's intentions are not lecherous, and she goes off with him just as much because she cares about him as because she is interested in his money. Joan credited Lionel for helping her be believable in that scene: "He was so appealing, so gentle and joyous, he all but broke my heart. Any wonder these scenes were believable?" Lionel could be moody, but she found him a joy to work with. A great deal of time was wasted by cast and crew members searching for the little fake mustache he wore, which was always dropping off his lip and disappearing. She also enjoyed acting with John, who was generally giddy or hung over, but a consummate professional once the cameras were rolling.

If Joan was not intimidated by the male stars of *Grand Hotel,* it was a different story with Greta Garbo, whom she admired and envied. Garbo was generally considered a much greater actress than Joan, but in *Grand Hotel* this is far from apparent. Garbo was at her best in *Camille,* but in *Grand Hotel* she seems artificial and "actressy." To be fair, she is playing a very airy and affected prima-donna type, and she does have some strong moments, but in general she does not come off nearly as well as Joan does. It is also true that Joan's Flaemmchen is perhaps an easier part. Joan's character merely had to latch onto a nice guy with money after the nasty guy with money is removed from the scene; Garbo's character had to fall in love, virtually at first sight, with a man—the baron—who entered her room to steal her jewelry! It would be tough for any actress to make that entirely believable. Playing a ballerina who fears she is losing her audience, talent, and youth, Garbo mostly fails to get across her character's desperation, exactly the characteristic Joan was so good at portraying. In *Photoplay,* James Quirk wrote, "The story is not all Garbo. Joan Crawford gives excellent competition and moves up along her ladder of successes."

The two actresses had no scenes together. Garbo even came in later in the day to shoot her scenes, after Joan had gone home. For the previous few years at the studio, Garbo had more or less avoided Joan entirely. Joan would greet Garbo from a slight distance, and Garbo would respond with the barest nod. Joan never pursued a friendship with Garbo. The two women were attracted to each other and were possibly afraid to get too chummy in front of studio gossips. Both also recognized that they were rivals. This competition erupted when Garbo demanded that Joan's scenes be trimmed—or else. As Garbo was the bigger star, this presented a problem. Although Mayer insisted that no cuts be made, it may explain why Joan's role seems underwritten, her time on-screen so limited. As it stands, the film is nearly two hours long, so there may have been some judicious cutting that had nothing to do with Garbo. Joan literally bumped into Garbo one day on the soundstage; Garbo finally deigned to speak to Joan, muttering something about what a shame it was that they were in the same picture, yet not working together. When she found out later what Garbo had tried to do to her scenes in the picture, Joan was furious. "That bitch thinks she's so much better than me, does she?" she screamed to Jerry Asher. "She's jealous because I'm a lot better-looking than she is. She doesn't even have breasts!" Joan appeared at the premiere of *Grand Hotel* to the delight of her fans, but when "Garbo" showed up, it turned out to be Wallace Beery in drag. "I didn't know he had a sense of humor," Joan said. "At least he has bigger boobs than Garbo."

In later years, Joan would alternate between high regard for Garbo as an artist and fellow star, and annoyance at her reclusive tendencies. Joan did not give up on pictures until they gave up on her. Garbo announced her retirement and simply disappeared. Joan even gently castigated her in her autobiography: "To this day I deplore the fact that she is unable to share herself with the world. What a waste! . . . If only she hadn't been so afraid, she wouldn't today be a lonely stranger on Fifth Avenue, fleeing before recognition." Joan was so much better able to deal with being a star and everything that came with it. In private, she could be harsher about Garbo. "She's let herself go all to hell. She walks along the sidewalk and runs across the street through the cars when somebody notices her, like an animal, a furtive rodent. It's a wonder anybody notices her—she looks like a bag lady. I heard that she's simply stopped bathing." Although *Grand Hotel* placed Joan in the top echelon of stars, making her every bit as acclaimed as Garbo (if not more so), she never forgave anyone who didn't want to know her, and Garbo had practically snubbed her. Although Joan got a handful of negative notices for *Grand Hotel,* reaction to Garbo was even more mixed. Joan came out the winner in what Jerry Asher once called the "*Grand Hotel* Bitch Fight of 1932."

Edmund Goulding helmed *Grand Hotel* and found that this time Joan hardly needed any direction. "You're thinking with your heart, Joan," he told her. Goulding obviously noticed how much the camera loved Joan. Even in the powerful bar sequence in which Kringelein confronts his employer Preysing and winds up collapsing into tears over his condition, Goulding uses a three-shot, the third actor being Joan, and eschews close-ups of the men, even of Lionel, minimizing the impact of this heartbreaking moment. *Grand Hotel* ends relatively happily for Flaemmchen (although one wonders what her fate will be, once Kringelein runs out of money and/or dies), but it is nevertheless a tearjerker par excellence. The compassionate baron is murdered, and the prima ballerina, for whom the baron represents a new beginning, goes off to meet him at the station, unaware that he is dead. Even the baron's dachshund Adolphus—"the only thing in the world he really loved"—gets walked out of the hotel lobby, presumably to the pound and eventual destruction. Anyone need a Kleenex?

Joan always loved *Grand Hotel* and regarded it as her career highlight up to that point. She loved her performance in it, as well as the fact that she held her own not only with the powerhouse male costars but even with the Great and Powerful Garbo.

If there were still any doubt, Joan proved that she was an expressive, poignant, and sensitive actress with her next performance, in *Letty Lynton* (1932). In this movie, she played the title character, who is pursued by her lothario of a lover Emile (Nils Asther) to New York. There she meets Hale Darrow (Robert Montgomery), a more respectable man who wants to marry her—until Emile shows up, threatening to ruin everything. Letty goes to Emile's hotel to plead with him, planning to drink poison in front of him if he doesn't relent. Instead Emile inadvertently drinks the poisoned potion himself—and Joan doesn't stop him! The surprising and somewhat immoral wind-up has Joan getting off scot-free (not even charged with involuntary manslaughter) due to the lying intervention of her fiancé and mother. This is a minor drama, but Joan's performances and those of the supporting cast certainly make the movie absorbing. It also helped that director Clarence Brown, with whom Joan had worked on *Possessed,* was again at the helm. As Joan was now playing not a shopgirl but a socialite, this time there could be no complaints about her impeccable diction or air of sophistication. The renowned designer Adrian came up with some exquisite gowns for her—one critic commented that they would be "the talk of the town." Years later, *Letty Lynton* remained one of Joan's favorite movies.

Joan had one of her best early roles in *Rain* (1932), although she later disavowed her performance. Based on a story by W. Somerset Maugham, *Rain* takes place on the island of Pago Pago, where a group of travelers are temporarily stranded due to a sailor becoming stricken with cholera. Among the group is one Sadie Thompson (Joan), a prostitute seeking a better life than the one she left behind in Honolulu, and a stern missionary couple, the Davidsons (Walter Huston and Beulah Bondi), who object mightily to everything the garish, fun-loving, excessively berouged Sadie stands for. Mr. Davidson tries to get Sadie deported back to San Francisco, where she claims she faces jail time for an unspecified crime she didn't commit. Sadie's naïveté and vulnerability are no match for Mr. Davidson's powers of persuasion, and before long she is "born again" and anxious to go back to the States to atone for her sins. Even a marine she calls "Handsome" (William Gargan) who wants to marry her can't divert Sadie from her new course. (This plot development—marine and all—is not in "Miss Sadie Thompson," the original Maugham story.) Then one night Mr. Davidson succumbs to temptation and enters Sadie's room with lascivious intent. The next day, Mr. Davidson is found dead by his own hand on the beach, and Sadie is back in full makeup and sexy costume, disgusted with all men but willing to give "Handsome" and his matrimonial offer a go of it.

Rain is a fascinating study of sexual repression and religious hypocrisy that still resonates, decades after its initial release. Joan's performance, both before and after her conversion, is generally outstanding. She has many powerful moments, such as when she tells Mr. Davidson off ("You'd tear the heart out of your own grandmother if she didn't think your way.") every bit as forcefully as when Mr. Davidson tries to scare the devil out of Sadie. Joan is especially impressive in her quieter moments, registering a sincere change in attitude when "Handsome" begs her to run away with him instead of returning to the States.

Joan always hated her performance in *Rain* because of the negative reaction of critics and some of her fans. For the first time in her life, she received hate mail. The shopgirls she had essayed before may not have been paragons of virtue, but they were not as cheap and common as Sadie and they were not prostitutes; some were outraged by this new portrayal. In other words, Sadie Thompson wasn't "a nice girl," and Joan's more sanctimonious fans objected to her in much the same way that the pious Mr. Davidson did. A harsh assessment of both Joan's performance and her makeup in *Variety* asserted that Joan was out of her depth and that "pavement pounders don't quite trick themselves up as fantastically as all that," leading wags to wonder exactly how the reviewer would know unless he hung out with streetwalkers. Joan truly feared that *Rain* might cause her to slip as a movie star.

It didn't help that she had little rapport with her costars, most of whom were from the New York theater. They all remembered Jeanne Eagels essaying the role on the stage, and Gloria Swanson in the silent film version. In fact, the character of Sadie Thompson had been the stuff of parody for years, and director Lewis Milestone had little faith that a new version would make anyone take the character any more seriously. Milestone also liked to plan many of the camera movements ahead of time, frustrating Joan, who wanted more spontaneity. Joan decided to let Milestone attend to the camera angles and basically direct herself as Sadie Thompson. Always preferring to rely on a strong director, Joan always worried that she had made some wrong decisions in *Rain*. She didn't make many.

Milestone did provide Joan with a great introduction. First we see a close-up of one of her hands pulling aside the beaded curtain over the entrance to her room; then the other hand. This is followed by a close up of one foot stepping forward; then the other foot. Then we cut to a full-length shot of Joan, complete with patented sneer, lustful eyes, provocative manner, and painted lips promising fun and fulfillment. Playwright Maxwell Anderson, who adapted Maugham's story, gave Joan and the other actors some trenchant dialogue, such as when Horn, the proprietor of the general store/makeshift inn where Sadie and the others hang out, remarks on rumors of Sadie's past: "We've all crossed thresholds we don't brag about." When "Handsome" asks Sadie to marry him, he hints that he knows all about her past by saying "knowing the worst to begin with isn't the worst way to begin."

Milestone "opened up" the story by filming many exterior shots of soldiers marching, natives dancing, and lots of rain: rain on leaves, rain on the sand, rain overflowing water barrels, rain cascading into puddles, all of which gave the picture a soggy but highly effective atmosphere. Although the camera is frequently in motion during the interior scenes, Milestone's use of long takes made some indoor scenes still feel stagebound. Joan's performance was clearly not crafted in the editing room, as she often has long stretches of dialogue in shots that go on for several minutes. Joan was so uncomfortable with the long takes—it was too much like being in a play—and with this kind of filming in general, that she never realized how good her performance was. In later years she could hardly bring herself to even look at the film and see why others found her so excellent. "Every actress is entitled to a few mistakes, and that was one of mine," she said. "I don't care what anybody says, I was rotten." It was decades before *Rain*—and Joan's performance—came to be more appreciated.

Although it should be clear from the performances, certain elements of *Rain* have often been misconstrued. For instance, some think that

Sadie's conversion to religion is a sham, simply a ploy of hers to gain control of Davidson, but this is not the case. If the idea were simply to outwit Davidson, all she had to do was run away with "Handsome." There is also confusion over the fact that Davidson does not actually drown in the sea where his body is found, but dies of an apparently self-inflicted throat wound. Could "Handsome" have followed Davidson and cut his throat? William Gargan's performance suggests that this is not the case, and that Davidson did commit suicide, as in the short story.

Some of the negative critical and fan reaction to *Rain* had more to do with its exposure of religious hypocrisy than it did to how much lipstick Joan wore as Sadie. The picture dares to present the missionaries as unloving, cold-hearted, intractable bigots who expect everyone else to live by their own religious tenets—or be damned. Conservative critics felt the picture failed to present honest, caring religious types who are much different from the Davidsons, but they missed the point of the picture. While it would certainly be simplistic to suggest that Joan's own conversion to Christian Science late in life was similar to Sadie's conversion in *Rain,* Joan's own animosity to the film may have had something to do with its deliberately one-sided, negative view of religionists.

Rain was filmed on Catalina Island, where Douglas Fairbanks Jr. would fly out to try to talk to Joan, who insisted that she needed to be left alone so she could concentrate on her part. In truth, she had had her fill of Doug Jr., and right then wasn't certain if she had a future with Clark Gable or not.

But a new man, an unexpected man, would enter the equation and throw Joan into a tizzy that would rock her emotions and have a disturbing effect upon her life.

Chapter Six

SKIN TONE

Whether or not Joan had fallen in love with Clark Gable, her marriage to Douglas Fairbanks Jr. was probably doomed from the start. In many ways Doug was a spoiled, isolated child of privilege who had married a comparatively sophisticated older woman who had pulled herself up by her bootstraps. For all his charm and levity, Fairbanks was, emotionally speaking, a boy who'd had everything handed to him at birth—by contrast, Joan had had to struggle for the same things. "Looking back," Joan remembered, "it would probably be unfair of me to say Doug was superficial and I was so world-weary, but frankly that's the way that it seemed sometimes. Doug didn't know anything about struggle, he'd never wanted for anything, he knew so little of the world outside his tiny sphere, and didn't seem all that interested. No wonder he was content. But I wanted it all. Sitting home waiting for the phone to ring and his vapid friends to come over was not for me." Although Joan wrote in her memoirs that it was Doug who wanted to go out all the time and she who wanted quiet evenings at home, Joan increasingly found married life at "El Jodo" a tiresome strain. The puppyish antics of callow Doug made him seem like an adolescent, especially when compared with the manly charms and unprivileged directness of Clark Gable, who had come from a background very similar to Joan's. Gable was the grown man; Doug, the emotional teenager. After a while, Joan grew tired of Doug, the way a child does of a pet that requires more care and attention than the child had bargained for.

Another bone of contention was that, despite the career inroads made by Doug Jr. resulting from the publicity lavished on his relationship with Joan, he was not as big a star as his wife. Doug was old-fashioned, suggesting that Joan give up her career and let him be the sole bread-winner—a sure sign that he never really understood his wife at all.

Then there was the lack of children. "I didn't need another child," Joan said, "I already had one in Doug." In her autobiography, Joan mentioned several miscarriages; privately she admitted that on at least one occasion she had had an abortion. She hid this fact from Doug, just as she hid her affair with Gable. By the time Doug learned of her involvement with her frequent costar, he was indulging in extracurricular activities of his own. It has been suggested that Louis B. Mayer forced Joan to stop seeing Gable, insisting that she make her marriage to Doug Jr. work—or else—but this is unlikely. The press of that era was not as rapacious as the supermarket scandal sheets of today. To be sure, there were blind items about Joan and Gable in some of the columns, but Mayer rightly figured that without solid evidence these stories would only serve to titillate most of their fans, not alienate them. In other words, publicity was publicity. Even when the columnists reported, in 1933, that Joan and Doug were divorcing, it meant still more publicity—plus sympathy for Joan, the working class heroine whose Cinderella marriage had failed. Indeed, the fans may have reasoned that Doug Jr. was, like his father, a little too "swashbuckling." Those pesky Gable rumors? Who could blame Joan if she turned to the manly arms of Gable for consolation and comfort? Too bad the handsome lug was married. Her fans wondered, would little Joan ever find happiness? Joan's father-in-law, Douglas Fairbanks Sr., who had always been pathologically jealous of his son (despite the show of closeness he had with him in later years), had actually counseled Joan to divorce Doug Jr., if she was that unhappy. Doug Sr. figured that if he couldn't keep his son from having a successful career, at least he could ensure that he didn't hold on to the hot number he himself wasn't man enough to handle.

As Doug Sr.'s own marriage to Mary Pickford was falling apart, Joan assumed that he was simply identifying with her situation and speaking from the heart, without ulterior motives, but in later years she began to wonder. It didn't matter. Even without her father-in-law's approval, she would undoubtedly have divorced Doug Jr. in time. Doug Jr. still spoke well of Joan months before his death in May 2000. "We remained very good friends for a long time, a very satisfactory friendship after the marriage, as such," he remembered. "I loved traveling, and people, and coming back to New York, going over to London and Paris. And she just liked to be, naturally, back at work—which was admirable. But she was only happy when she was at MGM studios, which was fine for her, but not for me." Asked by interviewer Steve Randisi if Joan was totally absorbed by her career, he replied, "Yes, which explains, in part, her great success."

While the columnists had a field day, Joan shrugged her shoulders and reported to the studio for her next picture. She was, for all intents and purposes, free of Doug Jr., and mostly free of Gable (physically, if not emotionally), by the time she met the next man in her life, Franchot Tone, who did not figure at all in Joan's divorce with Doug.

Today We Live (1933) marked the only time Joan ever worked with Gary Cooper. Joan played Diana Boyce-Smith, an English playgirl during the World War I period. Diana is carrying on with British naval officer Claude Hope (Robert Young), but falls for American pilot Richard Bogard, played by Cooper. Franchot Tone, a serious Broadway theater personality, was cast as Diana's brother Ronnie. The storyline has Ronnie and Claude sacrificing their lives in order to save Bogard, who has volunteered for a suicide mission, because they realize how much Joan has come to care for him. Joan got good reviews for the picture, which was met with mixed notices and didn't do well at the box office. The general consensus was that Joan didn't look at all like an English "Boyce-Smith" type, but that her portrayal was, as one critic put it, "steadfast and earnest." Joan remembered that she was "extremely uncomfortable with a British accent." The screenplay was based on a short story and screen treatment by William Faulkner, but there was little Faulkner left by the time the other screenwriters got through with it. The character of Diana was written in late to inject some romantic interest to the story. The studio, which had to pay Joan whether she worked or not, wanted to take advantage of her services. Joan was not crazy about the assignment, and director Howard Hawks wasn't happy with Joan's involvement either. Hawks had conceived of *Today We Live* as a "man's movie," but the two agreed to make the best of it and got along very well. Joan had pleasant memories of the movie, chiefly because of her costars and director. The man who made the biggest impression on her, of course, was her future husband, Franchot Tone.

Franchot Tone, as of 1933, represented everything positive to Joan, everything she aspired to, everything she felt would give her life ultimate meaning and purpose: fulfillment and a kind of peace she had never known and, at times, had felt she never would know. She was 29 years old in 1933, she had failed at one marriage, and Gable's married status was, of course, one of the factors that had rendered his involvement with her an unstable situation at best.

And here was Franchot, handsome, sexy, accomplished, cultivated and—she knew without feeling in the least threatened by it—a far finer actor than she. (In this, she was ultimately to be proven wrong, for her performances in the 1940's would establish her own credentials as a fine artist.) She loved Tone's theatrical bona fides, his impeccable manners, and his distinguished collegiate background. And, of course, that she found his famous voice romantic and sexy and masculine was the proverbial icing on the cake. Tone was a completely different type than either Doug Jr. or Gable. Doug had tried to be a mentor to Joan, but he was too young to carry that off, and he was certainly not as sophisticated as she was. Joan loved Gable, but she couldn't look up to him because he came from a background similar to hers and was too rough-hewn and uncultured. Franchot Tone was the mentor/father figure she had been seeking in Doug Jr., but at the same time he was the experienced lover and adult that Gable was. In other words, the complete package.

But Joan proceeded cautiously. Thinking of what had happened to her and Doug, as well as to Doug's father and Mary Pickford, she wondered if it were even possible for a marriage between two actors to succeed, especially when the female partner was as ambitious as she was. Joan and Tone did several pictures together and she became thoroughly conversant with his splendidly honed acting style. Two years passed; they did well together before the cameras, and the chemistry was right. They became lovers, and the chemistry was eminently right there as well. Finally she decided to take the plunge. On October 11, 1935, they were married.

Later there was speculation that she had stepped up the marriage plans because she feared competition from Bette Davis, who costarred with Tone when he was on loan to Warner Brothers for a picture aptly titled (from Joan's perspective, anyway) *Dangerous*. She was not blind to the chemistry between them that raged during the *Dangerous* shoot—in spite of Davis's marriage to Ham Nelson—nor was she (or anyone else) unaware of the great crush Davis had on Tone. Tone would join Joan for lunch in her dressing room on the adjoining set, and return to his own set smeared with her lipstick, as if Joan were marking her territory. As Davis later wrote, "I was jealous, of course." Joan knew that Davis was as sexually aggressive as she was and was afraid she would get ideas. According to Harry Joe Brown, the producer of *Dangerous*, she did: Brown swore he saw Davis and Tone in a compromising position one time when they left the door to Bette's dressing room unlocked. "And when they saw me they didn't seem to give a damn!" he recalled. Whether Joan believed the rumors of Davis fellating Tone or not, she knew that marriage might convince Davis that her relationship with Tone would never amount to more than a quickly forgotten fling. She and Tone tied the knot before *Dangerous* was released.

Before the marriage took place, Joan did several pictures, both with and without her lover. In *Dancing Lady* (1933), she was teamed with Gable and Tone. She plays Janie Barlow, a burlesque performer who is torn between wealthy paramour Tod Newton (Tone), who starts a romance with her after he bails her out when her club is raided, and Broadway dance director Patch Gallagher (Gable), who, as expected, can't stand rich, entitled fellows like Newton. Joan gave a snappy, mostly excellent performance, vividly conveying Janie's vulnerability, her resentment over her lot in life, and her anger at Newton's condescension. However, in the scene in which Gable informs her that she's out of the chorus, Joan's reaction isn't strong enough.

Joan was less successful as singer and dancer, as usual. She remembered, "I never worked harder than on *Dancing Lady*,"—and she had to. Her singing voice at this time was mediocre and unpleasantly deep. She also had the misfortune of being teamed with none other than Fred Astaire—in his first movie—for a couple of dance numbers. Joan's dancing is adequate, but she doesn't have anything like the natural rhythm, flow, or grace that distinguishes a genius like Astaire from a somewhat talented amateur. Some say that she was dancing on a broken ankle against her doctor's advice during these scenes, as if to explain her inferiority to Astaire, but not even Joan would ever have suggested that she was in Astaire's league. And it was very unlikely she would—or even could—dance on a broken ankle, despite her claims in her memoirs. "I was knocking myself out to dance as well as the chorus girls," Joan recalled. Earlier in the film she does a solo dance, which is, similarly, adequate but unspectacular.

Gable acted with his usual charisma, and Newton's fascination with Janie reflected Tone's true feelings toward Joan at the time. A bit player who walks angrily out of a producer's office was Eve Arden, who would later have a major role in *Mildred Pierce,* one of Joan's most famous movies. And the fellows who accompany Janie when she auditions for Patch Gallagher's Broadway show are, incredibly, The Three Stooges—making for what must be one of the most bizarre juxtapositions of Hollywood types in motion picture history!

Dancing Lady offers mostly show business clichés and hardly goes into any of the realities of life in the chorus, although it is on the mark in depicting how girls with well-heeled boyfriends often find a sexual shortcut to stardom. Robert Z. Leonard's often interesting direction helps make it all palatable. There's a wonderful below-the-knee montage of Janie following Patch through the busy city streets, and the extravagant production pulls out all the stops in the handsome, elaborate, and expensive musical numbers. In a scene that could only happen in an old MGM musical, the platform on which Janie is dancing on opening night rises up, seems actually to pass through the ceiling and leave the building, floats through the clouds over bustling Manhattan, and lands in a village which is apparently, somehow, still on the stage of the theater. Remarkable. This kind of cinematic license was typical of Hollywood musicals in that era, as if Hollywood were anxious to offer effects that weren't possible on Broadway. The pleasant songs, which Joan found only "pretty fair," were composed by Burton Lane, who would later have major successes with Broadway musicals like *Finian's Rainbow* and *On a Clear Day You Can See Forever.*

In *Sadie McKee* (1934), Joan played the title character, who loses out on love when Tommy (Gene Raymond), a handsome singer, leaves her to go on the road with Opal (Jean Dixon). On the rebound, Sadie marries Jack Brennan (Edward Arnold), an alcoholic millionaire she likes but for whom she feels no true passion. Mike Alderson (Tone), for whom Sadie had worked as maid, looks on disapprovingly as she carries a torch for Tommy. Although certain sections of *Sadie McKee* have bite and sparkle, the script, by Viña Delmar and John Meehan, and Clarence Brown's direction are both too perfunctory to make the movie anything more than a mediocre divertissement. Joan isn't bad in the film, and Tone and the others supply good support—Arnold is especially memorable. Joan thought that the plot was too similar to so many others she'd done—"the Crawford formula," she called it—and made sure that at least Adrian would make her look different (if still glamorous), with slicked-back hair, simple but effective clothing, and, oddly, untweezed eyebrows. Over the years, Joan's initial dissatisfaction with the film gave way to a perhaps time-distorted appreciation. "That one just worked, didn't it? Everything worked."

In *Chained* (1934), also helmed by Clarence Brown, Joan played Diane Lovering, the mistress of her employer Richard Field (Otto Kruger), who, wanting to marry her, sends her on an ocean voyage to think it over. There she meets and falls in love with nice-guy rancher Mike Bradley (Gable). She winds up in an untenable and poignant situation, torn between a kindly, loving older man and Gable, who represents all-out passion and youthful abandon. The effective (if minor) drama is watchable and entertaining, with fine performances, some good scenes and funny moments, and a rather pat and convenient conclusion, with the older man turning out to be improbably understanding. Years later, Joan thought

Chained worked because of the "Crawford-Gable sex magnetism." Otto Kruger recalled that "it wasn't easy being in a picture with those two and expecting to get any share of the attention, but they both were marvelous, fun to work with, and not at all into upstaging or hogging the action. Purely professional."

Another reason *Chained* may have worked, at least as far as Joan was concerned, was how she was shot. *Chained* began her association with cinematographer George Folsey, who lit her beautiful bone structure for seven films after *Chained*. Folsey highlighted what he thought were Joan's best features: her eyes and her cheekbones. He photographed her from slightly above and instructed her to keep her head high, using a 500-watt key light coated with oil to get the desired effect. To Joan, the effect was breathtaking.

It was while Joan was working on *Chained* that she finally met her biological father, Thomas LeSueur, who got in touch with her once she'd become a star. Once it was verified that he actually was who he said he was, Joan entered into a correspondence with him. Then she invited him to the set and he told her how proud he was of her. But it was too little, too late. By this time, Joan did not trust fathers, or for that matter father figures. After a few minutes of awkward conversation, Joan was called back to work and her father went off on his way. "The man was a complete stranger," Joan said. "When I was an innocent baby he couldn't be bothered with me. I accepted that he had to find his own path, but he had to accept it too. I have no idea what he was hoping to get, or if he was hoping to get anything as 'Joan Crawford's Father,' but it never came to that. He went out of my life a second time as quickly as the first."

Although *Forsaking all Others* (1934) again combined Joan and Gable for more romantic fireworks—with the added bonuses of Robert Montgomery and Rosalind Russell—the picture was a major disappointment. In this comedy of errors and mismatched emotions, the leads couldn't be faulted; a poor script was to blame, despite some snappy dialogue and tasty situations. Even the brisk pacing of "One-Take" Woody Van Dyke couldn't save it. It didn't help that Montgomery tried too hard to come on like Bob Hope, who was a completely different kind of actor. The stars did have a lot more fun, as Montgomery confirmed. "We all did our best to keep the darn thing afloat," said Montgomery. "You couldn't ask for better costars. Lots of laughs on the set, I remember; maybe not in the audience." According to Joan, "That one wasn't very good but the cast helped."

Her first 1935 feature, *No More Ladies,* was similarly helped by a strong cast, which included Joan, Tone, and Robert Montgomery. Here she played Marcia Townsend, a society gal who marries Sherry Warren (Montgomery), who turns out to be unfaithful. Jim Slaston (Tone) begs Marcia to dump Sherry so that he can marry her and treat her the way she deserves, but she is determined to stick with her marriage. Marcia organizes a party to which she invites every person she can think of that her husband wronged—especially cuckolded husbands and jilted ladies—then pretends to have an affair with Jim. Marcia winds up back with a chastened and reformed Sherry at the film's conclusion.

No More Ladies was mainly notable as the first time Joan would work with a former dialogue director named George Cukor, who would later direct some of her more interesting pictures. He took over as director of *No More Ladies* when the original director, E.H. Griffith, came down with pneumonia. Joan regarded the occasionally caustic and condescending Cukor as a "theater person" who looked down his nose at movie people—in the beginning, at least. "Later I really loved George," she said. "But it took me a while to warm up to him. And vice versa." Her relationship with Cukor would become extremely important to her career later on, although at the time Joan thought that the best thing about making *No More Ladies* was the chance to work and be with Tone. It was during this film that Joan really began to fall for him—he obviously reciprocated her feelings, as he asked her to marry him when the shoot was over. Joan agreed and the two became officially engaged.

"It was illuminating to watch [Franchot] work with Cukor, both of them from the theater, speaking the same language," she would say. As for *No More Ladies,* Joan would admit that Edna May Oliver as Fanny, the tippling grandmother, stole the movie. She would criticize her performance in later years, coming to agree with those critics who saw her as being overly mannered and artificial. She claimed that Cukor tried to help her but that she wouldn't listen, having at that time much more motion-picture experience than he did. She recalled with amusement how she read a speech for the director, confident that she was delivering it with the required forcefulness; completely unimpressed, Cukor told her to "put some *feeling* into it, please!" Joan did not like being criticized by comparative cinematic neophytes. "He took me over the coals until I gave every word *meaning*," she remembered.

I Live My Life (1935) is an above-average Joan Crawford comedy in which she played Kay Bentley, a saucy heiress who is engaged to her stiff boyfriend, who might bail her father (Frank Morgan) out of a financial jam. While vacationing in the Greek Isles, Joan has a playful dalliance with archeologist Terry O'Neill (Brian Aherne), who follows her home to America, much to her surprise. Complications ensue before the two of them finally make it to the altar—although one wonders how long this marriage will really last. This spirited picture hasn't dated at all, featuring terrific comic performances by the two leads. Frank Morgan and Jessie Ralph score as Crawford's dad and her formidable old tigress of a grandmother, respectively. While Joan was making the film, Tone was in Catalina appearing in *Mutiny on the Bounty*. Joan dismissed *I Live My Life* as "another formula film."

For the first year or so, the Crawford-Tone marriage went well, at least as Joan remembered it. Tone got Joan interested in "treading the boards," and they opened a small informal theater behind her garden, where they performed both classical and popular pieces. Tone also encouraged her singing efforts. Reports that she was considering opera, however, seem absurd, as her voice did not begin to qualify for such artistry, but she nevertheless studied with vocal coaches, and Tone praised her dedication and hard work. At one point, they hired Romano Romani, vocal coach of the legendary soprano Rosa Ponselle, to give them voice lessons. "Our house resounded with arias," she wrote in her memoirs. "When Rosa Ponselle visited from the east, she and I sang a duet from *Tales of Hoffmann*." One can only imagine what the great Ponselle made of Joan (or, indeed, what Romano made of her, but at least he was handsomely paid for his efforts). Joan's "singing" was unfortunately encouraged by Tone, who also fancied himself a distinctive vocal presence. Joan fell for Tone's flattery, seeing this as another way of distancing herself from her déclassé past. If singing opera would make her respectable and classy, then she would sing opera—not very well, alas. This is made all too clear by a 1938 private recording of Joan singing a duet of Verdi's "Recordatus" with an unnamed operatic soprano who sounds like (and probably is) Ponselle. Joan's warbling on the recording seems surprisingly acceptable, but then the professional soprano joins in, and the difference between real operatic singing and ersatz imitation becomes plain. However, their social life was rewarding and pleasurable, and Joan enthusiastically met her husband's friends from the world of the theater.

But there was one major problem: Tone's career was not keeping pace with Joan's. She was a major star, with a major star's devoted following. Her name always appeared above the title, joined at times with costars like Clark Gable, William Powell, and Robert Montgomery. Franchot never got past supporting-actor status, at least in Joan's films.

On loanout he did slightly better, even qualifying as leading man at times, as in the 1936 *The King Steps Out.*

Back at his home base MGM, Tone was still Mr. Also-Ran. His fan mail was there, to be sure, in decent numbers, but Mayer simply did not consider him to be major star material. He was not conventionally handsome in the Robert Montgomery style, or sexily charismatic in the raffish Gable mold. His head was oddly shaped, at least for a potential star, and his aristocratic good looks did not register on-screen as much as people expected. Tone became acutely aware that his Hollywood career would always have certain built-in limitations. This dawning frustration eventually grew into resentment. His wife's far greater fame galled him; he hated being second fiddle. Joan tried to help, urging Mayer to cast Tone in more ambitious roles, but in his usual blunt, forthright way Mayer forced Joan to accept the realities about her husband. He was registering pleasantly enough with the fans, but the response to him was just not major. The sum of Mayer's advice was: Franchot is a fine actor, but when it comes to major stardom, there was something lacking.

Tone knew it, too. He became increasingly bitter.

Joan's next film, *The Gorgeous Hussy,* began what might have been a rewarding association with producer Joseph L. Mankiewicz, who had been a dialogue writer for early talkies. He was one of the writers on *Forsaking All Others,* which had originally been planned for Loretta Young. (He also worked on *I Live My Life.*) When producer Bernard Hyman decided to use Joan instead, he dispatched Mankiewicz to Joan's house to read her the script. Mankiewicz was in awe of the glamour surrounding Joan at her Brentwood estate, which he likened to a film set. Of course Joan appeared beautifully coiffed and made up, as always. She didn't warm up to the script until he said the line "I could build a fire by rubbing two boy scouts together." Joan always credited Mankiewicz with saving many of her scripts with his intelligent revisions, and she felt that they got along so well because Mankiewicz understood that she had different moods and simply let her run with them. How he dealt with her depended upon the mood she was in.

"I was madly in love with him," said Joan, referring to a later period of their relationship when Tone was out of the picture. "I don't know of any woman who knew him at all who wasn't in love with him. He gave me such a feeling of security, I felt I could do anything in the world. . . . He relaxed me, teaching me to have fun in my work. I'd had joy, not fun. He brought that out of me, frothy or not." Joan's relationship with Mankiewicz was one of several factors that broke up his marriage to socialite-actress Elizabeth Young. At a dinner party at the Mankiewicz home, Young became hysterical when she noticed that her husband had been missing for quite some time—as was Joan. However, it turned out they had only gone to look at their new baby. Joan was overheard telling Mankiewicz that the baby should have been hers.

"I would never have married Joseph Mankiewicz," she said years later. "He knew me too well. I don't think he had any interest in marrying me, either." Mankiewicz also claimed that he enjoyed Joan's varying moods and the way she seemed to be acting even when she was not on the set. Reportedly, he once said, "I could put up with Joan when I was making a picture with her, but living with her would be another matter. Joan for twenty-four hours a day, seven days a week? Not me, brother!" Mankiewicz eventually veered from Joan to other actresses, among them Loretta Young. Years later, Mankiewicz would declare Joan "the consummate movie star: she dressed the part, played it off screen and on, and adored every moment of it."

It was Louis B. Mayer who decided that Mankiewicz would stop writing Joan's features and begin producing them. Mankiewicz noted that most of the MGM producers had a patronizing attitude toward Joan, but he wasn't much better. "She is not demonstrably a proficient actress," he said. While her major performances might still have been ahead of her, the Joan Crawford of the 1930's was still a very skilled motion-picture actress. Mankiewicz didn't see her as being especially sexy, at least not a "sexpot," but he thought she had a certain appeal to "lower-middle-class audiences." No matter how hard she tried, many of her co-workers still saw Joan as "common."

Which makes it doubly strange that the first picture Mankiewicz produced for Joan was her first and last costume drama, *The Gorgeous Hussy* (1936)—hardly something for the shopgirls that supposedly made up Joan's audience. Joan always blamed herself for this picture, for at the time she had much more clout at MGM than Mankiewicz did, and she wanted to do the film very badly. Her desire to do *The Gorgeous Hussy* had everything to do with her competitive spirit toward Greta Garbo and Norma Shearer, her two chief rivals at the studio. She knew that they were considered real actresses and she "merely" a movie star, because they did "serious" pictures and she didn't. Norma had recently appeared in nothing less than Shakespeare (*Romeo and Juliet*), and Garbo had done pictures like *Anna Karenina* and *Camille*. Joan felt there wasn't any reason that she couldn't appear in a period drama herself and silence her critics for good. She also agreed with the critics that she seemed to be making the same film over and over again. *The Gorgeous Hussy* would certainly be different from what had gone before. To his credit, Mankiewicz came to see Joan's side of it and encouraged her desire to broaden her range and style of picture.

In *The Gorgeous Hussy,* Joan played Peggy O'Neill, an innkeeper's daughter and niece of presidential hopeful Andrew Jackson. Peggy is in love with Senator John Randolph (Melvyn Douglas), who doesn't return her affections—at first. She marries a handsome Lieutenant Bow Timberlake (Robert Taylor), who is unfortunately killed shortly after. Finally Randolph realizes his love for her, but their divergent political convictions—he favors states' rights, she the union—keep them apart. Peggy marries Secretary of War John Eaton (Tone) and decides to leave Washington with him because her reputation as a "hussy" would embarrass Jackson's administration.

Watching Joan in *Gorgeous Hussy* for the first time can be a bit disconcerting. In her ringlets, oversized bonnet and frilled puffy sleeves, she appears slightly grotesque, like a younger version of Jane Hudson, Bette Davis's character in *What Ever Happened to Baby Jane?* In her close-ups, however, she is quite beautiful. Although she was criticized at the time of the film's release for being too "modern" in the role of an innkeeper's daughter of 1823, the problem with the movie isn't Joan but the script, or rather, the overall conception. Joan's performance is confident, strong, and completely professional—she is especially good in her love scenes with Melvyn Douglas—but the movie alternates in tone between historical drama and a typical Joan Crawford romance. It's a hybrid that never quite jells, an A-movie with a B-movie script.

A significant complaint about *The Gorgeous Hussy* is that while Joan may have been gorgeous, she wasn't much of a hussy. While married to Eaton, Peggy has a tender moment with Randolph at his deathbed, but while Jackson's political opponents turn it into a scandal, we know that she is merely saying a final good-bye to an old cherished love. Critics charged that the character and storyline had been severely watered down. On the other hand, the character was never intended to be Julie Marsden, Bette Davis's character in *Jezebel*; the whole point is that it is only the gossip of jealous biddies that creates her false image as a trollop, and paints her warm, loving aunt as a moronic hillbilly.

The Gorgeous Hussy was the kind of "historical" picture that only Hollywood could make; one wonders why the publicity department at MGM didn't release it with the tagline "History, yes! And Joan Crawford, too!" The executives at the studio figured the only way they could make this slice of American history palatable to a paying audience looking for escapism was to focus more on Peggy's romantic troubles than on the tumultuous events in Washington D.C.—this was, after all, a Joan Crawford vehicle, and her fans expected something more melodramatic. There are, however, some lively sequences, including one in which Jackson's supporters storm an inn, only to learn that the man they despise has just won the election. Jackson climbs down a trellis and knocks out a man who dares insult his wife Rachel (the wonderful Beulah Bondi, who got an Oscar nomination), whom the Washington elite regards as déclassé. The supporting cast, including Lionel Barrymore as Jackson, Tone as Eaton, Robert Taylor as Timberlake, and James Stewart as another persistent suitor, all offer flavorful performances, and there are many amusing moments. But the movie is never as much fun—or "important"—as it should have been. There was plenty of MGM gloss to the handsome production, and Clarence Brown's direction was brisk, if uninspired: none of this was enough to prevent the picture from ultimately becoming rather dull. The script gives the impression that the reputation of the president's niece is more important than the entire cabinet, or indeed the fate of the country.

Tone was not thrilled that he had so few lines in *The Gorgeous Hussy,* appearing only in some brief sequences late in the picture. Joan once again appealed to Mayer—could he give her husband a larger part in another important picture? Mayer insisted that Secretary of War Eaton needed to be played by an "important actor," saying that "Joan Crawford can't walk off into the sunset with a complete unknown, you know." Joan didn't learn who would play the part until filming had already begun, as Mayer knew she would hit the roof when she found out. "Franchot did it for my sake," she remembered. "It was a major mistake. It was the breaking point in his career, and the breaking point in our marriage, although we didn't realize it at the time." There are those who insist that Tone had an important part and several big scenes in the movie, but Eaton was really a minor supporting role. Tone was so bothered by the situation that he began to show up later and later for his calls, until finally Joan exploded at him in front of the crew and much of the cast. Tone was humiliated, but Joan felt that he was asking for it. By contrast, director Clarence Brown broke his arm one morning, but he managed to arrive at the set only a few minutes late. "There was no good reason why Franchot couldn't have arrived on time like the rest of us," she said. "I know it was a difficult period for him but by not acting like a professional he didn't do himself any good."

Joan practically disavowed *The Gorgeous Hussy* in later years, feeling that she was completely miscast, and that she had only herself and her grand notions to blame. As she told one interviewer, "I think that's where the term 'credibility gap' originated." She ruefully remembered that David O. Selznick had laughed at her suggestion she be cast as Peggy O'Neill, telling her that she was all wrong for the role. At least everything was done to make her as comfortable as possible on the set. For her dressing room, an entire New England–style cottage was erected behind the cameras. And a man was hired to play her favorite records between takes.

The Gorgeous Hussy marked the first time Joan worked with Melvyn Douglas, who was to appear in three more of her films. In his memoirs, Douglas was rather uncomplimentary toward Joan, albeit in a gentlemanly way. He made fun of what he called her "'method' preparation," having noticed that she used different recordings to put her in the mood for certain scenes. This may be true, but Joan liked to listen to music between takes in general, and if a certain piece suggested a particular emotion to her, then there was nothing wrong with that. This did not mean she used records to do her acting for her. Douglas was yet another of her early co-workers who attacked her as a mother with scant evidence but for the publication of Christina's book. Douglas may have been stung by a well-intended but tactless comment in Joan's autobiography to the effect that although he was a fine actor, he would have been an even bigger star had he been better-looking. Another problem was that Douglas and Joan never bonded, possibly because she was not attracted to him and her jealous husband was always nearby. Joan surprised Douglas during the filming of *The Gorgeous Hussy* by being more ladylike than the stories he had heard would have led him to expect. The reason for this might have been that, as this was her first costume drama, she found it necessary to concentrate on the set more than usual and had less time to mingle with the other cast members.

Douglas noticed that Joan, Robert Taylor, Lionel Barrymore and others in the famous cast each showed up on the set every day with an entourage of hairdressers, cosmeticians, and so on. One day he brought some friends, family members, and a couple of dogs with him to the studio, just as a joke. No one got it. But when Joan started wearing sunglasses to hide black eyes and enlisting her makeup crew to cover the bruises on her face and arms, everyone eventually "got it." According to Jerry Asher, "Tone was one of those guys who thinks it's perfectly okay to take out his problems on his wife and smack her around. I think Joan put up with a lot because she felt sorry for him and his situation, and she'd been mistreated by a lot of men in the past. But believe me, when *she* had bruises, *his* bruises were even worse. Joan would only take so much before she'd hit back. I don't just mean throw things, but smack him right back, which he deserved."

Joan was caught in another lousy marriage, but she was determined not to give up on her second union as easily as she had the first. She made excuses for Tone. He hit her because he drank, she rationalized, and he drank because he felt like "Mr. Joan Crawford," a role he detested. Even many years later, she continued to defend Tone, writing in her memoirs, "I don't believe Franchot ever for a moment resented the fact that I was a star. Possibly he resented Hollywood's refusal to let him forget it." Unlike her feelings for Doug Fairbanks Jr., Joan still felt at this time that Franchot was the one and only man for her, her true soul mate. She was in a quandary as to what to do about the whole sorry situation.

And then fate stepped in.

Fate and a sexy starlet.

J.C. Archives, Inc.

Chapter Seven
LOVE ON THE RUN

The Crawford-Tone combination still had a couple of years to self-destruct, but Joan did her best to concentrate on her work and avoid the sullen Tone when he was drinking. Things seemed to be looking up a bit when both were cast in another film together, with the added attraction of Clark Gable. Tempting as it might have been for Joan to seek shelter in the arms of Gable, she was wise enough to know that doing so would only make a bad situation worse. She still hoped her marriage to Tone would magically improve; his becoming as big a movie star as she was would certainly not do their union any harm.

Although Joan always liked *Love On the Run* (1936), the second of her MGM films produced by Joseph Mankiewicz (perhaps because Gable was again her costar, with the added bonus of having her husband around), it was a major disappointment after some of her successes. *Love on the Run* is a distinctly poor imitation of *It Happened One Night*, which Gable had made with Claudette Colbert two years before. *It Happened One Night* had ushered in a sub-genre of "reporter romances runaway heiress" movies—and *Love on the Run* was one of the worst. Although Joan established herself as a skilled comedienne in many other pictures, *Love on the Run* didn't showcase this side of her as well as it might have. The talents of Jean Harlow would have been more appropriate, but the script might have done even Harlow in.

Love on the Run opens with a long shot of a couple in bed. The covers flip up and we see that it isn't Joan with either of her male leads, but rather Gable and Tone, platonically sharing the mattress. It turns out that they are Mike Anthony and Barnabus "Barney" Pells, reporters and friends who are always trying to one-up one another. Barney lords it over his rival when Mike is bound and gagged—a viewer who knows the background can take it as Tone chortling over having snatched Joan away from Gable. Joan stars as Sally Barker, who runs out on her wedding to the Prince of an impoverished nation when she realizes that the groom values her money more than he does Sally. Trailing her from the church, Mike befriends Sally, concealing his profession from her. The twosome impersonate a baron and baroness who are famous aviators, and take flight in their plane, after a nearly catastrophic take-off. Unbeknownst to Sally and Mike, the real aviators are spies who want at all costs to get their hands on an important map on the plane. Meanwhile, rival reporter Barney follows Mike and Sally all over the globe trying to undermine Mike's deceptions.

While the story is efficiently told by director "One-Take" Woody Van Dyke, it simply never catches fire, and the movie eventually becomes quite tedious. The performances are all very professional and adept—just not very amusing. Tone especially lacks the light touch his part requires, and, surprisingly, Joan isn't much better. When Sally finally learns that Mike, with whom she's falling in love, is just another reporter after a story, Joan's reaction isn't strong or funny enough. While no one could accuse Joan of being a brilliant comedienne along the lines of Lucille Ball, she was certainly capable of better than this. Donald Meek temporarily enlivens the picture as the batty caretaker of a palace in which Joan and Gable briefly take refuge; first he dances a minuet with Joan (he thinks she is a ghost haunting the palace), and then he does a snappy jazz number. Aside from this, *Love on the Run* is a comedy virtually devoid of laughs. Joan liked her performance in the film, however, and had a great time making it. In fact, Joan, Gable, and Tone had a ball together.

Love on the Run may not have been stellar, but it made a lot of money. During filming, a crew from *Motion Picture* magazine came to do a photo spread on Joan and Tone on the movie set. *Life* magazine had christened her "Queen of the Movies," and the film journals were not about to be outdone in covering "the queen." Joan had been named the top box-office star for the third year in a row. Joan gave the reporters and photographers from *Motion Picture* the full-glamour treatment. Joan was used to such treatment and could take it in stride, but her husband, less used to being in the limelight and blatantly jealous of the attention paid to his wife, came off a little full of himself. At one point, when he was tired of the flashbulbs directed at his wife (and not himself), he curtly ended the interview and ordered a rug to be unrolled from where Joan was holding court over to her dressing room. Taking her hand, Tone escorted the queen of the movies to her dressing room and closed the door in everyone's faces. They did not emerge for quite some time. But then, dressing room trysts were nothing new to the Tones.

Making *The Last of Mrs. Cheyney* (1937) was not an especially happy experience for Joan. First, in this adaptation of a Frederick Lonsdale play, Joan was again teamed with Robert Montgomery, neither of whom particularly cared for the other. Both Joan and the studio had hoped that teaming Joan with one of their top male leads, William Powell, would generate sparks, but the chemistry just wasn't right. In this tale, Fay Cheyney (Joan) poses as a society gal so that she can rob wealthy social-ites. Joan was arguably better in the part than Norma Shearer in the 1929 adaptation of the material, but then Shearer never had a particular flair for comedy. But not even Joan was a match for Powell, who was entirely in his element. As usual, Joan and Montgomery played well to-gether despite their mutual dislike, which may have helped imbue their interchanges with a peppery acidity. Most critics agreed that this was a story that may have been told once too often, and it does not loom large in the Crawford canon. Crawford herself was always critical of her per-formance in the film, blaming personal problems. "My mind wasn't on it, not one hundred percent. I wasn't embarrassed by my performance, but it's not one I want to be remembered for, either." When asked about the picture many years later, Montgomery snapped, "I barely remember the thing. Joan was fluttering all over the place, as usual. I just came in and did my work and went home at night until it was over. I liked work-ing with Bob [*sic*] Powell, though." Many viewers wondered why Powell had not been teamed with his usual leading lady Myrna Loy, and, in fact, Loy was originally assigned to do *The Last of Mrs. Cheyney*. The trouble was that Joan did not want to do another costume drama—*Parnell*, with Clark Gable—after *The Gorgeous Hussy*, so she and Loy switched parts, with the studio's blessing. *Parnell* turned out to be a bigger bomb than *The Last of Mrs. Cheyney*.

The director, Richard Boleslawski, was terminally ill while making the film, and couldn't muster the needed energy to remedy the problems; sadly, he died before filming was completed. "We knew he was ill," Joan remembered, "but had no idea how really serious it was. I came into the studio one morning and was told he had died during the night. What a shock. Most of the picture had been shot. I think an A.D. [assistant director] finished what was left [it was actually completed by Dorothy Arzner and George Fitzmaurice]. It was not a happy experience for any-one. I think it showed on screen."

Joseph Mankiewicz was not involved in *The Last of Mrs. Cheyney* in any capacity, but he did produce Joan's next feature. In *The Bride Wore Red* (1937), Joan plays Anna Pavlovitch, a broke gal who goes on vacation at a ritzy resort in Turano (financed by an admirer who gives her two weeks to change her life) and finds love and confusion when she falls for two suitors: wealthy Rudi Pal (Robert Young), and Giulio, a poor postman wonderfully played by Tone. Anna knows that Rudi could change her life for the better (and gives little thought to the other woman who's in love with him), but she's more simpatico with Giulio than with rich Rudi. When Anna meets up with an acquaintance, a former B-girl, who (improbably) seems perfectly happy as a hotel maid, she wonders if chasing rainbows is the answer. Still, she continues to resist her attraction to Giulio . . . until she finally gives in. Anna scandalizes everyone late in the picture with the titular red dress, a year before Bette Davis would do the same early in the superior *Jezebel*. With fine supporting performances from George Zucco (as the patron who sends Joan off on her excursion) and others, excellent direction from Dorothy Arzner, and a good Franz Waxman score, *The Bride Wore Red* is certainly not one of Joan's misfires—except for her performance, which is one of her worst. Joan remains on the surface throughout the picture, self-conscious, overrehearsed, and perfunctory, rushing through her lines as if she'd forgotten everything she'd ever learned about acting. She and Tone were not having the easiest time of it during shooting, and then there was the presence of the director, Dorothy Arzner, who had finished the few remaining scenes of *The Last of Mrs. Cheyney* after Boleslawski died.

Joan had thought it would be interesting to have a woman direct one of her films, but with Arzner she got more than she bargained for. Despite her relationships with women and her bisexual nature, Joan never thought of herself as a lesbian, certainly not the stereotypical "dyke" so disdained by homophobes of every generation. Arzner fit that stereotype, unfortunately, which made Joan quite uncomfortable. Joan was also made uneasy by the fact that Arzner was obviously very attracted to her. "I knew she found me sexually desirable, and in a way I felt bad for her," Joan said years later, "but I swear she just made my flesh crawl."

A bigger problem was that despite Arzner's obvious talent, she was simply overawed by Joan, and didn't tell her when she was overdoing things or not doing enough. Despite her talent, there were times, especially when she was preoccupied, that she needed a guiding hand, someone like George Cukor, for instance. Arzner was not in the same league when it came to helping shape a star performance. It didn't help that she didn't want Joan in *The Bride Wore Red* to begin with.

The film was originally to star Luise Rainer. According to Arzner, Mayer himself got down on his knees to beg her to use Joan when Rainer was put on suspension "for marrying a communist." It is unlikely that Mayer would have to beg Arzner to use Joan; he simply would have told Arzner that Joan was in and that was that. It was less that Arzner objected to using Joan, whose participation she feared would make the movie "synthetic," than that the switch in female leads would necessitate major script changes, which is what ended up happening. It is ironic that her attraction to Joan, combined with her resentment that she was in the movie at all, helped bring about precisely the synthetic quality that she was so worried about; in a sense, it was a self-fulfilling prophecy. Things got so bad that by the time the filming was nearing completion, Joan and Arzner refused to talk to each other. Studio publicist Maxine Thomas would carry a written note from Arzner to Joan, wait for Joan's reply, then take the reply to Arzner—and so on.

Joan told one writer that *The Bride Wore Red* was "a waste of time for everyone; what a botch!" On another occasion she denounced it as "just a fashion show; a lot of those early things were fashion shows. The plots didn't matter. After a while, they all seemed alike." One admirer of Joan's, writer Fred Lawrence Guiles, credited Arzner with doing "what no male director could have done as well: she fashioned its thin plot around costumes, or the way Joan dressed—a tactic perhaps appropriate to a film career as dependent upon what the star wore as upon the story or her performance."

Evaluated on its own terms, *The Bride Wore Red* was actually a good movie; it just didn't showcase Joan at her best. It attracted her fans, but not much of a crossover audience. Moviegoers who thought that a little of Joan Crawford went a long way voiced their opinion—by staying away from the theater. When the picture failed to make much money, it helped Joan qualify for inclusion on a prestigious list of fellow professionals labeled "Box-Office Poison." Louis B. Mayer's faith in Joan's durability was unshaken, however, and she was signed to a new five-year contract.

Mannequin (1938) is a slightly above-average movie in which she costars with Spencer Tracy. Joseph Mankiewicz was good friends with both Tracy and Joan (somewhat more than just good friends, in the latter case), and he thought the two would make a good team. In *Mannequin*, Joan played Jessie Cassidy, a factory girl living with her sweet, bedraggled mother and ne'er-do-well father and brother in a tenement on Hester Street in New York. She marries handsome but unworthy Eddie

Miller (Alan Curtis), who then notices that a wealthy shipping man named John Hennessey (Tracy) has his eye on Jessie. Eddie suggests that they get divorced so that Jessie can land Hennessey, divorce him after six months, and then return to Eddie with a large settlement. Repulsed by this plan of her husband's, Jessie walks out on him and the two soon divorce. As fate would have it, Jessie eventually does wind up marrying Hennessey, but when Eddie reappears and tries to cause trouble to raise cash, she decides to walk out on her second husband with just the clothes on her back. When Hennessey's business goes belly-up, however, Jessie decides to prove her love by staying with him and helping him rebuild their lives.

In *Mannequin* we again see the Joan Crawford who won legions of fans, as she plays with simple sincerity, rather than artificiality. Under the sympathetic direction of Frank Borzage, Joan gives one of her finest early performances. Affecting, touching and completely convincing as Jessie, Joan manages to outact the legendary thespian Tracy, who overall gives a good performance but is also at times rather perfunctory. For the most part, Joan and Tracy play very well together, although of course they lack that Gable-Crawford chemistry. Joan is wonderful as she pours out her hopes and fears to her first husband on the subway: "Sometimes I feel kind of old, responsible for everything." Surely the actress was thinking back to the vicissitudes of her own early life. "I took one look at those poor Delancey Street sets and knew I was back home; I *was* Jessie," she wrote in her autobiography. Once again, some critics insisted that Joan was too polished and spoke too well to be a truly convincing tenement-dweller; however, it was precisely this quality that always made her inevitable conversion to wealthy woman more believable.

An interesting aspect of *Mannequin* is that the script by Lawrence Hazard (based on a story by Katherine Brush) is often especially sympathetic to women, at times almost feminist and definitely ahead of its time. Jessie's friend Beryl (played by Mary Phillips, the second Mrs. Humphrey Bogart) tells Tracy, "I'd say you deserve Jessie but I don't believe any man deserves any woman." When Jessie tells Beryl that at least "Eddie Miller took me away from Hester Street," Beryl snaps, "A streetcar coulda done that and cost you less!" Jessie's mother has a sad speech about her past, and the need for Jessie to strike on her own and to get what she wants out of the world, rather than live "a man's life" with her husband, like most women do. Large sections of *Mannequin* are intelligent and literate, but the picture becomes too pat and contrived by the time the movie wraps up.

In her autobiography and early interviews, Joan focused on the positive side of Spencer Tracy. She said that acting opposite Tracy taught her how to underplay (which she did very well in *Mannequin*), but this may have had as much to do with director Borzage as it did Tracy. Tracy was not yet a big star, and perhaps for that reason he was supposedly unimpressed by big stars. He was amused and a little irritated with the way that Joan played the "star game" so obsessively. But Joan also had a steeliness about her that he admired. At first, Joan found Tracy's practical jokes during filming to be relatively harmless and even somewhat amusing, but things changed once the two began an affair. They were both still married and had many clandestine encounters during the shooting of *Mannequin*. Now that Tracy had slept with Joan more than once, he saw her not so much as a strong personality as simply a woman who could be "had," like any other. For her part, Joan found herself turned off by the very things she had first found attractive: his macho appeal and his charming boyishness. Joan was as susceptible to such things as any other woman. Tracy's jokes became more and more obnoxious, as did his behavior when he was drinking, which was often. "He would show up for romantic scenes with beer and onion breath," Joan complained. "I was supposed to act all lovey-dovey with him when I wanted to gag. He was like a big child who needed to be spanked." In later years, Joan rarely spoke well of Tracy in private, although she always felt he had a lot of talent. "His drinking really was the problem," she'd say. "It put an end to any relationship we might have had." Mankiewicz did not seem to mind that Joan and Tracy had become intimate while making *Mannequin*; in fact, the two men exchanged observations about Joan during more than one drinking session.

Joan was set to do two new projects for Mankiewicz after *Mannequin* wrapped, but she changed her mind about both of them. *Three Comrades* was an adaptation of Erich Maria Remarque's best-selling novel, and *The Shopworn Angel* was a remake of a 1929 semi-silent movie. The official story was that Joan was afraid that the three male costars of *Three Comrades* would dominate the picture (she was to play the woman that all three love). While this was true, she also did not relish working yet again with Tone, cast as one of the three comrades. The role of the kept woman and actress in *The Shopworn Angel* smacked to Joan of something she had done too many times before; reluctantly, she bowed out. Margaret Sullavan played both parts, and was more appropriate for them.

Joan worked with Sullavan in her next project. She was excited when she learned she had been cast in the film version of Keith Winter's successful Broadway play *The Shining Hour* (1938); it was she who urged the studio to acquire the rights to the play. She always enjoyed working with Robert Young, with whom she had acted twice before, and was happy to be working with Melvyn Douglas and Sullavan, both of whom she admired. Mankiewicz again produced, and Borzage of *Mannequin* directed. With all of that talent both in front of and behind the camera, Joan was sure that *The Shining Hour* couldn't miss. This turned out not to be true: *The Shining Hour* didn't work at all. Years later, Joan would blame this picture for starting her on her downward spiral, observing that the audience could only sit through so many bad movies before they stopped wanting to see her.

In *The Shining Hour*, Joan again played the rags-to-riches type who gets involved with a rich, proper guy from a ritzy background. The difference is that Olivia Riley doesn't need anybody's money, as she has become successful as a dancer in Manhattan. However, she grows tired of her frivolous life and agrees to marry Henry Linden (Douglas). This does not sit well with Henry's stern sister and brother, Hannah (Fay Bainter) and David (Young), both of whom are not only snobs but are convinced that Olivia will inevitably cheat on Henry, marriage or no marriage. Instead, David falls for Olivia himself; afraid she'll come to return his feelings, Olivia convinces Henry to depart for a belated honeymoon for six months. Olivia has become close to David's wife, Judy (Sullavan) and has no desire to hurt her or Henry. For her part, Judy realizes that her love for David is less than fully requited.

Up until this point, *The Shining Hour* is a literate, polished, well-acted romantic drama whose snappy, intelligent dialogue and intriguing situations lift it above mere soap opera. After that, unfortunately, it becomes more and more ludicrous. Hannah inexplicably burns down the home that Henry is building. (For Hannah, the home represents Olivia, whom she despises, but since Olivia and Henry were going away for months, there seems little point to the destructive act.) Judy runs into the fiery conflagration—not to commit suicide because her husband loves another woman (which would at least have made sense), but to sacrifice herself so that David and Olivia can be together. ("I wouldn't have believed it if I read it in a book," Olivia says of this development.) If that weren't enough, we are then asked to believe not only that Henry would still be on speaking terms with his sister, but also that Hannah would suddenly accept Olivia into the family, rather than blame her for Judy's near-death experience. Judy does survive, however, and David's love for her is finally awakened. Olivia realizes that Henry is the only one she truly loves. Meanwhile, in the bedroom upstairs, Judy's head is completely covered in bandages like a mummy, even though it is clearly seen in the preceding sequence that the fire never actually touched her and all she could possibly be suffering from is smoke inhalation. Such slipshod attention to detail ultimately undoes *The Shining Hour.*

The shame of it is that Joan is very good in the picture, in every way a match for Margaret Sullavan, considered by many the superior actress. Whether Sullavan could out-act Joan or not is beside the point. Sullavan made only a handful of movies, and obviously didn't appear in as many bad ones as Joan. When the two are on the screen together in *The Shining Hour,* they come off as equals. Joan is especially effervescent and delightful as Olivia, as believable in the emotional scenes as in the comic ones (such as when she socks Frank Albertson on the jaw when he makes a drunken pass at her). In her dance number early in the picture, Joan does more of her faux dancing, but she is fairly graceful. It is very clear, however, that while her male dance partner's movements are effortless, Joan is concentrating on every step.

As for her costars, Sullavan and Bainter are superb, Douglas is adequately smooth (and sometimes better than that), Hattie McDaniel is delightful as always, and Robert Young, in hot young pursuit of Joan, is simply miscast. *The Shining Hour* is handsomely produced, and the proceedings, believable or not, are bolstered by a lovely Chopin-esque score by Franz Waxman. There are so many good things about *The Shining Hour* that it is too bad that it fails as a whole. The picture did not do very well at the box office, either. "It should have worked but it didn't," Joan remarked ruefully years later. "When it finally sank into me that we'd put so much into a movie that offered the public so little in terms of story value, I was ill. We should have thrown the script into the fire instead of Maggie Sullavan!" At 76 minutes, the movie is so short, much like a silent movie, that one senses that a lot of footage must have ended up on the cutting-room floor. Joan remembered that certain sequences were never filmed, but after so long she couldn't recall precisely what had been excised. "Another half an hour may not have done it any good in any case," she said. It also didn't help that the action was shifted from England, with its strongly held traditions and class-consciousness, to Wisconsin.

On the set, relations between Joan and Margaret Sullavan were cordial but not warm. Apparently each was a bit envious of the other. Joan knew that Sullavan was considered the better actress of the two, and she was anxious to prove that she was Sullavan's equal. Meanwhile, Sullavan was envious of Joan's stardom. As Sullavan once described her status at MGM, "There were too damned many bitches in that kennel for my taste. In the middle of all that noise, I had to yap the loudest to even get myself heard!" Sullavan later said she found Joan "affected" and "pretentious" and "caught up in a Hollywood dream world." Sullavan was not as driven as Joan, and she didn't understand how important the success of *The Shining Hour* was to a woman who'd been labeled "box-office poison." Ever the perfectionist, Joan didn't just want the picture to succeed—for her, it had to be *quality*. When Joan tried to explain this, Sullavan's dismissive response annoyed her. Far more laid-back than Joan, Sullavan felt that it was pointless to lose sleep over such matters. Joan felt Sullavan was "cold . . . not a sympathetic person." According to Fay Bainter, everyone on the set was concerned that one of the women might eventually blow up at the other. Joan's knitting between takes nearly drove Sullavan crazy. But the two were very professional, and when all was said and done they even managed to become friendly in a casual way.

There was another reason for Joan to envy Margaret. Sullavan was happily pregnant, and Joan was constantly reminded of her various miscarriages and two bad marriages. "She's such a tiny, small-boned thing," Joan complained to Jerry Asher. "How come she can have a child and I can't?" It wasn't long after finishing *The Shining Hour* that Joan began mulling over the possibility of adoption. Her assorted miscarriages (and abortion or two) had made it impossible for her to have any children of her own. Or so Joan always claimed.

Margaret was not above playing jokes on Joan. She felt that Joan's occasional nervous tension ought to be playfully punctured now and then. When Joan has to carry Sullavan out of the burning house at the end, she was concerned because of Sullavan's pregnancy. At one point Joan stumbled, and did her best to break the fall by dropping to her elbows and knees. Sullavan kept her eyes shut and waited until Joan endured a few frantic moments wondering whether Sullavan was injured; she then opened her eyes and shouted "Boo!"

Relations between Joan and Melvyn Douglas had not warmed up much since *The Gorgeous Hussy*. "I didn't think Joan really appeared to advantage in it," he recalled. "She was challenged by the superior acting skills of Maggie and Fay, and to her credit she did try to rise to the challenge. But Borzage, fine director that he was . . . was not the director to bring out the best in *her*." Douglas accused Joan of "attitudinizing all over the place," adding that "she had to watch the happily married and happily pregnant Sullavan achieve maximum effects with relatively little effort and it put her off no end."

Joan was still determined to stick it out with Franchot Tone, even though the situation at home was as bad as it had ever been, despite some loving moments and happy times. Tone's drinking was sometimes out of control, making him late for work and depriving his performances of spontaneity. Joan decided to surprise him at the studio one afternoon when she was in between film commitments. She opened his dressing room door and discovered him being fellated by one of the bit players in the film. Jerry Asher remembered Joan's account:

> Joan was livid. I don't know if she'd slept with Joseph Mankiewicz by this point—probably she did, and I know she'd been to bed with Tracy—but what was good for the goose wasn't necessarily good for the gander. She told me she went in and literally *pulled* him out of the poor girl's mouth. She slapped the girl around until she fled out of the dressing room like a hive of bees was after her. Joan could be funny. I think she was angrier that he was letting a *nobody* do him than she was that he was cheating on her. When Joan cheated on her husbands, she cheated with the best. Gable. Mankiewicz, and so on. The costars, the director, the producer, maybe a supporting player or two, but a bit player—never!

Joan may have forgiven this and other of Tone's indiscretions—she was well aware that she would have been a hypocrite not to, under most circumstances—had it not been for Tone's attitude afterward, and even right then in the dressing room. "He was so *contemptuous,*" Joan said many years later, still trembling a bit at the memory of her fury at Tone and her hurt feelings over his words in the dressing room. "I'd really tried my damndest to make that marriage work, to build up his career, to get him good parts, to do everything for him because I loved him. And the way he spoke to me. I don't remember the exact things he said to me; I just remember they were vile and hateful and unforgivable." Driving home from the studio after the fateful encounter, Joan decided then and there to divorce Tone. There was a trial separation at first, and according to the columnists there had been some chance of a reconciliation, but that marriage was over on that very day—and Joan knew it. Tone did his best to smooth things over, he said it was only hurt male pride that made him lash out at her and have affairs, but Joan wasn't having any of it. The physical blows, the tongue-lashings, the drunken beratings, and the infidelities had finally combined to make Joan fall completely and irrevocably out of love with Tone. It wasn't long before Tone was out of her home in Brentwood, then out of her life for good.

For their next project, Mankiewicz wanted to team Joan and Gable in the film version of Margaret Mitchell's *Gone With the Wind*. It wasn't that the studio had a problem with Joan as Scarlett O'Hara—although in retrospect she would have been an odd choice for the part—but that, according to Mankiewicz, Irving Thalberg assured Louis B. Mayer that Civil War pictures never made any money. *Gone with the Wind* would not be made at MGM.

Gone With the Wind, of course, was produced by David O. Selznick and went on to make motion-picture history, with Vivien Leigh unforgettable in the role of Scarlett. While she probably suited the part better than Joan would have, Joan would hardly have been terrible as Scarlett. Joan could have done the character's determination and anger full justice, and she had already shown how well she worked with Gable. Would Joan have been *too* strong as a Southern belle? That we will never know.

Hollywood—and life—had other things in mind for Joan Crawford.

J.C. Archives, Inc.

Chapter Eight

JUNGLE RED

Considering the hit-or-miss quality of the films that came before, it is perhaps not surprising that Joan wound up in *Ice Follies of 1939* with Jimmy Stewart, who'd had a bit part in *The Gorgeous Hussy,* instead of *Gone With the Wind.* ("Talk about going from the sublime to the ridiculous!" commented Joan.) The two leads had very different styles, but they played well together as Mary McKay and Larry Hall, an ice-skating duo who break up when Mary becomes a movie star. By now, Stewart was a major player in his own right. The two are at their best in a sequence in which Mary comes home late from a premiere drunk and tells Larry how rich and successful she's going to become: "I'm gonna be a star, a *star,* darling; they lent me that [dress] for the preview, but after this I'm gonna *own* all my nice clothes." As Joan does a splendid drunk routine, Stewart skillfully expresses jealousy and resentment underneath his affection. Larry tries to continue the act with a male partner, Eddie Burgess (Lew Ayres)—naturally this doesn't work out as well. Although many have commented that Joan and Stewart used doubles for long shots in the skating sequences, such doubles were hardly needed because the two only appear on skates once, coming off the ice at the end of a show. We never do see their characters do any fancy footwork on the ice.

Ice Follies is fun and the performances perfectly charming, but it's not the uninteresting details of the plot that stand out in the memory, but rather the movie's raison d'être, the terrific ice acts performed by the International Ice Follies (including a drag queen on skates!), the pleasant musical sequences, and a striking shot of a boat on the Hudson River sailing past the Statue of Liberty as a plane passes overhead. *Ice Follies* ends with a film within a film, the latest picture starring "Sandra Lee" (Mary's new name), which turns out to be a campy *Cinderella,* only with ice-skating acts. The Cinderella sequences were in Technicolor—Joan's first appearance in a color movie. Joan manages to get out a few bars of "It's All So New to Me" as well, first in the aforementioned drunk scene and then in the *Cinderella* sequence. Joan also made a recording of the song, which was released commercially. An interesting feature of *Ice Follies* is how Mary McKay is turned into "Sandra Lee," much the same way that Harry Rapf turned Lucille LeSueur into Joan Crawford.

"This represents the nadir of the bad assignments Miss Crawford has gotten from Metro-Goldwyn-Mayer and if she stages a cataclysmic rebellion after this, no one can blame her," wrote one reviewer, who was certainly telling it like it was. "Everyone was out of their collective minds," Joan said years later. Joan was out of her mind with anger. She despised the assignment, but she figured that it wouldn't hurt to do a light, breezy comedy after the heavy emoting in *The Shining Hour*. What she couldn't know was how bad *The Shining Hour* would turn out, and how little it would do for her career. She also did *Ice Follies* as a favor for Rapf. Joan was also told that she would sing several numbers in the picture; as she still fancied herself a real singer, this helped her approach *Ice Follies* with a degree of optimism. Of course, Joan had been working with Romano Romani, but his emphasis on operatic material meant that Joan's voice in *Ice Follies* didn't sound any different than it did in *Possessed*.

When the studio publicity department learned of Joan's training with Romani, and discovered that Joan had even recorded operatic duets with actor-baritone Douglas McPhail as well, the bullshit factor roared into high gear. Joan wasn't just studying opera, the flacks reported to the papers, she was going to *make her debut at the Met in the fall!* Even Joan must have had a good laugh over that one. After all, celebrities did not impress the powers that be at New York's famous Metropolitan Opera; even Grace Moore had a hell of a time getting onto the stage at the Met. Joan would never have had a chance. Perhaps figuring that if she no longer had Tone she at least still had her singing voice, Joan whined when most of her numbers were dropped from *Ice Follies* due to overlength and even put forth the ludicrous suggestion that MGM singing star Jeanette MacDonald feared that a singing Joan would be too much competition. (For the record, the Met never invited the talented but rather shrill MacDonald to sing, either.) Joan was always able to delude herself when she needed to, and she deluded herself a great deal about her singing voice in these early years. A line she spoke as Sadie Thompson in *Rain* best describes her singing voice: "My voice ain't so bad if you don't listen too hard."

Joan needed something else to occupy her attentions when she wasn't in front of the camera, and she noticed that Jimmy Stewart had gotten a bit cuter since his appearance in *The Gorgeous Hussy*. Or perhaps it was just that his new star status filled him with a confidence that made him sexier. Stewart wasn't really the type that normally got Joan's juices flowing (neither was her other *Ice Follies* costar, gentlemanly Lew Ayres), but she had neither husband nor boyfriend at the time, and Joan was always on the prowl for an intriguing encounter in the sack. Jerry Asher and Billy Grady were certain that Joan managed to snare Stewart at some point during filming, although probably not in her dressing room but at her home. Neither Asher nor Grady was surprised when the affair ended even before shooting did. For his part, old-fashioned Jimmy liked to be predator more than prey, and Joan simply made him nervous. Neither Joan nor Stewart ever went on record about their affair, but in later years whenever Stewart's name came up, Joan would speak of him fondly. Apparently he came along just when she needed him and disappeared when she was through with him, without any tiresome melodrama. In other words, he was just what the doctor ordered, and Joan was grateful for that.

Her feelings toward MGM and Mayer were another matter. She told Mayer in no uncertain terms that he had better find her a picture that would showcase her talents better. "I deserve better than this and so do my fans," she told him. "You've got a valuable commodity in me— why throw it away on crap like *Ice Follies*?" She demanded a choice role in *The Women*.

And she got it.

Although her screen time in the film was comparatively brief, Joan had one of her snappiest roles in *The Women* (1939), and she ran with it. She is absolutely superb as the tramp Crystal Allen. What made the movie unique was the gimmick that, as the title suggests, no man is ever seen on-screen. Accordingly, most of *The Women* takes place at a dude ranch in Nevada where women can establish residency in the state in order to get their divorces. The movie starts with housewife Mary Haines (Norma Shearer) reluctantly deciding to divorce her (of course, unseen) husband when she finds out that he's been carrying on with Crystal. Mary winds up at the ranch in Nevada, where she encounters new friends Peggy Day (Joan Fontaine) and Miriam Aarons (Paulette Goddard) among others, as well as old friend Sylvia Fowler (Rosalind Russell), who is divorcing her husband because of his affair with Miriam. Naturally, the entanglements inevitably lead to some good catfights. Afterward, the marriage between Mary's ex-husband Stephen and Crystal doesn't proceed very happily, and Mary wins him back. In the final scene, Mary rushes out of a restaurant ladies' room into his arms. When someone asks her whether she still has any pride, she replies "pride is a luxury that a woman in love can't afford."

Nowadays, *The Women* certainly has its dated aspects—all the catty, bitchy, conniving obsession with menfolk seems a bit stereotypical after women's liberation—but the picture is still grand entertainment, beautifully acted and amusingly written by Anita Loos (from the play by Clare Boothe Luce; F. Scott Fitzgerald also worked on the script). And even today there are women who worry endlessly about men and compete with other women for the ones they want. Affairs are commonplace, and two-faced friends still easy to find. One can enjoy the picture as if it were an ancient time capsule that still contains a few truths for the contemporary viewer.

The Women was essentially Norma Shearer's picture. Never a great comedienne, Shearer's usual conviction works superbly in the straight central role. But Joan knew that she had a chance to make a splash in her flashy supporting part, which sets the interlocking plot strands in motion. Highlights of the film include the bitchy interchange between Joan and Russell at the perfume counter where Crystal works, as Sylvia teases Crystal about her relationship with Stephen. Even better is the confrontation between Joan and Shearer in the former's dressing room, tiny Mary standing up to homewrecker Crystal, who sneers down at her and refuses to apologize or show any compassion. According to Anita Loos, it was Norma Shearer's idea to have Joan play Crystal Allen. "Norma knew that she and Joan," Loos recalled, "highlighted as love rivals, complete with the juicy, catty scenes I wrote for them, would bring them into theaters. I think it helped things along a great deal." Originally only Shearer and Joan were supposed to be above the title, but Rosalind Russell caused such a fuss—and called in "sick" so often—that her name was added to the credit card, albeit in smaller type.

George Cukor, who directed the all-female cast, years later had reservations about the picture. "At the time it probably wasn't as silly as it seems now, because it came from a different world. 'Kept women' and marital break ups were big moral questions then. Now, of course, everybody would be screwing everybody, and everybody would know about it. Crystal wouldn't be a kept woman, she'd be carrying on with another girl." Cukor inexplicably thought that the "central story . . . didn't fit with the rest," an odd comment as everything else revolves around this central story, Mary and Crystal fighting for Stephen. Cukor also hated the studio's insistence that a long color fashion show sequence be inserted into the middle of the black-and-white film, about which he was certainly right. The fashion show seems to go on forever and stops the movie dead in its tracks. Actually, Cukor had not been first choice to direct *The Women*. Ernst Lubitsch originally got the assignment, but when Cukor was replaced on *Gone with the Wind* by Victor Fleming, Cukor was in on *The Women* and Lubitsch was out. Cukor was seen as one of the few directors who could handle, as Hedda Hopper put it, "that feminine kennel" of MGM egos.

Considering the negative reaction to her portrayal of Sadie Thompson in *Rain* seven years earlier, it was risky for Joan to take on the role of hard-as-nails Crystal Allen, who is scarcely better than a prostitute. Louis B. Mayer told her he thought of her like a daughter and that he was afraid it might not be good for her to play a bad gal. Cukor also needed convincing. As Joan told Mayer, "If I can't have a good picture of my own, let me sneak into someone else's." Privately she kind of liked the idea of taking attention away from Shearer with the less sympathetic— but showier—role.

Joan got away with it. She didn't steal the picture from Shearer, but she did get a lot of attention, and she didn't alienate any of her fans or the critics. Why the difference? For one thing, *The Women* wasn't really a "Joan Crawford movie," it was an all-star extravaganza. Second, Crystal was far removed from the essentially kindly shopgirls she had played in the past. Joan got higher marks from some of the critics than Shearer did, because she was trying something different, unlike Norma, who was perceived as playing it safe. The irony is that the public accepted Joan as Crystal but not as Sadie, when of the two, Sadie was the much nicer character, despite her occupation.

Joan always loved the film and had an honest admiration for her own work in it. She thought that Rosalind Russell stole the picture (she never had terribly kind things to say about Shearer), and she recalled how much fun it was to work with Russell, Mary Boland (as an older woman perpetually—and foolishly—in love), Butterfly McQueen (she played her maid in this, as she would in *Mildred Pierce*), and Paulette Goddard, who was much more Joan's speed than the somewhat pretentious Joan Fontaine. "Cukor did a great job, I did a great job, Roz was sensational," she remembered. "I think the only one I could have done without was Joan Fontaine. She wasn't a bitch, she wasn't nasty—there was just something about her. She had the smallest part of all of us and maybe she was just a little jealous."

Joan had always been a little jealous herself—of Norma Shearer. Her oft-quoted comment about Shearer went, "How can I compete with Norma when she's sleeping with the boss," meaning, of course, Irving Thalberg. Joan felt that Shearer was given the choicest assignments out of nepotism. She didn't deny Shearer's talent—after all, Thalberg couldn't get up there on the screen and act for Shearer—but she fumed at the way she was considered, and seemed to consider herself, queen of the lot. By the time of *The Women,* Thalberg had passed away, but Norma still had a lot of clout at MGM.

The studio publicity department wanted *The Women* to be known as "the catfight of the century," and they did their best to drum up stories about the alleged feuding and fussing on the set, in particular about how much Joan and Shearer hated one another. Howard Strickling, head of MGM publicity, engineered and was overjoyed by a *Look* magazine cover featuring Joan and Shearer glaring at each other in mock hatred. The caption, which read "They don't like each other," referred to the characters the two women played, but Strickling didn't mind if the public believed it was more personal. After all, insiders knew that it was.

Nevertheless, Joan and Shearer got along for most of the filming. They pretended to be feuding for the columnists, but underneath the pretense there was genuine dislike. "Norma and Joan could never have been personal friends," remembered Anita Loos. "They came from different worlds—Norma thought Joan crude and pushy and Joan considered Norma overbearing and uppity—but they both knew the 'feud' was good copy, and so they helped it along. And why not?"

Hedda Hopper passed along the true story of the famous on-set incident between Joan and Shearer. Joan was off camera feeding lines to Shearer for close-ups. Joan always considered it the mark of professionalism to feed lines to a costar, and was annoyed if a costar didn't return the compliment. To indicate the antipathy she felt for Shearer, Joan fed her the lines, but sat in a chair doing her knitting, needles clicking all the while. She would momentarily stop knitting so that Shearer's lines could be recorded, but the minute it was her turn to talk the needles would begin clicking again. Finally Shearer lost her patience and shouted at Joan to go back to her dressing room if she couldn't be professional. Joan got up, savagely stuck her knitting back into a bag, and stormed off the set, calling Shearer a bitch. Outwardly incensed by (but secretly relishing) Joan's behavior, Cukor ran after her to reprimand her, but Shearer ordered him back to her side *"that instant."* Back in her dressing room, Joan fumed and, according to Loos, drafted a nasty telegram to Shearer at the urging of Howard Strickling "just to keep things percolating for publicity purposes." "So many people say Norma and I dislike each other," Joan told Hedda Hopper, "who are we to disagree with the majority opinion?" Many years later, when Lawrence Quirk was interviewing Joan about *The Women,* he made the mistake of mentioning that he hoped one day to do a book on Norma Shearer. "*Someone* should!" Joan snapped gleefully. "She's all but forgotten!"

Joan was back with producer Joseph Mankiewicz for *Strange Cargo* (1940), Joan's eighth and final pairing with Clark Gable.

The two of them were teamed for sizzling results in the picture, which unfortunately didn't make the most of their sexy pyrotechnics, focusing instead on suspect religious symbolism. *Strange Cargo* deals with an escape by several prisoners from Devil's Island. The escapees include tough guy Moll (Albert Dekker), wife-killer Hessler (Paul Lukas), pious Cambreau (Ian Hunter), and Verne (Gable), incarcerated for un-stated reasons. Joan played Julie, the bar entertainer Verne meets up with; having had an abortive dalliance with her earlier in the film, he takes her along for the ride. Their adversarial, purely sexual relationship gradually softens into warm affection as they struggle to stay alive on a boat without fresh water. Cambreau's compassionate, often sanctimonious musings eventually stir up kindly feelings of self-sacrifice in the escapees. Verne eventually realizes that Cambreau is actually God—that's right, God—in human form. After everything he goes through to escape the hellish prison, Verne winds up turning himself in; he will serve out his sentence until, presumably, he begins a new life with Julie.

Joan offers a vivid and convincingly "hard-boiled" portrayal as Julie. At times she even seems a bit psychotic, such as when she knocks down and nearly stabs a man who is making demands of her. Sometimes regarded as a superficial glamourpuss, Joan proved in *Strange Cargo* that she could deglamorize herself as much as Bette Davis or any other actress when she allowed herself to be photographed without elaborate makeup, as in the jungle sequences. When she remarks to Cambreau on his religiosity, "I know that routine; it starts with a prayer and winds up with a bible in one hand and me in the other," she could be a sadder-but-wiser Sadie Thompson sizing up her latest pious hypocrite. Gable finishes a distant second to Joan in the acting department. Although he had played plenty of tough guys in his career, Gable's portrayal of Verne never delves below the surface or seems especially convincing.

Strange Cargo is the kind of dopey hybrid that results when the popular motion picture industry finds religion and decides to offer a message to the "Great Unwashed." What could have been a perfectly good adventure story and romance is turned into a dubious vehicle for alleged enlightenment. It is the kind of film that seems devout and profound only to Hollywood illiterates. It is a shame that *Strange Cargo* couldn't have jettisoned the Cambreau character or at least made the religious overtones less heavy-handed, for the picture has a good deal of tension and suspense and there are many arresting sequences. Never confident in the audience's intelligence, Mankiewicz was probably the one who decided to have Cambreau spread out his arms, Christlike, onto a floating piece of wood behind him so that he could appear to be mock-crucified after Verne throws him off the boat—just in case the audience didn't get it. The picture momentarily becomes clever when Verne shouts at Cambreau that since his life is in his hands, he, Verne, is God, but then it blows it when Verne has a sudden epiphany: "I'm God, he's God, *you're*—" It is amusing that throughout the film nobody ever bothers to ask Cambreau, if you're so great, what were you doing locked up in prison with the rest of us? Of course, as Cambreau is not a real person but God on a mission, he simply fades into the shadows at the end of the movie.

"It was almost a good film," Mankiewicz remembered. Referring to the censorship problems the film encountered, he said, "I wish it could have been made later." Any and all intimations of sexual intimacy between the characters played by Joan and Gable had to be scrupulously avoided. Incredibly, the character of Cambreau was considered blasphemous by the Catholic Legion of Decency, who condemned the picture, which severely affected its performance at the box office. It was banned outright in Boston, and other cities demanded cuts before allowing it to be screened. This was all ludicrous, especially when one considers that the film is about how bad people can change, if they take the influence and spirit of God into their hearts. But Joan and Gable were simply too sexy in their playful banter to appease the prudes, who cared more about their hypocritical version of morality than about any so-called "decency."

While Joan and Gable were no longer hot and heavy offscreen—Gable was enjoying a happy marriage to Carole Lombard at the time, for one thing—their relationship was still friendly and comfortable. There was a slight behind-the-scenes contretemps when several people twitted Joan about Gable's name being above hers in the promotional materials. Joan knew that Gable was now as big a name at the box office as she was—perhaps bigger, thanks to *Gone with the Wind*. But her competitive nature was challenged when someone unwisely reminded her that only rival Norma Shearer had gotten top billing over Gable for *Idiot's Delight,* made the previous year. What was good enough for Norma was good enough for Joan, who lobbied for—and got—top billing in *Strange Cargo.* Gable only shrugged and went about his business. Both of their names were above the title, what difference did it make? It made a lot of difference to Joan, not so much due to pettiness or megalomania, but rather because she saw any sign of diminishment as a sign that she was slipping, letting somebody else (not Gable, of course, but the higher-ups) chip away at what she had worked so hard for. She also did not see why the male star, even someone on Gable's level, always had to have top billing. So it was not just a cosmetic victory, as far as she was concerned. Although Gable may have been her nominal leading man in so many of her early movies, everyone knew that *he* had been supporting *her,* in what the public perceived as "Joan Crawford movies." His status in Hollywood may have changed, but hers had not. She would not be "supporting" him in *Strange Cargo*—or any other movie. His name could go above the title, but it could not go above *hers.*

Joan liked *Strange Cargo* well enough, and enjoyed working with Gable. "That certain chemistry was still there between us," she remembered. "Making a picture with Clark was always so energizing in one sense, and relaxing in another. He was effortless at what he did, with wonderful results." She told one interviewer that Gable came up to her one afternoon and told her that they'd play each scene exactly the way she wanted it. "You've become an actress and I'm still Clark Gable," he told her. There was talk that Gable was a more "natural" actor than Crawford and should not be teamed with her any longer, but Joan was arguably the more talented of the two.

Joan got a kick out of working with Peter Lorre, who played her nemesis, Monsieur Pig, who promises not to turn Verne in, as long as she agrees to go off with him—and everything that that implies. "Peter had a tremendous sense of humor," she remembered. "A really wicked, impish wit, and he always had Clark and me in stitches. I had to say the most terrible, degrading things to him when he was playing Mr. Pig, of all things, and he always had an even nastier comeback, which of course had to be cut because it wasn't in the script." When asked if Moll and the younger man he befriends were intended to be homosexual characters—Moll cries and commits suicide after the younger man dies—Joan replied, "We had enough trouble with a Christ figure, for Pete's sake, let alone homosexuals. Frank [Borzage] didn't say anything about it, but it really wasn't played that way. I think the Albert Dekker character just thought of the kid as the son he never had, someone he wanted to save from the kind of life he had had. But who knows?"

Strange Cargo was partially filmed at Pismo Beach, where Joan wore the same dress constantly until it was in realistic tatters. Her career, on the other hand, was in pretty good shape.

Susan and God (1940) was based on a Broadway show by Rachel Crothers that had starred Gertrude Lawrence, and Joan picked up some pointers on how to play the title character (Susan, not God) by watching Lawrence play the role on Broadway. Director George Cukor also helped her with the role. Joan plays Susan Trexel, a frivolous woman who has allegedly "found God" and wants everyone to follow in her righteous path. She neglects her husband Barry (Fredric March) and her daughter Blossom (Rita Quigley), and spends most of her time espousing a new brand of religion she picked up in Europe. Ruth Hussey plays Charlotte, a woman who has always secretly loved Barry, who drinks too much. While *Susan and God* is often hilarious and certainly lands some (relatively safe) points about religious hypocrisy ("Your *own* life is a mess," one character tells Susan), it veers back and forth between drama and comedy, never settling comfortably into either. The sentimental ending, wherein Susan realizes the error of her ways, is also not believable.

On one hand, Joan is sensational in *Susan and God,* really dominating the screen. On the other hand, despite some of the self-delusionary pretensions of her own life, she was simply too down-to-earth an actress (think of all those shopgirls she portrayed) to fare entirely well as such a flighty bird as Susan. But Anita Loos's often witty screenplay does little to make Susan much more than a caricature. Some find the picture very funny and entertaining; others, talky and long. It's both.

The rights to the play were originally bought for Norma Shearer, who passed on it, possibly because she wanted time off to spend with her family, or maybe it just wasn't what she was looking for. It is amusing that Joan wrote in her memoirs that "Norma didn't want to play a mother," when Norma had done just that in *The Women*. (Of course, it's possible that Norma just didn't want to play a mother twice in a row.) Then Greer Garson was the front-runner for the role, until Cukor suggested Joan, who jumped at the chance to work with him again, in what she hoped would be an "important" picture. However, as the first day of shooting approached, Joan began to get a bit panicky—she didn't have a clue to Susan's character, didn't understand what made this odd woman tick, and the screenplay wasn't giving her any help. On the first day of shooting, she went to Cukor, nearly hysterical. Cukor sat her down and spent half an hour or so discussing the part with her. When they were through, she knew just how to approach the role. Joan always gave credit to costar Fredric March for helping her give a good performance. March understood that she had the showier part and wisely underplayed in counterpoint. To some viewers, this makes him seem a bit bland as Susan's husband.

Although the movie was successful at the box office (both play and movie are largely forgotten today), the real payoff was that the studio and its directors began to take Joan more seriously again. There were those who thought she was more interesting in the first half of the film, but found the later scenes too much in the traditional "Joan Crawford" mold. Cukor took the blame for that, remarking to interviewer Gavin Lambert that Susan "should have remained a foolish woman all the way through, even when she was coming to her senses. I should have talked to [Joan], we should have understood together. . . . Put a black mark against me." As always for Joan, it was three steps forward, two steps back. The role of Susan was different from what she had played before, and as most critics felt she was quite good in the movie, even the public began to see her as more versatile and gifted than they had previously imagined. This led to her next picture.

After which many people would never see Joan Crawford in quite the same way again.

Chapter Nine

SCARRED

A Woman's Face (1941) turned out to be one of Joan's best movies. She played Anna Holm, scarred in childhood by a fire caused by her alcoholic father. Reactions to her disfigured face have made her cold and bitter, although deep down she still desires love and pretty things. She owns a roadhouse, from which she and a gang of confederates blackmail the indiscreet. When some love letters written by a married woman named Vera Segert (Osa Massen) fall into Anna's hands, she goes to her home to demand payment for their return, but winds up being treated by Vera's husband Gustaf (Melvyn Douglas), a plastic surgeon who restores her facial beauty after a series of painful operations. In thrall to her lover Torsten (Conrad Veidt), Anna takes a job as governess to a four-year-old boy whom Torsten wants her to murder so that he can claim an inheritance. Realizing that Torsten is a monster, Anna kills him instead and winds up facing the music with a now-smitten Dr. Gustaf at her side.

    A Woman's Face offers another thoroughly accomplished performance from Joan under the tutelage of Cukor, who by now had clearly become one of her most sympathetic directors. With Cukor's help, Joan created three separate phases for her character: the merciless bitch with a hidden romantic side we first meet at the roadhouse; the happy but emotionally stunted woman with the pretty, unscarred face; and the softer woman who realizes that she is not the monster others regard her as and that she is worthy of a good man's love. The story is told primarily in flashbacks during Anna's trial for Torsten's murder in Stockholm. At first we only see her from the other characters' point of view. In her first appearance in the courtroom, we see the "soft" Anna she has become, even though the audience isn't yet aware of what will happen to her or even if the operations on her face were successful (during this scene she is photographed only from one side). Cukor does a fine job of building up the suspense over whether Anna's face was properly healed.

Although the premise of the film—that physical scarring can make a person "evil" or even excuse their actions—is psychologically dubious, the script is rich with ironic humor and wonderful dialogue. After Gustaf repairs her facial damage, he tells Anna "I've created a monster—a beautiful woman with no heart." To which Anna replies "Indistinct from other women with beautiful faces?" Confronting Vera about her indiscreet letters, Anna sneers, "Such silly letters. Such childish writing. Such cheapness. Have you read any real love letters? George Sand. Keats. Browning. Do you know anything about love in that miserable soul of yours that dribbles itself out of these letters? Can you imagine loving a man so greatly, so completely, that you surrender everything you have just to be near him, just to have him near you. That's love as I know it."

Then follows one of the great sadomasochistic scenes of classic film: During this speech, Vera notices the disfigurement on Anna's face and, in a fit of incautious malice, deliberately raises the shade of the lamp near her and flicks the switch so that the hideous scar is fully illuminated. "So *that's* love as you know it," she snickers cruelly. Humiliated and outraged, Anna repeatedly slaps the childishly whining Vera and shouts at her to "Get the rest of your jewels!" Photos of Osa Massen jeeringly forcing the lampshade up as Joan's eyes bulge in fury are prime collector's items, but the forceful, harpy-like figure of Joan with her half-gargoyle, half-glamorous face hovering over the cringing doll-like Massen remains an even more indelible image. Osa Massen never had such a good part again, and she was absolutely perfect in the role.

In another memorable scene, having fallen for sinister Veidt, Anna comes back to headquarters wearing a pretty new hat. One of her co-blackmailers, Christina (Connie Gilchrist), has spitefully placed a forbidden mirror on the wall. When Joan spots her scarred features in the mirror, she grabs for her gun in the drawer, fully intending to shoot everyone in the room, but she is disarmed. The supporting players in the film were particularly well chosen: Donald Meek and Gilchrist as two of her partners in crime; Marjorie Main as a no-nonsense housekeeper who takes a dislike to Anna; Conrad Veidt, particularly in a wonderful scene with Joan when Anna returns from the hospital—Torsten realizes that her face is now normal and begins to laugh with her as they sit at the piano. Playing not merely a sociopath after money, but a truly demonic figure who hopes to use wealth apparently (in an uncharacteristically silly moment) to take over the country or even the world, Veidt's Germanic characterization was clearly influenced by the belief that the United States would soon be entering the war. (The Japanese attacked Pearl Harbor a few months after the film was released.)

Little Richard Nichols, who had appeared with Bette Davis and other stars in some significant films, is adorable as Lars-Erik, the boy who is nearly murdered—a real charmer. There is a very suspenseful scene when Anna takes Lars-Erik in a kind of open cable car over a rushing waterfall, fully intending to push him to his death. There is also an exciting chase in which Torsten takes off with Lars-Erik in a sleigh, with Anna and Gustaf in frantic pursuit. While it is fascinating to imagine what Hitchcock might have done with this script—not to mention how Hitch and Joan would have gotten along—it must be stated that Cukor's direction is top-notch all the way.

At first, Cukor had trouble getting Joan to play the part the way he wanted her to. It's not that she was doing Anna Holm as if she were still flighty Susan, but she was simply exhibiting too much personality for such a bitter, utterly miserable and conscienceless woman. Cukor made her recite multiplication tables, among other tricks, to shed her voice of excess emotion, so that she could create this twisted creature, so different from anything Joan had played before. Cukor's techniques helped, and Joan's effects in this are appropriately muted. She is allowed one moment of unbridled happiness—after her successful surgery, a little boy smiles at her instead of looking away in horror—but that unemotional blankness informs her performance almost until the end.

Joan spoke well of *A Woman's Face* her entire life; it was her high-water mark at MGM during this period. As with Fredric March in *Susan and God,* she thanked Melvyn Douglas for what she called his "consummate underplaying that made me look good." In this she was being overly generous; she was glad that Douglas was bland enough (a competent but unmemorable performance) not to steal attention away from the star. "I think that was the picture that finally made people sit up and notice that there was a lot more to Joan Crawford than what they thought, that I could be given a strong *dramatic* assignment and really come through. Too bad I was given such shitty movies afterward. It was so damn frustrating." Douglas noticed that Joan's demeanor on the set was completely different from her refined manner during the filming of *A Gorgeous Hussy.* "She had again become rough, bluff and hearty," Douglas recalled.

Joan's reviews for *A Woman's Face* were generally excellent; the critics and public now thought of her as an actress, not just a movie star.

There were those who felt that, as in *Susan and God*, Joan was a real character in the first half of the movie and reverted to her movie-star mode in the second half—but this is not really a fair assessment. Cukor, who usually defended Joan's acting in his films, once stated that "When she becomes pretty, she becomes . . . Joan Crawford." But he meant this more as a deficiency of the script than of Joan's work. The picture was also criticized by some for turning into a conventional thriller, which is odd since it is made clear from the very outset (at a *murder trial*, no less!) that *A Woman's Face* is not a straight drama. Many years later, Cukor said of the film:

> I may have reservations about the picture, but all in all I think it turned out very well, and Joan was wonderful. We weren't trying to do *The Snake Pit* or *Possessed* [the 1947 Crawford film, not the 1931 one], something along those lines. Joan really gave her all in that picture. She never complained about the heavy, disfiguring make up, she let me direct her and do special exercises to help bring forth the performance I knew she could give, I really think she put one hundred per-cent into it. I think she got across the struggle she was under-going in the second half of the film, the love she felt for Conrad Veidt versus her love for the boy, her need to feel whole and decent. She was very compelling. I think it remains one of her best performances.

Indeed, Joan's performance in *A Woman's Face* (along with her Oscar-winning turn in the later *Mildred Pierce*) has stuck even in the minds of people who weren't necessarily big fans of hers—and in strange ways. Premier special-effects wizard Ray Harryhausen was thinking of Joan in *A Woman's Face* when he created his Medusa for the fantasy film *Clash of the Titans* in 1981. The sequence with the Medusa (a model brought to life with 3-D animation) was photographed with special light-ing inspired primarily by *A Woman's Face*: "I say 'Joan Crawford light-ing,'" Harryhausen explained to *Cinefantastique* magazine, "because this Medusa is a woman with fine bone structure and films of Joan Crawford like *Mildred Pierce* and *A Woman's Life* [sic] always photographed her in interesting ways, putting shadows in, just showing her eyes, or part of her face stepping from shadow into light." As Joan died four years be-fore *Clash of the Titans* was released, we can only wonder what she would have thought of inspiring the depiction of a gorgon. It must be said, however, that Harryhausen's "stop-motion" Medusa almost "acts" with the flair and star quality of the real Joan Crawford.

So far Joan had taken on Greta Garbo, Margaret Sullavan, Norma Shearer, and even Bette Davis (offscreen, marrying the man Davis was after), and triumphed over all of them, as if she really were the mythical gorgon whose stare could turn people into stone. For her next assignment, Joan would find out if she had what it took to take on studio newcomer Greer Garson—a woman with true polish and sophistication.

Joan was to become disillusioned about her next assignment, *When Ladies Meet* (1941). She played Mary Howard, a best-selling novelist who has fallen in love with her married publisher Rogers Woodruff (Herbert Marshall), who also functions, improbably, as her editor. Her old beau Jimmy Lee (Robert Taylor) schemes to bring Mary together with Rogers's glamorous but long-suffering wife Claire (Greer Garson) during a weekend in the country. This leads to a marvelous sequence with the two women confessing their romantic hopes and fears, unaware that they're discussing the same man. The engrossing comedy-drama may have had old situations (it was a remake of a 1933 picture with Myrna Loy and Ann Harding), but it put a fresh twist on them. Although the movie is talky at times, there is some excellent dialogue. Although Joan was playing the "other woman," she got a lot of competition from Greer Garson in the looks department: Garson made sure that she had never looked sexier or more luscious than in *When Ladies Meet*. The character Garson plays seems almost too masochistic and noble for words, but she makes good points as she expresses compassion for all of her husband's many romantic cast-offs. For the most part, the acting by all of the players, Joan included, is quite Hollywood-ish—theatrical and superficial. Joan is often "actressy" and artificial, if effective—as this is a very theatrical piece, it works. The picture survives the stylized acting, but toward the end it becomes rather conventional. Also, we get the point of view of both wife and mistress, but we don't hear enough about the husband's motivations.

Joan didn't especially enjoy making the movie, and would give out a little trembling "yuchh" whenever it was mentioned. "I got to wear some beautiful Adrian gowns and that was it! It was a real comedown and letdown after *A Woman's Face*. Talk about going from the sublime to the ridiculous!" (As already mentioned, she said the same thing about doing *Ice Follies of 1939* instead of *Gone With the Wind*. It was one of her favorite phrases.) Joan had wanted to star in *The Spiral Staircase* as the deaf-mute eventually played by Dorothy McGuire in 1946, but the studio felt she'd done enough deformed "stunt" performances and should concentrate on being glamorous again.

Joan had had enough clout to take the starring role in *Susan and God* from Greer Garson, who was an import and a newcomer to MGM. Garson had done *Pride and Prejudice* instead; it ended up being a much better picture. Still, Garson was hardly a major star, so Joan accepted her as the love rival in *When Ladies Meet*. She also accepted that it would seem like unfair competition if Garson were not also allowed to look beautiful; audience sympathy would be entirely with the less attractive wife and not with the mistress. She and Garson had a perfectly cordial relationship, but things soured a bit when Garson received an Oscar nomination for *Blossoms in the Dust* and Joan was, to the surprise of everyone, passed over for *A Woman's Face*. (At the time, Joan had never been nominated for an Oscar.) Joan was furious that, as she saw it, MGM had used its considerable clout to back a Johnny-come-lately—part of the "British Invasion"—instead of herself.

Some of Joan's anger understandably spilled over toward Garson, but she didn't really blame her. She blamed the MGM executives, especially Benny Thau, a top Garson booster. "After all the money I made those miserable bastards," she fumed to Jerry Asher and others. "I've got nothing against Greer, but why couldn't they let her pay her dues, the way I did?" Joan was bitter that she had made so many movies for the studio and Garson was nominated for an Oscar for only her fourth American movie.

Joan was capable of honest admiration for talented costars, among them Garson. But she had fought for many long years to get where she was, and she couldn't help but see other prominent actresses at the studio as legitimate threats to her career, and therefore her livelihood—not to mention to her stardom and to her life itself, all of which were practically the same thing to her. She was determined never to be labeled "box-office poison" again. This made it all the more remarkable that, despite her competitive feelings, Joan was quite often kind and helpful to younger actresses like Gail Patrick and Betty Furness, among others. True, she did not see them as competition—yet—but that could always change, indeed perhaps in part because of her advice. As for major stars (Shearer, Sullavan), or newcomers with big studio clout behind them (Garson) Joan knew that they were quite capable of fending for themselves.

Over the years, Joan and Garson maintained a cordial but not warm relationship. According to Garson, Joan invited her to a dinner party in her home several years after the completion of *When Ladies Meet*. "Joan sat herself at the center table, surrounded by the most desirable men, including a certain Buddy Fogelson, whom she knew I was dating," she wrote. "She placed me at the studio electricians' table, with the words, 'Oh Greer, dear, you get along with everyone.' Our table had more fun than any other." When dessert was served, Garson moved her chair from the electricians' table to Joan's, seating herself next to Fogelson. "There was nothing Joan could do about it."

One senses there is more to the anecdote. Joan would probably not have been quite so deliberately insulting if she hadn't felt that Garson was looking down on her. Sensing Joan's competitiveness, Garson had always kept her distance, which may in turn have made her seem remote and haughty to Joan, which would certainly have irked her. She may well have wanted to charm the pants (literally) off Buddy Fogelson, while Garson sat watching in a snit, unable to do anything about it. It is unlikely that Joan would have achieved her objective, as Garson and Fogelson later got married. "Joan was just completely nonplussed that I refused to feud with her," Garson stated. As Garson related the story about Joan and the dinner party in 1991, many years after Joan's death, when it was open season on her reputation, it should perhaps be taken with a grain of salt.

In *They All Kissed the Bride* (1942), Joan played Margaret Drew, a very unpleasant businesswoman who doesn't brook incompetence in any form. She's mad as a hornet at reporter Michael Holmes (Melvyn Douglas), certain that he will libel her in a piece he's working on. This was the movie that Carole Lombard was planning when she died in a plane crash in January 1942; Joan took over for her, but it's doubtful that even Lombard would have been any better in the part. Another candidate, Myrna Loy, could never have played a tough businesswoman as convincingly (although she would probably have been funnier). Once again Joan demonstrated her underrated acting ability; she was also very beautifully photographed in the film, but then during this period she was at the height of her beauty. Her hairstyle—very bushy on top and at the sides—was also rather sexy. Douglas gave a nice performance as her adversary/love interest, but as leading man he was hardly "dreamy" enough to set the screen on fire. Douglas resented having to do the picture during wartime; he wanted Harry Cohen to release him from studio commitments so that he could work full-time for the government. Cohen refused, claiming that Joan would not do the picture without him.

Overall, *They All Kissed the Bride* is rather dull and dreary, despite the actors' game attempts to inject life into it. The mediocre script makes much too little of the premise, although there are a couple of good scenes, which the supporting players certainly helped punch up. The most amusing and energetic scene occurs when Joan enters a dance contest with employee Johnny Johnson (Allen Jenkins), who doesn't know that she's his boss. As they frantically jitterbug their way across the floor—Margaret getting dragged along and swept around, finally emerging a little worse for wear—the picture briefly comes to life. Joan also has a fine drunk scene a bit later. The other notable scene features Nydia Westman as Margaret's secretary; she tells her boss what it's like to be married, how one becomes attached to—and then lonely without—one's partner for life. She tells movingly of lying in the dark, listening to her husband sleep, telling God to "please take me first . . . take me first." As Marsh, one of Joan's executives, Roland Young has a funny bit in which he and Johnny Johnson take turns punching each other, and the always reliable Billie Burke is fine as Joan's mother. When Margaret's sister Vivian (Helen Parrish) gets married early in the picture, the anxious Burke says "I do" along with the bride!

Joan met her third husband, Phillip Terry (né Frederick Kormann), when a press-agent friend brought him to her home for dinner. Terry was under contract to MGM, and was handsome, pleasant, and gentlemanly—just the kind of man Joan was looking for. After her divorce from Franchot Tone, she dated many men—Glenn Ford, Cesar Romero—but as husband material, no one had ever jumped out at her. Joan was becoming convinced that she and marriage just didn't mix. But something new had entered the equation. When it was clear that her union to Tone was going to dissolve, she applied to adoption agencies for a baby, and she continued to do so after she was single. Joan had become convinced that a child would allow her to share the love she had bursting inside her without the complications of marriage, with its tricky questions of sex and compatibility. Babies gave love, they didn't get jealous over your stardom, expect you to give up your career, or have nasty quickies in dressing rooms. There was more to it than that, of course. Despite her active career and social life, Joan was lonely, and she was always haunted by the fear that the absence of children may have contributed to the dissolution of her marriages. There is good reason to believe that Joan wasn't so much unable to have biological children as that she preferred to adopt in order to keep pregnancy from interfering with her career. On top of everything else, she was genuinely grateful for her success and the advantages she enjoyed, and wanted to share them with another. She truly looked forward to having a child whose life she could enrich beyond measure, someone whose early life would be entirely different from hers, because of her own generosity. Joan may or may not have had great parenting skills, but her motives were pure. The first baby Joan adopted was a blonde girl named Christina. A year later she adopted a blond baby boy, which she at first christened Phillip Jr.

Joan had two reasons for marrying Terry after knowing him for only six weeks. She thought that he would make the perfect husband— and even more important, the perfect father. Christina arrived quite some time after Tone had departed, so Joan had the baby but no father. Joan desperately wanted her daughter to have a father figure, and when little Phil also entered her life, it became even more important for the presence of a male role model.

Phillip Terry was a thirty-three-year-old actor who'd had small parts in minor pictures before meeting Joan. During their marriage, which lasted from 1942 until 1946, his career moved forward—he had good supporting roles in *The Lost Weekend* (1945) and *To Each His Own* (1946)—but he never really made it to the big time. After he and Joan divorced, his film career deteriorated until there were often several years between film assignments; he eventually wound up in movies like *The Leech Woman* (1960) and *The Navy vs. the Night Monsters* (1966).

But in 1942 he had every reason to be hopeful, and whatever his true feelings toward Joan at the time of the marriage, he saw the union as the start of something exciting and glorious. What Joan liked about Terry—and what made him good father material—was good breeding, kindness, a quiet masculinity and a gentle passivity, all of which made it easy for Joan to picture him reading to the children and bouncing them on his knee. Joan's decision to marry Terry after only six weeks was not a mature one, but at the time she felt certain that Terry was the man she needed, if not wanted. Terry had the requisite good looks and charm and was dependable enough in bed, he made an attractive escort, so on that level Joan was satisfied enough with him as a husband. It felt like love, it looked like love to those around them. Joan was sure that if it wasn't love, it would be eventually. "It was perhaps the greatest mistake I ever made," she would say years later. Until that realization hit her, she did her best to make the marriage—which began on July 20, 1942, in her lawyer's office—work.

In the early '40s, the studio made Joan make two war-related duds, *Reunion in France* and *Above Suspicion*. Joan was completely ill-suited for both. In *Reunion in France* (1942), her last, ignominious picture with Mankiewicz as producer, she was happy to be teamed with John Wayne;

she had always had her eye on him. The studio had to promise her Wayne as costar or there would have been hell to pay. Joan later regretted letting her hormones make her decisions instead of her brains. As she told one interviewer, "If there is an afterlife, and I am to be punished for my sins, this is one of the pictures they'll make me see over and over again." Joan was angry at herself for not putting up more of a fight over the script due to her preoccupation with her new marriage and babies, among other things, and even angrier that her designs on Wayne came to nothing.

Joan plays a Parisian designer named Michelle de la Becque, who is so utterly apolitical—on the eve of World War II, no less—that she comes off like a complete moron. She doesn't even seem to get it when she returns to Paris and finds that the Gestapo has taken over her townhouse! Michelle's lover, industrial designer Robert Cortot (Philip Dorn), is apparently collaborating with the Nazis. Michelle meets up with Pat Talbot (Wayne), an American who joined the Royal Air Force and was downed in French territory, when he hides out in her pied-à-terre and, with some trepidation, she decides to help him. Then Michelle and Pat, enjoying a growing affection, have to flee Paris and make it to the border, with Robert and his German associates in hot pursuit. It turns out that Robert is only to be pretending to be helping the Nazis, and he and Joan are reunited after Wayne makes the "ultimate sacrifice." Joan wasn't anybody's idea of a Frenchwoman, and the very concept of a super-glamorous and elegantly attired Joan Crawford versus the Nazis was glossy and unreal, and the trivializing combination of the Nazi oppression of Paris and haute couture almost offensive. The script had its moments, but director Jules Dassin was not able to make the most of them. The film rarely evokes a sense of menace, and both Joan and the film are extremely superficial. Joan has some good moments such as the scene in which she stands up to a German officer and the one in which she argues with clothier patron Natalie Schafer over a coat in which information has been secreted. Schafer recalled:

> I think Joan was just about at the end of her rope. She wasn't brutal or offensive to me or to anyone else—just tightly wound. I think she knew her days were numbered at MGM, she was smarting over the assignments they had given her. *Reunion in France* was not right for her and she just did not want to be [on the set]. But she remained very professional in spite of all that. That was Joan. Whatever was going on in her mind, you might see glimmers of it in her expression, in her

off-camera mood, but she was always about getting the work done, being a pro. She thought of her colleagues who were there to do a picture, fair or foul.

Despite that tension, Joan was on the prowl for John Wayne, who wasn't on set very much, as the movie was nearly completed before he even put in an appearance. She made her move on him in the dressing room, and Wayne rebuffed her with as much charm as he could muster. He was married and in no mood for a dalliance. Joan didn't take no for an answer so easily, and she threw herself at him more than once. Wayne would quickly wipe off her lipstick and get himself out of the dressing room as fast as he could. She was a bigger star than he was at the time, but there was only so much he would do for his career. Wayne stayed out of Joan's dressing room, but he would tell people that for years afterward he would get come-hither looks from Joan, as well as salacious little notes expressing the wish that they could "get together" at her house. Wayne was more amused than angry by it all. Even in later years Joan would fume about the man who got away and the terrible picture she made because she'd been so hot for him. "That lousy movie! Just because I wanted to get Wayne in the sack! And the only thing he could play was cowboys. We hit it off like filet mignon and ketchup!"

Philip Dorn, who played Robert, was not Joan's type. Stories that she threw Dorn out of a two-shot on a Paris street by flinging her hips at him because he had rejected her, and that she and Dassin nearly traded punches because of it, are amusing but more than a little exaggerated. Joan was highly sexed, perhaps even oversexed, but she didn't throw herself at every single man she encountered, and she was too professional to get into fistfights with her director over such a casual incident. Shouting matches, occasionally—punching matches, no. It is true that she and Dassin did not get along well, but Dassin's comments about her later should not be taken too literally.

Above Suspicion (1943), her last film at MGM for many years, was a poor suspense movie taken from a Helen MacInnes novel. Joan and Fred MacMurray play Frances and Richard Myles, a newlywed couple honeymooning in 1939 that gets drafted by the British Secret Service to go on a mission for them inside Germany. They have to obtain "magnetic plans" but don't know who has them. The foolish clues and directions the pair receive only ensure that they can be certain of no one that they meet. One senses that the entire affair could have been handled much more straightforwardly; at times *Above Suspicion* seems more like a parody of a spy film. The running around becomes so ludicrously con-voluted that at one point Frances even says, "We climb through train windows, fire a shot in a theater, sing 'Annie Laurie' backwards, and Boris Karloff will fall out of the closet with an apple in his mouth." ("Unfortunately, neither Joan Crawford nor Fred MacMurray look quite bright enough to unravel the tangled skeins of this screen melodrama," wrote one wag at the *New York Herald Tribune*. "Much ado about noth-ing," wrote another.) Alas, Karloff doesn't turn up, but Basil Rathbone, at his most sinister, does play a Gestapo chief. A murder in a hall during a concert is lifted from the first version of Hitchcock's *The Man Who Knew Too Much* (Hitchcock improved upon the scene in his second ver-sion), but in *Above Suspicion* the murder is utterly impossible: the assas-sin fires from an angle from which he couldn't possibly hit his target.

Joan enjoyed working with Fred MacMurray, whom she found lik-able and charming, if not necessarily her cup of tea sexually. Also in the supporting cast was Bruce Lester, a young actor who had been Bette Davis's lover for a time. Director Richard Thorpe remembered that while he found Joan professional, much of the time she listlessly went through the motions. "I think she knew that she was living on borrowed time at the studio. There were no explosions of temperament; she just had her mind on other things." Thorpe would occasionally ape Hitchcockian tricks like subjective tracking shots, close ups of significant objects, and so on, but to significantly lesser effect. Like *Reunion in France,* the movie is generally devoid of the requisite tension. Movies like this without The Master of Suspense himself at the helm are almost always far less effective.

Joan was at her best portraying women having man trouble, women suffering emotional crises, situations she could plumb with her expres-sive face and often intense acting. While *Reunion in France* at least gave her some opportunity to do that (what with desperate Wayne and al-leged traitor Dorn in the picture), *Above Suspicion* was a real slap in the face; it presented her as a happily married woman struggling not for anyone's love but simply to stay alive. Not her métier. Not her meat. Not Joan at her best.

Which is how MGM wanted it. They thought she was done for good.

They couldn't have been more wrong.

Chapter Ten

MILDRED

By 1942 Joan was so dismayed with her assignments at MGM that she felt she would do better as a free agent or at another studio. Despite fine performances in films like *A Woman's Face,* the studio was no longer giving her the kind of buildup and support that she knew she deserved. She never blamed Mayer for this. She knew there were higher-ups who felt that she was simply getting too old to maintain her hold on Hollywood stardom and remain a profitable performer for the studio. She'd had a good run; now they wanted to put their money on somebody younger. Mayer tried to talk her out of leaving, but she was adamant. Years later, she would say, "If you think I made poor films at MGM after *A Woman's Face,* you should have seen the ones I went on suspension *not* to make!" Leery of becoming a completely independent agent, in 1943 Joan signed a contract at Warner Brothers for one-third the salary that MGM had paid her. It was a disappointment, to say the least, but she was determined to survive.

Joan's first picture for Warner Brothers was the forgettable *Hollywood Canteen* (1944). This was an all-star salute to the Canteen, with dozens of actors playing themselves. The "plot" was a pretext to showcase Warner Bros. stars; it involved two servicemen on leave (Robert Hutton and Dane Clark) spending time at the Canteen before returning to duty overseas. At one point the soldier played by Dane Clark gets to dance with the real Joan Crawford. Other Warner Brothers stars in the picture included Bette Davis, Barbara Stanwyck, John Garfield, Jack Benny, the Andrews sisters, and Roy Rogers and his horse Trigger. For what it's worth, Joan had no scenes with her friend Stanwyck or her nemesis Davis. Some reviewers, such as Kate Cameron in the *New York Daily News,* found the whole project objectionably patronizing. "The players in the picture seem constantly awed by their own gracious and hospitable entertainment of the servicemen," Cameron opined. Movies in which ordinary people mingle with dozens of self-absorbed movie stars (who are fully aware that said vehicle will do little to move their careers ahead) are always rather painful to watch.

At first it was suggested that Joan do a song number in the film, but her high regard for her own voice had finally waned by this time, and she asked to do a dance and dialogue scene instead. Joan was gratified that so many people on the Warner Bros. lot showed up on the day they shot her cameo, clustering around her after she was finished. But her brief foray in front of the camera only reminded her of how stalled her career had become. It almost seemed as if she spent more time actually working at the real Hollywood Canteen than she did making movies. One or two nights a week, Joan would report to the Canteen, where she would make sandwiches, serve coffee, and write notes home to the families of servicemen. She also became a member of the American Women's Voluntary Services, and was one of several women who started a daycare center and school for the children of women working in war factories. Years later, Joan would completely dismiss *Hollywood Canteen*, even wondering whether she actually appeared in it—considering the triumphs that came immediately afterward, it's no wonder.

Warner Brothers had trouble coming up with good scripts for Joan. They still seemed to see her as a singer or dancer and even suggested she costar with James Cagney in *Yankee Doodle Dandy*. Joan turned that down, as well as many third-rate scripts that had been offered to and rejected by Bette Davis and other actresses at Warner Bros. Meanwhile, Phillip Terry's career at RKO seemed to be on the rise. RKO had high hopes for Terry, and they let it be known that they were grooming him to be their answer to Clark Gable. Without a film of her own and bored at home, Joan would often accompany her husband to the studio, where she'd coach him or go over lines in his dressing room. Terry had starring roles in minor movies such as *Pan-Americana* (1945), in which he played a photographer who falls for a writer when they are sent to Latin America for a story. There were several "hotcha" musical numbers, and Eve Arden stole the show, as she so often did, with her acerbic delivery as the leading lady (but not the love interest) of the picture. In his next film, *George White's Scandals* (1945), Terry romanced Martha Holliday and was support for stars Joan Davis and Jack Haley. And then his option was dropped by RKO.

In a sense, both Mr. and Mrs. Phillip Terry were unemployed. Joan was still drawing a salary at Warner Bros., but she was turning down picture after picture. She was determined not to get caught in the same rut she'd been in at MGM. Despairing of finding work at another studio, Terry went to work at a war plant, brooding over the fact that his wife was turning down scripts when he would have taken a part in anything. By this time they had adopted a young baby boy they named Phillip Jr. After Joan divorced Phillip, the child was rechristened Christopher so that his name would match his sister Christina's and no longer remind Joan of her ex-husband.

Jack Warner was furious that Joan could not settle on a picture. He came up with a vehicle that he thought would be perfect for her, an Edmund Goulding project named *Never Goodbye*. Warner knew that Joan had always enjoyed working with Goulding and was certain she would approve of the storyline. But Joan gave the script a careful reading and decided that it had "loser" written all over it. When she turned it down, Warner told her that she couldn't expect to draw a salary from Warner Brothers when she refused to appear in any of the pictures they chose for her. Warner was flabbergasted when Joan agreed with him and told him to take her off salary until she and Warner came to an agreement over a project, however long it might take. No other star had ever made such an offer. But it suggested to Warner that Joan was a very determined lady, that she guided her career and guarded her screen image very carefully, and that she truly cared about quality. *Never Goodbye* was never made. Instead Joan did *Mildred Pierce*.

Joan wanted to star in the film version of *Mildred Pierce* very badly. Warner Bros. queen Bette Davis had turned it down, and the front-runner for the role was Barbara Stanwyck, who had already triumphed in another James M. Cain adaptation, *Double Indemnity*. Stanwyck also wanted to play Mildred, and director Michael Curtiz, who had won an Oscar for *Casablanca* in 1943, gave Stanwyck his backing—that is, until Joan agreed to test for the role, changing Curtiz's mind. Until he saw the test, Curtiz was adamantly opposed to casting Joan as Mildred. For the first couple of weeks of filming, he and Joan frequently argued, disagreeing about everything from clothes to screenplay revisions to other matters of interpretation. Producer Jerry Wald, who had been eager for Joan to take the part all along, refereed as often as he could until a mutual respect finally developed between Joan and Curtiz. It did not, however, develop into a warm friendship. *Mildred Pierce* was the first film Joan did for producer Wald, who would produce six more films with Joan from 1946 to 1959. "Jerry always had faith in me," Joan was to say years later.

Mildred Pierce is the story of the eponymous housewife and mother

(Joan), who has a pathological need to win the love and approval of her older daughter Veda (Ann Blyth). Mildred asks her unemployed husband Bert (Bruce Bennett) to leave their home when he begins spending way too much time with a Mrs. Lee Biederhoff (Lee Patrick). Mildred takes a job as a waitress, afraid that snobbish Veda will find out what she does for a living and think less of her. She enlists her husband's unctuous former business partner Wally (Jack Carson) to help her open her own restaurant. Mildred throws herself into her work after the tragic death of her younger daughter Kay (Jo Ann Marlowe), who she knew loved her unconditionally. Mildred becomes involved with Monte Beragon (Zachary Scott), the owner of the property she buys, but she sends him packing when he turns out to be a parasite. When she has a falling-out with Veda, however, she marries Monte in the hopes that the people he knows and the elegant world he inhabits will attract Veda into coming home. This she does, but she and Monte have an affair, which ends when Veda shoots him after Monte tells her that he never loved her. Mildred tries to cover up for Veda, but the police see through her story. Veda is taken away, and it is implied that Mildred and Bert, their love rekindled, will see each other through the coming hard years.

Considering its importance to Joan's career, it is worth taking a look at the property that Warner Bros. had originally acquired. A "serious" book as opposed to a mere crime thriller, Cain's novel is generally excellent. In the book there is no murder, which was created for the movie. The Mildred of the novel is in many ways ahead of her time, a woman determined to make it on her own terms when her husband leaves her. She is a fascinating character, although as one reads the book, one doesn't quite see Joan Crawford in the role—Barbara Stanwyck is probably closer. Some of the changes made for the film make sense; others are inexplicable. In the novel, there is a fascinating scene in which Veda learns from a famous music teacher that she has no real talent as a pianist; she is unable to explain to her mother why this revelation is so devastating to her (this scene partly explains Veda's nastiness). Later, in a moment as contrived as anything in a film script, Veda coincidentally encounters this same teacher as she walks in a park one night singing out loud after hearing a concert, and he somehow recognizes genius in her *voice*. This improbably leads to Veda becoming a kind of Eileen Farrell, an opera singer who makes her name singing on the radio as well as on the stage. The screenwriter, Ranald MacDougall, wisely grasped how ludicrous and convenient all this would play on the screen and left it out altogether.

In the book, Mildred discovers Veda in bed with the husband that she only married to appease Veda in the first place, and she loses her temper so violently that she begins to strangle Veda. This apparently causes Veda to lose her precious voice, but in a gesture that is totally out of character, she agrees to live with Mildred and Bert, her father, when they decide to reconcile. But this is all an act; Veda has not really lost her voice, and the reconciliation was a ruse as well. Veda goes off with Monte, and Bert and Mildred agree that the proper response is "to hell with her!" They take comfort in the fact that they still have each other, and decide to "get stinko." End of book.

It is strange that the filmmakers left one scene in the novel out of the film. In the book, Mildred and Monte break up in highly dramatic fashion; Mildred drives away from his mansion during a storm and her car gets caught in a flood. Monte races after her and tries to drag her out of danger, but she is so anxious to get away from this man that she has come to loathe that she repeatedly struggles out of his clutches and is nearly swept away by the rising waters. After her car is ditched, she manages to walk miles home, sopping wet and miserable. This would have made for quite a vivid sequence for the movie. (Incidentally, Eve Arden's humorous lines, "Leave something on me, I might catch cold," and "Alligators have the right idea; they eat their young," are clever inventions of the screenwriter—they do not appear in the novel.)

As for the film, *Mildred Pierce* is almost perfect moviemaking. The picture is imbued with real cinematic know-how (albeit in a style not as showy as Hitchcock's), and the dialogue is often priceless. Michael Curtiz's direction is crisp, smooth and highly efficient, his handling of both players and props taut and assured. Curtiz and the brilliant cinematographer Ernest Haller ensure that *Mildred Pierce* is filled with expert camerawork, interesting angles, and evocative lighting schemes. Max Steiner may have recycled some music from his score for *Now, Voyager*, but his opening theme for *Mildred Pierce* is excellent.

It is a question if *Mildred Pierce*, like *Double Indemnity*, can truly be classified as "film noir." It shares many of the same elements—sleazy men supported by women, too-young women with hot bodies, illicit love affairs, murder in ritzy quarters on a moonlit night—but it lacks one of the most essential ingredients: a hard-boiled anti-hero, unless one counts Veda.

Joan is wonderful in *Mildred Pierce*, although there were critics of the time who suggested that she didn't have the requisite emotion in certain sequences. Joan does seem to hold back a bit after the death of

Mildred's other, younger daughter; she was afraid that if she overplayed the hysteria and abject grief most mothers would feel at such a moment, she would be accused of chewing the scenery. More important, Curtiz felt strongly that she should underplay the scene to emphasize her character's obsession with Veda. "Please, God, don't let anything happen to Veda," Mildred says significantly at the end of the scene. Mildred's over-the-top desire to do everything and anything to please Veda can be attributed to her overcompensating because of the death of her other child, but Mildred's obsession with Veda actually begins long before her younger daughter's death. When she asks God not to let anything happen to Veda, it's as if she's saying, "I can deal with *this* child's death, barely, but *Veda's—never!*"

There are moments in *Mildred Pierce* when Joan seems to be striking attitudes, or "indicating" an emotion rather than embodying it, but they are few and far between, and occur at appropriate junctures. In general, her performance as Mildred is accomplished and understated. Henry Hart of *Films in Review* wasn't the only one to suggest that there were many elements of Joan in Mildred. "Crawford gave *Mildred Pierce* a reality it might have otherwise lacked," said Hart, "because it was her own life in some ways, a strong woman struggling against misfortune and the wrong men." Because of this, Joan made her Mildred Pierce seem real despite the melodramatic and even far-fetched aspects of the plot, and despite the bravura and charismatic "star turn" that Joan's performance is (one suspects that the more "naturalistic" approach of a 21st century actress wouldn't be nearly as interesting). In other words, Joan worked hard for her Oscar and thoroughly deserved it. True, the role was not new territory for her (as other roles were); everything she did in *Mildred Pierce* she had always been capable of doing, but she was at the top of her form, bringing to bear everything she knew in order to fit herself into the required image and then bring it vividly to life. James M. Cain was delighted with Joan's portrayal; he inscribed a copy of his novel to her, "To Joan Crawford, who brought Mildred to life as I had always hoped she would be and who has my lifelong gratitude."

Joan was complemented by an extraordinarily effective supporting cast in *Mildred Pierce*. Jack Carson was born to play Mildred's sleazy real estate friend Wally. It was the role of a lifetime for Carson, who is natural, believable and altogether excellent in the part. Zachary Scott, who came to prominence earlier the same year in *The Southerner,* was never considered a Hollywood heavyweight, but he was a fine actor who played up to Joan with great ease and knowing aplomb in their many scenes together. Bruce Bennett's performance as Bert is solid and appealing, and Ann Blyth crackles with youthful sensuality and almost sublime bitchiness in her broad put perfect turn as Veda. Eve Arden is as pungent and amusing as ever as Ida, Mildred's business manager and Veda's chief detractor. Butterfly McQueen, who also played Joan's maid in *The Women,* also offers a flavorful and nuanced performance. In her few scenes as Lottie, she exudes a certain poignancy under her dizzy, likable surface that makes you wonder what Lottie's life might be like when she isn't on screen.

Eve Arden had had a bit part in *Dancing Lady,* but she didn't really get to know Joan until she appeared in *Pan Americana* in 1945 with Phillip Terry. Arden knew that Phillip and Joan had adopted children, and since she wanted to do the same, she solicited advice from Phillip, who told her that he would ask Joan, who knew more about it than he did, to give her a call. Arden never expected to hear from Joan, but Joan called her at six forty-five the next morning. "This is Joan Crawford! I have a baby for you!" she cried. Joan and Arden met for lunch and discussed the possibility of adoption, but for some reason it never happened. However, six months later Joan did prove instrumental in getting a child for Eve. This cemented the bond of casual friendship between them, more than their picture work together, which was limited to two films (not counting *Dancing Lady,* in which they had no scenes together). Once, however, Arden did get annoyed with Joan, when after a couple of martinis at a party at Arden's home she went in to wake up and play with the new baby. Arden wrote in her memoirs that "Joan and I got along well together" when they were making *Mildred Pierce.* Joan was nominated for a Best Actress Oscar, which she won. Arden received a supporting nomination, but lost to Anne Revere in *National Velvet.* Arden theorized that she and Joan got along so well together because "she didn't consider me a threat, neither as an actress nor as a rival with men." (In her memoirs, Arden also trots out a tiresome anecdote regarding Joan's alleged cruelty to her children, citing an incident during a visit with her daughter to Joan's house. Christopher got bored with the company and wanted to go out to play, but Joan wouldn't let him. Parents who want their children to be polite and stay and talk to visitors—especially if one of the visitors is another child—aren't generally classified as child abusers, but Joan was afforded no such luxury.)

On the other hand, Ann Blyth remained a friend until Joan's death and a supporter afterward. After doing a reading with her, Joan thought that Blyth had potential, and they rehearsed together in the dressing room before the screen test was shot. Curtiz and Wald had doubts, but again the test convinced them Blyth would be marvelous as Veda. Jerry Wald's first choice to play Veda was none other than Shirley Temple, who had played some good supporting roles since becoming a teenager. Curtiz would have none of it: "And I suppose we'd get Mickey Rooney for the part of Monte?" he snickered.

With the benefit of hindsight, there are many parallels between the monstrous daughter Veda and Joan's real-life adopted daughter Christina. Like Veda, Christina made self-centered and unrealistic demands on her mother that Joan could not possibly meet, and, like Veda, Christina grew to despise her mother. Veda manipulated her mother for money; Christina destroyed her mother's reputation for money.

Joan had a panic attack the night of the Academy Awards and came down with a cold and sore throat that many considered psychosomatic. She was unable to attend the ceremony. Her competition for the evening seemed formidable: Ingrid Bergman in *The Bells of St. Mary's,* Greer Garson in *The Valley of Decision,* Gene Tierney in *Leave Her to Heaven,* and Jennifer Jones in *Love Letters.* If nothing else, Joan gave a performance that was much more striking than the other four: it was pure Hollywood at its best. Joan told others that she was certain Bergman would win. She was surprised and overjoyed when she was announced as the winner.

Good friend Van Johnson, costar Ann Blyth, and many others rushed over to Joan's house to offer their congratulations. Old boyfriend Ray Sterling sent a telegram, as did many, many others. Michael Curtiz brought her the Oscar statuette and was photographed handing it to his bedridden star. Joan conceded that the Oscar might have been given to her for her cumulative efforts, not just for her performance in *Mildred Pierce.* "Frankly, I thought it was *about time,*" she said many years later. She thought she was just as good in such films as *Susan and God* and *A Woman's Face,* among others, which she was. But there was something especially irresistible about *Mildred Pierce* and Joan's vital portrayal of the long-suffering title character.

It was after the premiere of *Mildred Pierce* that Joan realized that her allegedly storybook marriage to Phillip Terry had gone sour. In truth, it had never been in such great shape to begin with. The two had not known each other very well when they got married, and what with their busy schedules at the studio, the children, and both attending a multitude of dinner parties and other official premieres and engagements, they had little time to get acquainted afterward. They also discovered that they had little to talk about. But the main problem was simply that Joan had gotten bored with Phillip.

The inertia set in during the months Joan was unemployed, when she first came to Warner Bros. She began finding ways to avoid Phillip, whose utterly placid nature she sometimes found unnerving. When she was making *Mildred Pierce,* she felt so alive in front of the cameras, and so wan at home with Phillip. She loved being with the children, but she didn't expect them to provide intellectual stimulus or excitement. A Stanford graduate who had attended the Royal Academy of Dramatic Art in London, Phillip was hardly unintelligent, but he couldn't compare to Tone. In fact, Phillip always came up lacking when compared with some of Joan's previous inamoratas. Through no fault of his own, Terry lacked Fairbanks Jr.'s outgoing, gregarious, showoffy nature, couldn't hold a candle to Gable's charisma, and was absolutely no good in a fight the way Tone was. "I think it got to a point where Joan would have welcomed those knock-down, drag-out fights with Franchot Tone over Phillip's bovine-like nature," said Jerry Asher. "He was an awfully nice man, but much too dull as far as Joan was concerned. He just lacked that inner spark that the others had. Joan eventually got bored with Fairbanks, as well, but Phillip was the one who really drove her crazy."

Joan was also afraid that Phillip was losing his drive and ambition. Not only did he not mind being "Mr. Joan Crawford," but he seemed to enjoy it—which Joan found unsettling. He was getting used to Joan being the breadwinner. In fact, in this regard he was altogether too much like Monte in *Mildred Pierce.* Joan had initially been attracted to Phillip's calm, placid, languid nature—it promised a peaceful atmosphere very different from the one she'd had with the abusive, drunken Franchot. Phillip would never beat her, she was certain—but Phillip was too far on the other side of the spectrum. Phillip's docility, the tranquil sterility of their marriage, eventually got on her nerves. For Phillip's part, he perhaps came to find the idea of a ready-made family equally unsettling. "I think he came to feel as if *he* were a baby who'd been picked out of a bassinet while Joan went on about how adorable he was," said Jerry Asher.

Although there had been professional gains during the time he was married to Joan, they might not have represented enough compensation, although most people who knew Phillip agree that he was not much of a predator. Rather, Phillip always took the path of least resistance. When Joan was done with him, he did not put up much of a fight. "Why should he have?" Jerry Asher said, "Joan paid him a very generous settlement which nearly cleared out her bank account. Joan thought Phillip could give her a life of serenity, but he was much too tame for a woman as vital as she was. He was easy-going, when she wanted *exciting*. Franchot may have beaten her, but he never bored her. It probably wasn't until Joan met Al Steele that she found a happy medium." About Phillip Terry, Joan would later write, "I realized I had never loved him. I think I've owed him an apology from the first." But she spoke very little about him, in public or private.

Joan landed in hot water with Hedda Hopper when she phoned Louella Parsons with the exclusive that she and Phillip Terry were getting a divorce. Hedda felt that she had been a big booster of Joan's in the pre–*Mildred Pierce* days, and the first columnist to suggest that *Pierce* should net her the Oscar. "I knew about Joan's early life," Hopper wrote in her memoirs, "her ambitions, loves, disappointments. Many lesser actresses, who hadn't given half her service, had received Academy Awards. I don't say my plugging got her the Oscar, but it certainly didn't hurt. . . . I will never understand why friendship isn't a two-way street." The sentences were carefully phrased, especially the bits about "Joan's early life" and "given half her service," to sound as threatening as they were flattering. Hopper was letting Joan know that she knew where the bodies were buried, and that there was a lot more she could say about Joan's early days—if she wanted to. Why did Joan risk Hopper's wrath and give Parsons the scoop about the divorce? Possibly she was just trying to maintain or establish her independence. Joan did not like anyone to tell her what to do.

This was not the last time Joan would cross swords with Hopper. Twelve years later, the two had a public brouhaha reported in Mike Connolly's column in *The Hollywood Reporter*. "Oh wow, that tongue-lashing between Joan Crawford and Hedda Hopper," Connolly wrote, but without providing any details. Joan was annoyed, to put it mildly, when Hopper insinuated that she and fourth husband Alfred Steele might be getting a divorce because a business commitment of Alfred's prevented them from attending a party William Haines had organized for the new-lyweds. After their verbal brawl, Hopper printed a quote from Joan: "I'm not about to divorce Mr. Steele, today or any other day." Five years after that Joan sat down for lunch with Hopper and Bette Davis as part of a publicity campaign for *What Ever Happened to Baby Jane?* Joan never really liked Hopper, who had had small roles in a couple of Joan's early movies, but felt that "she had her uses. We got along as long as she didn't go too far." She would send Hopper nice notes after every favorable mention in her column, and upbraid her in no uncertain terms after every unfavorable item. Hopper would fume and obliquely mention some little bit of Joan's past that she might someday reveal, in the hopes of getting Joan in line again. But Joan knew that Hopper wouldn't dare. When push came to shove, Hedda Hopper was a little scared of the tenacious Joan Crawford, who was in many ways even tougher than she. In her heart of hearts, Joan Crawford was the woman Hopper, failed actress turned gossip hen, always wanted to be.

After Phillip Terry was out of her life, Joan began dating a handsome lawyer named Greg Bautzer. Bautzer became her main escort to parties and premieres, and the two ran hot and cold for several years. Bautzer enjoyed being in the limelight and relished his status as "celebrity lawyer to the stars." (The "Greg Savitt" character in the movie version of *Mommie Dearest* is probably based on Bautzer.) Most chroniclers of their relationship (including daughter Christina) paint Joan as the villainess, with her purported expectations that Bautzer bow down and worship her, be her slave and carry out her every whim. The truth was that Bautzer, like most men Joan met, expected Joan to bend to *his* will as the natural order of things: men were the bosses, women did as they were told. This would certainly not sit well with an independent female like Joan Crawford. The story generally goes that Joan booted Bautzer out of her life—indeed, her car—because he paid too much attention to younger women at parties, and that aspect may well have been true. But mostly Joan got tired of constantly battling with Bautzer, who regarded it as his male prerogative to be in control at all times. He wasn't a placid doormat like Phillip Terry, which is one reason he lasted as long as he did; neither did he end up at the other extreme, and beat Joan, as Tone had. The trouble was that Joan didn't like taking orders from anyone—and why should she have? She had made it to the top on her own. No man was going to tell her what to do.

The title of *Humoresque* (1946), Joan's next film, of course comes from Antonín Dvořák's famous piano composition. It begins as the story of Paul Boray (John Garfield), who as a child nags his father for a violin and surprises everyone by practicing every day when he does get one. Years later he becomes a talented musician, but has trouble holding down a job until his friend and mentor Sid Jeffers (Oscar Levant) takes him to a society party run by Helen Wright (Joan), a patron of the arts. Helen and Paul are rather rude to one another, but Helen is intrigued by Paul's ability and rough-hewn appeal. She becomes Paul's sponsor, but both Helen's husband and Paul's mother are afraid that something more will develop between the two—which then happens. Her husband having agreed to a divorce, Helen is willing to commit to a relationship with Paul; even though she knows that he is totally committed to his musical career, she can't accept playing "second fiddle" to anyone. Drunk, alone, and afraid that she will never find happiness with anyone, Helen walks into the ocean as Wagner's "Liebestod," played by Paul in a concert hall, blares from the radio.

Helen Wright is perhaps Joan's most glamorous role, and the movie has a gloss normally associated with MGM rather than Warner Brothers. Thirty-five minutes elapse before Joan appears, dressed in an elegant gown by Adrian and surrounded by men vying to light her cigarette. When we first meet her, Helen comes off as somewhat insolent and "superior," but when she finally notices Paul she becomes intrigued and even a little intimidated, leading to the verbal sparring match between them. Some felt that neither Joan nor costar John Garfield were always up to the challenges of playwright Clifford Odets's wonderful dialogue, but if the star duo—who enjoyed splendid chemistry together—can be accused of anything, it's an occasional lack of spontaneity. Joan's line readings are always on the money, and her performance is generally assured and charismatic. A few times, she gets the most out of the pungent dialogue, such as when Helen tells Paul about her two previous husbands: "One was a crybaby, one was a caveman; between the two of them I lost my girlhood." If her performance is somewhat artificial, it is understandable insofar as Helen is essentially a "drama queen" who drinks too much and clings to intense emotions; she's wealthy, entitled, and accustomed to having her own way. In other words, Joan plays Helen just the way she ought to be played. In the climactic scene, in which Joan expertly pantomimes her confusion and anguish as she listens to Paul play on the radio, every note rings true. The scene is moving even before the "Liebestod" starts, this despite the fact that Helen is not a terribly sympathetic character. There is a moment during Helen's final phone conversation with Paul when Joan responds too quickly, but otherwise her timing and technique are flawless. She also pulls off some expressive pantomiming when Helen sits in the concert hall in an earlier scene and listens to Paul play—her eyes close, her glistening lips part, her head goes back as she abandons herself, not so much to the music, one suspects, but to Paul's sensuality. "What do you *think* I was thinking about?" she jokingly responded when asked about this sequence. In later years, Joan wasn't entirely pleased with her performance in *Humoresque*, lumping it with *Rain* and feeling that she had overacted. "There are some scenes where I think I just did too much," she said, but the film itself doesn't bear this out. Helen was, after all, a rather neurotic character, and her reactions were generally outsized.

Any movie that uses the "Liebestod" from Wagner's magnificent *Tristan und Isolde* for musical background is, of course, hedging its bets, but at least *Humoresque* uses it more appropriately than *Blume in Love* and others. The suicide sequence is artfully put together, and it works beautifully, although some have criticized the way the camera follows Helen into the water and sinks toward the bottom, as air bubbles rise to the surface. It is clear that Helen's suicide is foolish and completely compulsive, a sudden irreversible decision fueled by alcohol and self-pity, as she faces the enormity of the ocean and the peace it represents. Helen's death is a tragic waste—but one can't help but feel that Paul is well rid of her. As Helen herself puts it, "You don't want me. I'm too wearying on the nerves."

Again Joan was surrounded by a top-flight supporting cast: J. Carrol Naish as Paul's grumpy but loving father; Ruth Nelson as his initially supportive and later disapproving mother; and especially Joan Chandler as Gina, the musician colleague who is unrequitedly in love with Paul. Oscar Levant was never much of an actor, but his personality perfectly fits the cynical, self-deprecating Sid, who continuously cracks jokes to hide his obvious despair over his lack of success in life. Paul as a boy is played with great sensitivity by little Bobby Blake, who decades later would be arrested (as Robert Blake) for allegedly murdering his wife outside a restaurant.

The dialogue by Odets and Zachary Gold lifts *Humoresque* above the usual soap-opera level, but not quite into the realm of "masterpiece." To its credit, the movie does delve into the difficulties of becoming an artist while also making a living and dealing with unsupportive family members, and it doesn't gloss the grim realities facing those who aspire to a career in classical music—the need for money, a sponsor, publicity, critical approval, and so on. Director Jean Negulesco makes excellent use of frequent close-ups, such as during a scene in the concert hall when the various characters react to the emotions brought out by the music. Of course, much of *Humoresque* should be taken with a grain of salt. Garfield, although quite good as Paul Boray, is Hollywood's stereotype of the rude, stubborn, temperamental *artiste,* and patrons of the arts don't always lust after the artists they promote, as Joan's Helen Wright does.

Producer Jerry Wald thought that Joan shouldn't do *Humoresque,* and at first he did not offer it to her. She might never have gotten the part if John Garfield had not objected to some of the other names being bandied about as leading lady. Wald thought the role was merely a supporting part, and besides, it was really a John Garfield movie. Joan thought that the role really suited her, and she wanted to work with Garfield, whom she admired as a "serious" actor. When everyone finally realized that Joan was genuinely anxious to play Helen, the role was beefed up into more than a supporting part. Joan got top billing; her name was placed above Garfield's, just as it had been above Gable's for *Strange Cargo*.

Joan and Garfield got along well during the making of *Humoresque*; Joan would never confirm whether or not she and Garfield (who was married at the time) had an affair, or even a Hollywood "quickie." It is hard to believe that Joan and Garfield, who certainly exuded sexual tension in the movie, did not get together intimately at some point during filming or shortly afterward. Garfield's wife Roberta was nervous about Joan, but Joan won her over when she had William Haines help her with some redecorating. Rumor has it that when they were first introduced, Garfield pinched Joan's nipple; initially furious, Joan later admired his audacity and sexual aggressiveness—and told him so. She got Garfield in her corner when she realized some of the concert scenes weren't showing him to his best advantage and suggested that Negulesco reshoot them. It gave the scenes the proper balance.

For her next picture, Joan was fully prepared to go mad—and she did.

Bernard Wohl Collection

Chapter Eleven

POSSESSED

"*Possessed* (1947) contained the best performance I ever gave," Joan told Lawrence Quirk in 1956. "I put so much of myself into it!" She added that she always regretted not fighting the Warner Bros. front office harder when they came up with the title *Possessed,* as it was the same as her 1931 film for MGM. "I wanted to call it *The Secret,* but they overruled me. Since the main character was supposed, mentally, to be 'possessed' by devils, that seemed the more logical title to them."

Louise Howell (Joan) is a nurse to a neurotic, bedridden woman who wrongly suspects that Louise is having an affair with her husband, Dean Graham (Raymond Massey). In fact, Louise is madly and unrequitedly in love with a neighbor, engineer playboy David Sutton (Van Heflin), who gracefully tries to rebuff Louise's advances, to no avail. After his wife commits suicide, Graham asks Louise to marry him, which she does after winning the blessing of his suspicious and hostile daughter Carol (Geraldine Brooks). Although Louise is not in love with Graham, all is set to proceed uneventfully, but then David boorishly crashes their wedding reception. Then David begins to court Carol, who falls in love with him. This all brings out the latent schizophrenia lying dormant in Louise, and she begins to have hallucinations. She goes to David's apartment and shoots him dead during a quarrel. This drives her into full psychosis, and she is picked up after collapsing in a coffee shop. Graham is called to her side at the hospital, determined to stick by her as she confronts an uncertain future.

A controversial aspect of the picture is Louise's murder of David. At the end of the film a psychiatrist tells Graham that Louise will have to go on trial, and also that he believes she was not responsible for her actions. "Whether a jury will understand that or not, I can't tell you," the doctor says. When Louise pulls the gun on David, telling him to stay away from Carol, David—wisely or unwisely, depending on how you look at it—says, "At least be honest about it. You don't care about Carol. You never did. I'd rather be killed by a jealous woman than a noble one." Of course he's right, something a prosecuting district attorney would certainly play up in his closing statement to the jury. Even if Louise's mental illness is legitimate (as opposed to being merely emotionally disturbed), one suspects she would have shot David no matter what her mental condition. Her actions are those of a perfectly lucid jealous woman—one thinks of Jean Harris, the "diet doctor" murderess, for instance—and not an out-and-out psycho. Nowadays it would all make for an interesting episode of *Law and Order*.

For the most part, *Possessed* was well directed by Curtis Bernhardt. The opening sequence, in which Louise wanders empty streets in shock looking for the man she has killed, is quite striking, as is the subjective camerawork during her arrival at the hospital. In later years, Joan was amused that the two doctors who first attend to Louise were both good-looking (we see them looking down at the camera, filling in for Louise's point of view). "Wouldn't you know they'd both be so handsome?" Joan joked. The actor playing the blond doctor had had a small part in the party scene of *Humoresque,* as one of the young men Helen Wright surrounded herself with. *Possessed* was scripted by Ranald MacDougall with Silvia Richards; he contributed the same wonderful dialogue that so enhanced *Mildred Pierce.*

Critic James Agee probably summed it up best when he wrote of Joan's performance in *Possessed,* "Though she is not quite up to her hardest scenes, Miss Crawford is generally excellent, performing with the passion and intelligence of an actress who is not content with just one Oscar." Indeed, Joan did receive her second Best Actress Academy Award nomination for *Possessed,* but lost to Loretta Young for her work in *The Farmer's Daughter.* Joan certainly wasn't alone in thinking *Possessed* featured her best work on film. *The Hollywood Reporter,* for example, wrote that it was "the greatest performance—bar none—of her brilliant career." Her fans, however, have always been divided as to the accuracy of that statement. Is Joan really better in *Possessed* than she is in *Mildred Pierce, A Woman's Face,* or *Rain?* Probably not. In 1947, it was considered daring for an actor to tackle the role of a character with severe mental problems, and *Possessed* scores points because it even takes us directly inside Louise's mind on several occasions. There's a whole sequence, in which Louise hits Carol and sends her careening down the staircase, that turns out to be a complete hallucination, only taking place

in Louise's distorted mind. (This sort of fantasy sequence is now obligatory in afternoon soap operas.)

Joan researched schizophrenia and the behavior of patients afflicted
with the disease, and she does convey her character's confusion and dis-
orientation. Because she didn't play "mad" with grandiose gestures,
clenched teeth, bulging eyes and distorted facial expressions, à la Dwight
Frye as Renfield in *Dracula,* her interpretation was seen by some as great
acting. In truth, her more restrained depiction of mental illness, using
only the occasional off-kilter look, was a fairly standard delineation of
psychosis for the period. For years afterward, Joan would congratulate
herself on her portrayal of a schizophrenic, but the script merely calls for
her to be either numb and unemotional (her hospital scenes) or biting
and sarcastic (when she finally goes over the edge and shoots David). She
doesn't really "go mad" with any particular finesse, but on the other
hand she doesn't chew the scenery either, as a lesser actress might have.
The doctors she interviewed and the patients she observed made it clear
to her that that would have been the wrong way to go about the role.
The next year, 20th Century Fox's *The Snake Pit,* starring Olivia de
Havilland (who wasn't any better than Joan but had many more scenes
in which she was required to play "crazy"), would take viewers into a
mental institution and into the psychotic mind; this was only one of
many other similar, but more intense and realistic, pictures. Joan's depiction has simply become dated.

But as Agee and others observed, Joan is fine in the rest of the
movie. It could be argued that she fails to create a sustained characterization, but she is, after all, playing a moody person (to put it mildly)
with more than one personality, and the film itself is schizophrenic as
well. Is *Possessed* a thriller, a drama, a "woman's film," a melodrama? It
goes in many different directions. At one point it even threatens to turn
into a ghost story, when Louise thinks she hears and sees her husband's
dead former wife. For some viewers all of these elements never quite jell,
but for others *Possessed* is absorbing, suspenseful, and—despite the fact
that the story is told in flashback—unpredictable. We know all we really
need to know about Louise in her first appearance in David's house,
when she reveals how much she loves and needs him, and hints at her
unstable nature. Her unrequited, obsessive love for David is a symptom
of her illness, not the other way around. It has been remarked that Joan
seems too cool, too much like a femme fatale, in the scene with the police
after Graham's wife is found dead in the lake, but Joan was directed to
act in that style, since Louise later erroneously comes to believe that she

killed the woman. Director Curtis Bernhardt wanted the audience to keep guessing: did she do it or not?

Joan's costars thought highly of her work in *Possessed*. Many years later, Raymond Massey told Lawrence Quirk, "I never realized until I did that picture with Joan what a naturally gifted actress she was. I had seen and admired a number of her earlier films, but I felt she had developed an expertise in purveying Hollywood artifice, and that her personality, rather than any real talent, carried her. *Possessed* changed my mind." Massey especially recalled the scene in which Graham asks Louise to marry him after David has just scornfully rejected her yet again. "I found myself electrified by the wild lightning in her ironic laughter, and the genuine passion and conviction with which she told my character how wonderful it was to be wanted, that she was through weeping, that 'terrible things happened to a woman when she wasn't wanted.' She had many other fine scenes in that picture, but that is the one that stays most vividly in my mind." In *Possessed,* Joan demonstrated more convincingly than ever how well her technique was working for her. She needed to feel the emotions of a scene so intensely that she would find herself living it, even an hour after the scene was over. "Actresses like Bette Davis may be able to turn it on and off at will," Joan said. "*I* can't do that, at least not with a role as complex and intense as the one in *Possessed.*"

Van Heflin, who was as blunt a critic of the performances of others as anyone, admitted somewhat sardonically in 1956 that Joan had also surprised him in *Possessed*: "Damn, I knew Joan had perfected the art of projecting her personality, but I never took her that seriously as an actress until I found myself up against her in *that*. She outplayed me, Raymond, everybody in the cast—and she was up against some experienced competition. Yet she carried the day." Heflin's own performance in *Possessed* is superb; he effortlessly creates a character who is simultaneously likable and unlikable, and his playing is consistently natural and believable.

Don McGuire, the young actor who played the medical assistant in the psychiatric sequences, always remembered Joan's intensity, both in *Possessed* and in *Humoresque,* in which he had played a bartender. "Even when she was lying prone and comatose on a hospital bed, as she was in one sequence, there was an electricity to her. She was not lying there like a log, no sir. You could sense the suffering and torment just beneath the knocked-out, silent surface."

In her first picture, Geraldine Brooks is excellent as well. She re-

Joan looking love-struck in *Paris* (1926). J.C. Archives, Inc.

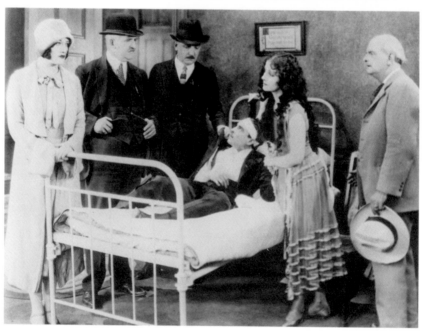

A tense scene in *The Boob* (1926). J.C. Archives, Inc.

Above, Joan found Harry Langdon a revelation to work with in *Tramp Tramp Tramp (1926). Below,* In costume with Tim McCoy in *Winners of the Wilderness* (1927). J.C. Archives, Inc.

With the tragic, later suicidal, James Murray in *Rose Marie* (1928). J.C. Archives, Inc.

Off-screen lesbian rumors circulated about Joan and Dorothy Sebastian, here in *Our Dancing Daughters* (1928). J.C. Archives, Inc.

Above, Joan and Johnny Mack Brown sparkle in *Our Dancing Daughters* (1928). *Below,* Joan and the guys clown it up in *Our Modern Maidens* (1929). J.C. Archives, Inc.

Joan and first husband, Douglas Fairbanks Jr., in an on-screen wedding in *Our Modern Maidens* (1929). Jerry Ohlinger.

Sheet music for *Montana Moon* (1930). J.C. Archives, Inc.

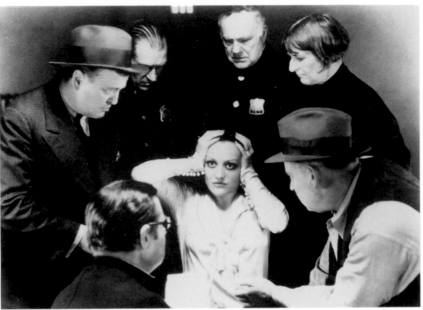

Joan under cop pressure in *Paid* (1930). J.C. Archives, Inc.

With Clark Gable, her first great love, in *Possessed* (1931). Bernard Wohl Collection.

Wallace Beery and Joan in advertising copy for *Grand Hotel* (1932). J.C. Archives, Inc.

Above, Relaxing on the set with the Barrymore brothers during the making of *Grand Hotel* (1932). J.C. Archives, Inc. *Below,* James R. Quirk of *Photoplay,* Crawford's mentor and one-time lover (1929). Lawrence J. Quirk Collection.

Right, Photoplay cover with Crawford, circa 1934. Jerry Ohlinger. *Below,* Joan and second husband Franchot Tone, 1933. J.C. Archives, Inc.

Above, Robert Young, Franchot Tone, and Crawford in a tense romantic moment in *Today We Live* (1933). *Left,* Joan gets the rough treatment from Gable in *Dancing Lady* (1933). J.C. Archives, Inc.

All dolled up in *Sadie McKee* (1934). J.C. Archives, Inc.

Loving it up with Robert Montgomery in *Forsaking All Others* (1934). J.C. Archives, Inc.

Above, Tone gives Gable the evil eye as Joan looks on in an ad for *Love on the Run* (1936). Bernard Wohl Collection. *Below,* Crawford greatly respected co-star Spencer Tracy for his acting talent, here in *Mannequin* (1938). J.C. Archives, Inc.

Above, Joan and on-screen hubby Melvyn Douglas take on the family (Fay Bainter, Margaret Sullavan, Robert Young) in *The Shining Hour* (1938). *Right,* There was no love lost between Joan and Norma Shearer, here in *The Women* (1939). J.C. Archives, Inc.

Above, Joan and Gable in their last screen appearance together in *Strange Cargo* (1940). *Below,* Joan puts on airs with Nigel Bruce, Bruce Cabot, and Rose Hobart in *Susan and God* (1940). J.C. Archives, Inc.

Above, In *A Woman's Face* (1941) with Albert Bassermann, Marjorie Main, and Richard Nichols, Joan's highlight performance at MGM. *Below,* Joan and Melvyn Douglas in a tense moment from *A Woman's Face.* J.C. Archives, Inc.

Above, Herbert Marshall and disillusioned Joan in *When Ladies Meet* (1941). *Below,* Joan and Greer Garson give each other the shoulder while Marshall and Robert Taylor look on with bemusement. J.C. Archives, Inc.

Joan clowns with her new husband Phillip Terry as her director Richard Thorpe looks on. The set of *Above Suspicion* (1943). J.C. Archives, Inc.

Joan found co-star John Wayne a sexy challenge in *Reunion in France* (1942). J.C. Archives, Inc.

Joan loved designer Irene's clothes; here on the set of *Above Suspicion* (1943).
J.C. Archives, Inc.

Above, Joan with Christopher and Christina on the set of *Mildred Pierce* (1945). *Below,* Ann Blyth, here in *Mildred Pierce* (1945) with Joan, always spoke well of Joan off screen. J.C. Archives, Inc.

Joan was sick in bed when she received her Oscar for *Mildred Pierce* (1945). Director Michael Curtiz delivered it. J.C. Archives, Inc.

Joan having man trouble with John Garfield in *Humoresque* (1946). Bernard Wohl Collection.

Joan makes like a designer in *Daisy Kenyon* (1947). J.C. Archives, Inc.

Joan looking radiant in *Goodbye My Fancy* (1951). J.C. Archives, Inc.

Showing off one of her favorite gowns, 1952. J.C. Archives, Inc.

Joan singing "You Won't Forget Me" in *Torch Song* (1953). J.C. Archives, Inc.

Left, Joan and Sterling Hayden had chemistry in *Johnny Guitar* (1954). Off screen, however, they came to despise each other. *Below,* Joan and Jeff Chandler tussle in *Female on the Beach* (1955). The two had had an affair before they made the picture together. J.C. Archives, Inc.

JOAN CRAWFORD
JEFF CHANDLER
Female on The Beach
co-starring JAN STERLING
A UNIVERSAL-INTERNATIONAL PICTURE

New husband Alfred Steele and Joan cut the wedding cake in Las Vegas in 1955. J.C. Archives, Inc.

Joan gave Cliff Robertson his big movie break in *Autumn Leaves* (1956). J.C. Archives, Inc.

Above, A bemused Jack Warner poses with Bette Davis and Joan Crawford at a party preceding the filming of *What Ever Happened to Baby Jane?* (1962). Reel Stills Collection. *Below*, Director Robert Aldrich referees Bette and Joan on the set of the movie. Doug McClelland Collection.

Above, Bette appears to give Joan a thorough kicking in *What Ever Happened to Baby Jane?* (1962). Bette's foot was actually nowhere near Joan's body. *Below,* Joan takes her gals through a routine of calisthenics in *The Caretakers* (1963). J.C. Archives, Inc.

Above, John Ireland sticks it to Joan in *I Saw What You Did* (1965). J.C. Archives, Inc. *Below,* Joan does a read-through for *Hush…Hush, Sweet Charlotte* (1964) with co-stars Bette Davis and Joseph Cotten (far left) and director Robert Aldrich. Joan later withdrew from the picture. Reel Stills Collection.

Above, Joan tries to stab Herbert Lom in part one of "The Five Daughters Affair" in *The Man from U.N.C.L.E* (1967). The episodes were released theatrically in Europe as *The Karate Killers;* Joan was killed off much too early. *Below,* At age sixty-four, still generating heat, this time with handsome Ty Hardin in *Berserk* (1968). J.C. Archives, Inc.

In her sixties, still enjoying a party. J.C. Archives, Inc.

Above, Visiting the set of *Rosemary's Baby* with Van Johnson (far left) in 1968. Mia Farrow stands next to Joan; director, Roman Polanski and producer William Castle are on her right. *Below,* Joan clowns it up with Joe Cornelius (in monster suit) on the set of *Trog* (1970), her last theatrical feature. J.C. Archives, Inc.

Joan was not thrilled with this candid shot taken at a party for Rosalind Russell in 1974. She was seventy years old at the time. *Reel Stills Collection.*

marked how helpful Joan had been to her during the making of the film. "It was my first real part—I had to do a lot of reacting, and rather intensely. Joan went all-out, explaining the mechanics of the scenes. When Curtis [Bernhardt] asked her once, in jocular friendliness, who was directing, he or her, and why was she cuing-in me on the side, Joan shot right back and said *she* was the one who had to act with me, and she wanted our interplay just right. Curtis later agreed that she was right, that she got the tone and style she wanted when we worked together." The only other problem Joan had with Bernhardt was that he had just come off working with Bette Davis on *A Stolen Life,* and occasionally referred to Joan as "Bette." Joan would playfully throw something at Bernhardt, but she was more amused than angry. Even though Joan was now working at Davis's studio, they were working on different projects, and they weren't interacting that much. At this point in time, there wasn't much of a "feud" between them.

The musical score by Franz Waxman makes heavy use of the somber and tormented "Chopin" section of Robert Schumann's *Carnaval,* a collection of sad, introspective piano pieces. It certainly complements Joan's performance well. The *Carnaval* theme grabs the viewer's attention during the opening credits and grows more sinister and insistent as the film progresses, aptly accenting the stages of Louise's mental disintegration. Waxman's original music is particularly effective in a horrific scene in which Louise suffers the delusion that she has thrown Carol down a flight of stairs, killing her. The musical nuances, combined with Joan's tormented facial expressions, make for a memorably disturbing effect.

Possessed was a very successful picture and won Joan a lot of positive attention. The executives at Warner's were thrilled with the results, especially in terms of its box-office grosses. A woman who had undergone shock treatment at a Pasadena sanitarium while Joan and others involved in the production were allegedly watching, however, smelled money, and even before the film was finished shooting she filed a lawsuit claiming invasion of privacy. Named in the action were the sanitarium, Warner Brothers, and Joan Crawford. The woman insisted that she had never given anyone permission to watch her treatment, and wanted $200,000 in damages. She settled out of court for far less than the amount she had been seeking.

Daisy Kenyon (1947) has always divided Crawford fans, but love it or hate it, it's one of the actress's most interesting pictures. Like many of Joan's films, it needs to be seen more than once to be fully appreciated.

The picture is indeed talky, which makes it dull for some, but the talk is mostly intelligent and psychologically astute. With handsome production values courtesy of 20th Century Fox, superior direction by Otto Preminger, and some fine acting from Joan and others, *Daisy Kenyon* has quite a lot going for it.

Joan played the unmarried title character, who has fallen in love with a supposedly unhappily married lawyer, Dan (Dana Andrews), but Daisy realizes that he will never leave his wife Lucille (Ruth Warrick) for her. She meets and marries an emotionally wounded widower and former soldier named Peter (Henry Fonda), and the two of them try to build a life together while forgetting their past loves. But Dan can't let go of Daisy that easily, and the situation explodes when Lucille learns of Dan's true feelings for Daisy and sues for divorce. Peter seems willing to step aside and let Dan and Daisy renew their relationship, but is unsurprised when Daisy sends Dan packing, realizing how much she loves her husband. "When it comes to combat maneuvers, you two are babies next to me," he tells her at the end.

As Daisy, Joan offers another professional, effective and generally realistic performance as a very conflicted woman. It's interesting that Joan did *Daisy Kenyon* for Fox, when she criticized Warners for putting her into too many stereotypical "Joan Crawford" films. In the naturalistic scene in which Dan comes to her apartment and tries to kiss her after she has broken off with him, Joan utterly embodies the appropriate emotions as Daisy pushes him away, beats him with her fists, and finally bursts into tears. Throughout her life, Joan tried to resist the alluring pull of men she knew were wrong for her. In making this scene believable, she had plenty of experience to draw upon.

She also had plenty of experience being in love with married men. In *Daisy Kenyon*, where the heroine is the mistress, the audience is asked to accept that the wife is undeserving of her husband, with precious little evidence but the implication that her own unhappiness has caused her to treat her children roughly. Daisy never wonders what Lucille may be going through: "I have more to be jealous of than she does," she tells Dan. Despite Joan's fine and incisive performance, it often seems as if her personality is solely defined by her relationship with the two men in her life. She seems to have no real characterization except insofar as it relates to Dan and Peter.

Still, Daisy doesn't completely let the men off the hook—for example, she's furious that the two men try to decide upon her fate together. There is reason to believe that the writer of *Daisy Kenyon,* David

Hertz, working from the novel by Elizabeth Janeway, had more in mind than just a simple soap opera. When Peter tells Daisy that since his wife's fatal car accident he has been emotionally numb, she informs him that if he were really numb he "wouldn't know it and wouldn't be here trying to convince me of it." When Dan complains that he's been humbled by losing his first case, Daisy tells him, "That's not being humble, that's being sorry for yourself." Daisy is an attractive, intelligent, in some ways modern woman, but she is not an especially warm one. In the case Dan loses, he was trying to help an (unseen) Japanese-American soldier who had fought bravely for the U.S. during the war reacquire the farm taken from him while he was overseas (this would have made an interesting movie all by itself). It is not surprising that the essentially selfish Dan would feel sorrier for himself than for the unfortunate soldier, but the script required that Daisy show as little real emotion over the whole matter as Dan does.

As Dan, Dana Andrews offers one of his best performances. It could be argued that Henry Fonda lacks the resources to convey his character's vulnerability, world-weariness, and pathos, but he quotes Robert Burns to Joan quite convincingly. Preminger keeps the otherwise talky movie lively with some interesting touches. As Dan leaves Daisy's apartment in the first scene, her smile turns to a frown, she sinks into a chair, and in the background a rainfall can suddenly be seen through the window. Theatrical, perhaps even clichéd—but it works. When the constant ringing of the phone—she knows it's either Dan or Peter bothering her at a moment when she needs to be alone—drives Daisy out of the cottage and into her car, Preminger keeps the ringing phone on the soundtrack even as she's driving hastily down the road. Preminger, who also produced the picture, hedged his bets by inviting two famous newspaper columnists, Walter Winchell and Leonard Lyons, to appear as themselves in a scene set at the Stork Club in Manhattan. This insured that *Daisy Kenyon* would get plenty of coverage in the press, but not all of the reviews turned out to be favorable.

There was some second-unit location shooting done in Greenwich Village to match sets built on a Hollywood soundstage. This is one of the few instances in which Greenwich Village in a movie actually looks like the real Greenwich Village. (Some of the worst offenders in this regard are *Greenwich Village* (1944), *The Seventh Victim* (1943), and—worst of all—Stanley Kubrick's final film *Eyes Wide Shut*.) The building where Daisy's apartment is located, 32 West 12th Street, still exists, and it looks just like it does in the movie. The Greenwich Village theater where Daisy and her friend go to the movies, and where Dan watches for them from a coffee shop across the street, was torn down in 2001 to make room for a gymnastic studio. The coffee shop has since been modernized and has re-opened under a new name.

Fonda and Andrews found the set of *Daisy Kenyon* too cold—literally. Joan wanted the air-conditioning turned up high during this particular shoot—she liked it around fifty-eight degrees—and they were constantly complaining about the temperature. At first they were pretending to shiver; after a while, they were shivering for real. Fonda wore a raccoon coat—and not just for show. Joan bought them pairs of long underwear and jokingly suggested they wear them underneath their clothing. Joan was attracted to both of the leading men, but she didn't get very far with Fonda at first. She went to the wardrobe department and asked them to make her what Dore Schary described as "a jockstrap of rhinestones, gold sequins, and red beads." She had the jockstrap gift-wrapped and presented it to Fonda, although it took him a while to figure out what the hell it was. Later, as they were shooting a scene requiring Fonda to carry Joan up some stairs, she whispered gently in his ear, inquiring whether he would model it for her later. "He almost dropped me down the stairs," Joan laughed. In his private life, Fonda was actually in a situation similar to that of his character's rival Dan, unhappily married to a woman who strenuously objected to his affairs and who would eventually commit suicide.

Otto Preminger always spoke respectfully of Joan. "I had a happy time making *Daisy Kenyon* with that remarkable, independent, and competent woman," he wrote in his memoirs. To Lawrence Quirk he said, "Joan was a pro who knew how to get the effect she was after. She did not need much help from me. By that time in her career, she'd appeared in dozens of movies and knew what she was doing, which was more than I could say about a lot of other actors I've worked with. I found her very pleasant, amusing, and generous." During filming, Joan bought new outdoor furnishings for Preminger's garden because she noticed that his existing ones were a little worn. Others would jump at this as proof of Joan's "controlling nature" or presumptuous behavior, but surely it was just a pleasant gesture for someone she liked. Joan often did impulsive things like that, usually with the best of intentions. She always credited Preminger with pulling off *Daisy Kenyon,* which she felt had a cliché-ridden storyline—"the usual triangle helped out by two very handsome young men."

Ruth Warrick, however, was never a fan of Crawford's. "She seemed to live in a crackle of tension one could almost feel like a physical thing around her," she wrote in her memoirs. Warrick was also annoyed with Joan because of the air-conditioning. Joan lost further points with Warrick when she saw Joan instructing her children how to behave in front of the press. Like many people, Warrick didn't understand that this was just common sense to someone as public-oriented as Joan. There was inevitable jealousy on both sides as well. Warrick was eleven years younger than Joan, but Joan was a major star, whereas Warrick's only noteworthy film credit was *Citizen Kane,* before she was banished to the relative obscurity of television soap operas. Warrick was only one of many lesser performers who sharpened their axes on Joan because of her success. Considering her opinion of Crawford, it is ironic that Warrick plays a child abuser in *Daisy Kenyon.* "You see [the children] for five minutes a day," Lucille tells Dan, "but interfere when I try to make better human beings out of my daughters!" As far as Joan was concerned, her disciplining of her children was intended for the same reason. The year *Daisy Kenyon* was released, 1947, was also the year Joan adopted two more children, little girls named Cindy and Cathy whom she always referred to as "the twins."

Flamingo Road was based on a novel by Robert Wilder (it was also a play); he would later write *Written on the Wind,* among other movies. He was hired to compress his sprawling story into an hour and a half of screen time. The story deals with a woman, Lane Bellamy (Joan), who stays behind in the small town of Boldon when the rest of the carnival employing her as a dancer has to flee from creditors. She's grown tired of hopping from place to place and wants to lay down roots in Boldon, hoping one day to make it to the ritzy part of town, Flamingo Road. The deputy sheriff, Fielding Carlisle (Zachary Scott), befriends and romances Lane, but marries his society fiancée when he decides to run for the Senate. Sheriff Titus Semple (Sydney Greenstreet) tries to throw Lane out of town so that she can't tempt Fielding; when that fails, he has her thrown in jail on bogus charges of prostitution. Lane not only gets out of jail, but winds up married to political boss Dan Reynolds (David Brian), and they live together—where else?—on Flamingo Road. But Titus still wants to make trouble for the couple and, in a bravura climax, Lane winds up shooting the rotund troublemaker as they tussle over a gun. Dan vows to wait for her to get out of jail. End of movie.

Michael Curtiz hoped to give the melodramatic *Flamingo Road* the same bite he had given *Mildred Pierce,* but this time around he was working with an inferior story. Although Curtiz suggests the interlocking of

Lane's and Field's fates by surrounding their silhouettes with a circle of light, the film loses the thread of this theme rather quickly. Worse, a half hour in, Joan seems no longer to be the focus of the movie—it's simply taken over by the convoluted chicanery of the portly, milk-guzzling sheriff Titus Semple. At least Greenstreet made for a formidable opponent for Joan, who remembered that "Sydney was a really fine actor, and it was a pleasure to have someone on that level to play off in our scenes together. He certainly gave me a run for my money. What a presence! And that girth of his!"

Underneath a more or less amiable nature, Greenstreet had an essential contempt for "movie stars and pretty people," but he respected Joan, whom he saw as "tough, professional, and a better actress than a lot of people realize. Her gifts may not have been natural, her talents may have been carefully nurtured or even manufactured over the years, but however she learned, she learned." In *Flamingo Road,* Greenstreet is given a speech about how fat people are always perceived as happy and harmless but underneath may be quite a different story, a perception Titus exploits to the hilt in the movie (although he seems malevolent from the very first). Lane's first comment on Greenstreet's Sheriff Semple: "We had better looking people than that in our sideshows."

Author Robert Wilder and his wife had first turned the novel into a play, from which some of the amusing dialogue was lifted. After Lane tells Fielding that she only has three dollars to her name, he replies, "that isn't much," to which she says, "That's a lot when I think of how many times I didn't have three dollars." Locked up in jail, she asks another inmate what she's in for. The reply: "My boyfriend cut himself on a knife I was holding." *Flamingo Road* keeps returning to the Crawford-Greenstreet duel of wits, which is where the movie really hums. Titus likens Lane to a rat that kept nibbling on his toes until he went about "plugging up all the rat holes." When he tells Lane that she's still acting like a cheap carnival girl, she slaps him in the face—twice. (This leads to her being framed for prostitution.) Lane gets even when she turns up as the now-wealthy Mrs. Dan Reynolds and tells Titus about a rogue elephant who went after his keeper and was shot. "You wouldn't believe how much trouble it is to dispose of a dead elephant."

Lane Bellamy is a typical hard-outside/soft-inside kind of character that Joan was essaying during this period. Joan looks very pretty with her hair lightened for the role and, as Lane, is insolent, smart-mouthed, and borderline bitchy. As usual in pictures of this sort, Joan identified with women born on the wrong side of the tracks who wanted to carve out a better life for themselves and felt bitter over their status and the condescension of others. "I'm sick of having people look at me like I was cheap," says Lane.

Joan had high hopes for *Flamingo Road,* and during filming she thought it would turn out to be a genuinely great movie. She enjoyed reporting to the set, despite a nagging cold that affected her throughout much of the filming. She thought the whole thing was a perfect illustration of her occasional lapses in judgment. "That one just didn't work, but for heaven's sake don't ask me why," she told Lawrence Quirk, who liked it much more than she did. "There was Curtiz working on it, and Wilder scripting his book. It seemed like it was a charmed project. Honestly, I don't think it's one of my better ones. I just thought it would turn out so much better than it did. I think a lot of good stuff that might have saved it was left on the cutting room floor. There's a lot of difference between the movie that emerges and the movie that might have been." In truth, had the picture remained more focused on Lane and Fielding, or been a half an hour longer, it might have amounted to more than it did.

Twice during the movie, Joan sings fragments of the saucy number "If I Could Be With You One Hour Tonight." While her voice still isn't great, by this time she had developed into a rather good vocalist, with an assured and insinuatingly sexy style. Zachary Scott, who had also been in *Mildred Pierce,* emerges as a rather odd-looking leading man without his trademark mustache, but his performance, especially during a drunk scene in which he eventually commits suicide, is first-rate. This was the first time Joan worked with David Brian, whom she liked. A solid but not great actor, Brian had a masculine confidence about him that Joan responded to, and she would work with him again on two other films. Joan had no problem sharing Brian with Eve Arden, who told Joan she had a big crush on him. Joan told Arden it would be easy for her to arrange a date. Joan, unfortunately, never told Arden that Brian was married, probably because it didn't matter to her and figured it wouldn't matter to Arden. Arden had a drink with Brian but resisted an affair.

In 1980, the movie was remade as a TV movie starring former model Cristina Raines, who played the part as a kind of disaffected hippie with excellent cheekbones. The ratings were strong enough for *Flamingo Road* to debut as a regular series in the early 1980's, but the soap opera only lasted for two seasons.

Joan next appeared with many other famous guest stars in *It's a Great Feeling* (1949). Much like the Norma Shearer short of the previous decade, *The Slippery Pearls* (also known as *The Stolen Jools*), *It's a*

Great Feeling featured oodles of stars doing cameos in a plot tied to the film business. The picture is a spoof of Hollywood with Jack Carson (playing himself) trying to direct a picture starring himself and Dennis Morgan (also playing himself) because no one else will helm it. In only her third movie, Doris Day plays a waitress who is discovered by Morgan and Carson and stars in their film. Encountering famous faces as they prepare to shoot the picture, the two men run into the real Joan Crawford in a dress shop. Joan was praised for her hilarious spoof of the kind of sophisticated, beautifully attired women she so often played.

Although she had some concerns about where her career was heading, Joan was fairly happy and more than confident that she had become a legitimate Hollywood survivor.

The next thing she knew, she had become a victim.

Bernard Wohl Collection

Chapter Twelve

VICTIM

Joan's next script was originally entitled *The Victim* and was based on the life of gangster's moll Virginia Hill, who had been involved with such famous criminals as Joe Adonis, Frank Costello, and Bugsy Siegel. The director, Vincent Sherman, was concerned that, at forty-six, Joan was too old to play a young girl at the beginning of the picture, but he thought it would work if she played a woman just a couple of years younger than she actually was. He felt that women in middle age still had ambitions and romantic dreams and that Joan's own romanticism and desperation as she herself approached fifty would imbue her performance with added authenticity.

Sherman had a somewhat chunky build and was not exactly handsome, but he was masculine and attractive in a rough-hewn way. He had already had an affair with Bette Davis when Joan put the moves on him as they watched a screening of *Humoresque*; Joan had suggested that watching the movie might help him decide which of the hairstyles she wore in it would work for the new film. Undergoing a rough patch in his marriage, Sherman responded to Joan's advances when he had dinner in her home one night and the two wound up having sex in the shower. Confronted by his wife, Hedda, he confessed everything. "I suppose it's too much to ask of any man that he turn down a chance to sleep with Joan Crawford," his very understanding wife replied.

When Hedda got to meet Joan at a party at the latter's house, she found to her surprise that she rather liked the actress. As she told her husband, "She's gracious and considerate, and if you can see beneath the Hollywood crap, you can detect a woman who refused to become a loser, who pulled herself up from nothing and made something of her life." It's ironic that so many people whom Joan never harmed felt it necessary to attack her after her death, but this woman, with the most legitimate possible grievance against Joan, actually felt sympathetic toward her. According to Sherman, Joan was convinced Hedda didn't really love him and wanted him to divorce her and marry Joan. In other words, Joan was playing Daisy Kenyon. Whether she was actually in love with the director or was just pretending out of some other motive is open to debate. In any case, in due time the picture was finished and its title was changed to the more dynamic *The Damned Don't Cry* (1950).

The story of *The Damned Don't Cry* unfolds in flashbacks, as police investigate the background of a supposed heiress who has gone missing at a scene of violence. "Lorna Hansen Forbes" is actually Ethel Whitehead (Joan), who left her husband and small town after the accidental death of her young son. Determined to get something out of life, she befriends an accountant named Martin (Kent Smith), whom she encourages to take a job in the outfit run by mobster George Castleman (David Brian). Martin is afraid he'll lose his self-respect. "Don't tell me about self-respect!" Ethel snaps at him. "That's what you tell yourself you got when you got nothing else!" Ethel eventually becomes the well-heeled and glamorously attired girlfriend of Castleman himself, and all goes well until Castleman suspects one of his subordinates, Nick Prenta (Steve Cochran), of plotting against him. Castleman gives Ethel a new identity and sends her to Prenta in order to get close to him and find out the truth. Ethel becomes a little too close to Prenta, and a shootout ensues, after which Ethel makes her way back to her childhood home. Castleman arrives to kill Ethel, but is shot dead by loyal Martin before Castleman can do more than wound his errant lover.

Joan looks properly plain and battered in the early "poverty" scenes, and the rest of the time is as glamorous as ever. Unimpressed movie critic Bosley Crowther labeled her acting "artificial," and while there's some truth to that assessment, it doesn't tell the whole story. Her performance has bite and commands attention, and she plays with passion—but, as Crowther noted, not with any particular subtlety or nuance. In other words, Joan is snappy but all surface. However, she does have her moments: she's very compelling in the brutal climax when Brian tosses Ethel around as she desperately tries to dodge his blows and get away. And throughout the movie she puts on the kind of performance that she knew her fans expected. But by no stretch of the imagination is any of it "bad" acting.

Of the supporting cast, Brian as Castleman and Richard Egan as her husband come off best. Stronger than usual in his portrayal of a jealous mobster desperate to defend his turf and wipe out his enemies,

Brian demonstrates a heretofore unrealized versatility. Whether engaging in sexy banter or telling each other off, Joan and Brian always worked well together. *The Damned Don't Cry* was Richard Egan's first movie, and he would go on to enjoy a long and varied career as a character actor. Joan tried to get her lover-director Vincent Sherman jealous by taking long walks with Egan, and with Steve Cochran.

The Damned Don't Cry is no masterpiece—Joan herself never cared for it—but it's much better than Joan's later "gun moll" movie *This Woman is Dangerous*. Thanks to Vincent Sherman, the film generates some tension and suspense, especially in its confrontational moments, and it's never dull. Some of the dialogue is amusing, such as when Joan listens to the different positions that a job counselor has to offer and asks, "Isn't there something better?" To which the counselor replies, "Well, there's the Republican Presidential nomination." The picture works in a lightweight way as a study of a woman in over her head, like many films of its type a cautionary tale. The movie ends with a conversation between two cops; one of them wonders if Ethel Whitehead will make another attempt to get out of her miserable environment. The other cop looks at the near-shanty Ethel grew up in and says, "Wouldn't you?"

Then again, *The Damned Don't Cry* is never far from the world of schlock. The death of Ethel's little boy on his bicycle is a heartbreaking scene, but it's simply the impetus that starts his mother on her heady road to ultimate damnation. Ethel should be completely numb on the day of her son's funeral, incapable of thinking or planning, let alone ready to take off on a new adventure, but that's what happens. Is the picture commenting on Ethel's cold nature? Is Ethel deliberately trying to commit slow suicide by taking up with dangerous people? You won't find out by watching *The Damned Don't Cry*, because it has little to say on the subject.

Warner executives were pleased with *The Damned Don't Cry*, and Columbia wanted Joan and Sherman to team up, on loan out, for a subsequent feature. Based on a Pulitzer-Prize winning play by George Kelly entitled *Craig's Wife*, it had already been filmed twice, once by Cecil B. DeMille's brother William in 1926, and once by Dorothy Arzner in 1936, starring Rosalind Russell and John Boles. A misunderstanding developed between director and star when Sherman told Joan he thought the script was badly dated and that neither of them should do it. Joan bowed out, and the assignment was handed to Margaret Sullavan, with Sherman attached as director. But Sherman had agreed to work with Sullavan without realizing that the project they would be working together on was *Lady of the House*. Joan contacted the film's producer, William Dozier, and got herself cast in it after all. In truth, Joan and Sherman were probably manipulated into doing the picture. It was highly unlikely that Sullavan would ever have accepted a part that was so patently wrong for her. Instead she made a film that was completely right for her, *No Sad Songs for Me* (1950), rejected all other offers, and retired from the screen for good until her death ten years later.

In this new version of an old play, now retitled *Harriet Craig* (1950), Joan played the title role, teamed with Wendell Corey, who played Harriet's husband Walter. The basic premise remained—a woman seems to love her home, furnishings, and gracious manner of living more than anything—but there were some minor changes to the supporting characters and to the storyline, including the elimination of a murder/suicide subplot involving friends of the Craigs. Harriet was now also much more multi-dimensional than she was in the earlier versions.

In all three versions, the heroine suffers terrible early privations in life because of her father's abandonment of the family for another woman; this accounts for Harriet's preference for possessions over men. In the 1936 version, Rosalind Russell played Harriet in a very icy, relatively unemotional fashion that left no room for sympathy, whereas Joan's Harriet is much more loving and affectionate to her husband, and a more well-rounded person. Perhaps because of Joan's more apparent sensuality and femininity, one can imagine her Harriet making love to her husband, whereas in the earlier film one supposes that the married couple have stopped having sex a long time ago. At the same time, Joan's Harriet is more monstrous than Russell's in her behavior. She destroys her cousin's relationship with her boyfriend by lying to her, and even goes to Walter's boss behind his back to intimate that he can't be relied upon, just to keep the boss from sending him to Japan for three months on business. Chic and handsome, Joan exhibits her wonderfully disciplined technique in every scene, although there are times when she could perhaps have exuded more vulnerability without betraying the veracity of the character.

Vincent Sherman recalled that the shoot went smoothly, and that Joan was the consummate professional. In her dressing room, the two had dinner and, presumably, occasional sexual encounters. Sherman was not alone in noting that Harriet and Joan shared certain characteristics: abandonment by their fathers (Joan's best scene is when Harriet recalls this) and a reverence for possessions and cleanliness. In truth, Harriet Craig was very close to some aspects of the real Joan, but the two women were more different than alike. For instance, Joan never had to rely upon any man to get her the good things in life. Also, Harriet is right about some things, such as the rose-carrying next-door neighbor who rather intrusively comes over all the time.

After the picture wrapped, Sherman took a vacation with Joan—with his wife's permission. According to Sherman, the two drove to Canada, stopping in motels along the way where they registered under assumed names. Sherman's wife was not overjoyed when a columnist got wind of the escapade. The trip was also cut short because, according to Sherman, Joan kept nagging him to divorce his wife and marry her.

Sherman and Joan continued their professional (and physical) association with their next picture, *Goodbye, My Fancy* (1951), which had originally been a Broadway play with Madeleine Carroll. In the film Joan played Agatha Reed, a congresswoman who goes back to the college that had expelled her when they offer her an honorary degree. There's a problem, however, when the administration is afraid to show Agatha's anticommunist film. The initially clever storyline eventually turns into a plea for freedom of speech that manages the remarkable feat of seeming both left- and right-wing at the same time. Joan is at her best in the second half of the film, when the script provides her with some righteous zingers. *Goodbye, My Fancy* may have seemed daring in its day (or, given the political climate, cravenly safe). Aside from Joan, a very young Janice Rule stood out, and Eve Arden was reliably good as a snappy colleague of Joan's. ("It was miscasting for Joan as an intellectual," Arden wrote in her memoirs.) The picture did not do well at the box office. "They watered it down so much," Joan said later, "that there was hardly any point in making it. A complete waste of time for everyone!"

Joan and Rule did not get along. Depending on whom you listen to, either Joan picked on Rule because she was jealous of her youth and the attention both the press and Sherman lavished on her in her film debut, or Rule provoked Joan with her total lack of professionalism. Both accounts may have had some truth to them. One afternoon, Joan snapped at Rule, "*You* certainly won't be in this business very long!" There's no doubt that Joan became jealous of younger costars on occasion—she was human, after all—but she was still the star of the picture. Rule's lack of experience and "theater world" arrogance made Joan impatient, but Rule's persistent refusal to listen to and absorb advice from the director and others made Joan outright angry. As Joan often said in one form or another over the years, "You can have all the talent in the world, but it won't do you a bit of good if you're an idiot." Joan never suffered fools gladly. At the same time, she was an honest admirer of talent. In her autobiography, Joan actually apologized to Rule because she found her performance in *The Subterraneans* (1960) so superb.

When Joan accepted the part in *Goodbye, My Fancy*, she assumed that it was only offered to her because the studio couldn't get their first choices, Katherine Hepburn or Rosalind Russell, both of whom Joan thought would have been better in the film. She gave credit for the relative success of the film and her capable performance to her director, who continued to accompany her to the bedroom frequently. Considering that her male costars in *Goodbye, My Fancy* were Robert Young and Frank Lovejoy—neither of whom sparked any romantic stirrings in Joan—it's no wonder that she continued to focus on the director. Neither the gentlemanly, placid Young—whom Joan only liked in a platonic sense—nor the rather crude Lovejoy was the type to get her motor racing. Sherman tried to get Lovejoy fired because he felt he wouldn't have any on-screen chemistry with Joan, although there are those who felt that Sherman and Lovejoy were similar "types" and that Sherman just felt threatened.

Joan's relationship with Sherman did not last long after *Goodbye, My Fancy* wrapped. In his memoirs, Sherman wrote that there was a melodramatic conclusion, with Joan alternately throwing him out, phoning his wife that she could "have him back," and then attempting suicide (or pretending to) so that he would come running back to her. Years later, Joan would not openly admit to an affair with Sherman, although she hinted at it. On one occasion, Joan seemed a little bitter about Sherman:

> Sherman was a user. I knew it. He knew it. We used each other. His wife was a masochist and I lost respect for her—I would never have let a man get away with the things he did. He wanted very much to be up in the big leagues and he figured I was his ticket. It didn't matter what his wife wanted. He would holler at me that he didn't like the way I tried to control him, but he never gave me back any of my gifts, did he? He made it clear that I was only a diversion, but he didn't understand that that was all he was to me. At times he could really be a prick.

However, she said more than once that she felt he was a good, sympathetic director and that she admired the independent stance he took with the studios.

As usual, Bosley Crowther had it in for Joan, although he did concede that she succeeded in making "the atmosphere . . . electrically charged." But, he added, "The lady is famously given to striking aggressive attitudes and to carrying herself in a manner that is formidable and cold. That is the principal misfortune of *Goodbye, My Fancy*. Miss Crawford's errant congresswoman is as aloof and imposing as the capital dome."

This Woman is Dangerous was Joan's last Warner Brothers film until *Trog*, nearly twenty years later. (Ten years, if one counts *What Ever Happened to Baby Jane?* in 1962, distributed but not produced by Warner Brothers.) Joan wanted to end her association with Warner Brothers so that she could get the lead in *Sudden Fear*. Jack Warner thought Joan's days as a star were coming to an end, and he wanted to end her contract. He offered her the script for *This Woman is Dangerous* in the hopes that she would realize how third-rate it was, and turn it down. Joan surprised him by taking on the assignment. Her price? To be let out of her contract. Joan was happy about that, at least. Unfortunately, the film still had to be made.

This Woman is Dangerous turned out to be a tired and inferior retread of *A Woman's Face*. In it, Joan plays Beth Austin, another tough gal with a soft heart who's fallen in with thieves after a brief stay in prison. Now she is the girlfriend of gangster Matt Jackson (David Brian), her former cellmate's brother-in-law. When she finds out that she will lose her sight unless she gets an operation, she goes to a clinic run by Dr. Ben Halleck (Dennis Morgan), who not only restores her vision but also falls in love with her. Beth is torn between the two men—the one rough and exciting, the other decent and romantic—but fate intervenes when Jackson is killed by the police during an attempt to murder his rival in the operating theater.

Done properly, *This Woman Is Dangerous* might have amounted to an intriguing piece of film noir, but instead it was turned into little more than a Joan Crawford formula film. Joan may seem excessively calm when she first learns that she may go blind in only a few days, but she's playing a very tough cookie who is all too accustomed to hiding her emotions. Some critics harped on this scene as evidence of her limited acting skills, even though her reaction is clearly explained in the dialogue: "I find it difficult to get emotional when there are other people around," says Beth.

Joan was back with David Brian of *Flamingo Road* and *The Damned Don't Cry*. By this time, Brian seemed to be cast in every Warner Brothers movie featuring a fading movie queen, as with Bette Davis in *Beyond the Forest.* Brian is effective in the same maniacal mode as in *The Damned Don't Cry.* Dennis Morgan is as pleasant and as superficial as ever as the surgeon; *It's a Great Feeling* was more his speed.

It was the only time she ever worked with director Felix Feist, who did inject a few arresting moments into the film. In one, Beth sits in the good doctor's automobile in the prison yard as he (improbably) attends to a dying woman in the prison infirmary. As she watches, several female prisoners are unloaded from a prison van. The matron realizes that one of them has been smoking against the rules and has them stand in a row while she looks at their hands. The offending party painfully crushes the lit end of her cigarette in her fingers, as Joan does the same in empathy. In this scene and others, Joan makes good use of her wonderfully expressive face. The climax in the operating theater is also quite tense.

The Joan Crawford of movies like *This Woman is Dangerous* was an easy target for any critic who had it in for her. Later, Joan would remember that she just didn't have the energy or internal resources at the time to try to make it a better picture. She was defeated by the script, by Jack Warner's attitude, by the unfamiliar director. What was the point of knocking herself out when nothing could save the movie from being formula schlock?

Sure enough, Bosley Crowther offered his most vicious sally in his review of *This Woman Is Dangerous.* He wrote that Joan's persona "has now reached the ossified stage" and theorized that the only possible reason for a movie like *This Woman is Dangerous* was "for the display of Miss Crawford's stony charm. [To her fans] the arrant posturing of Miss Crawford may seem the quintessence of acting art. But for people of mild discrimination and even moderate reasonableness, the suffering of Miss Crawford will be generously matched by their own . . ."

Crowther had never been too keen on Joan, and his contempt for drivel like *This Woman is Dangerous* was understandable. But no one, least of all Joan herself, exactly expected her to get an Oscar nod for this film. In his contempt for Joan, Crowther willfully overlooked the good points in her performance. Joan was intelligent enough to realize that the script for *This Woman is Dangerous* was so theatrical and artificial that the only thing that might salvage it was a colorful, theatrical performance by the star. To play the role of Beth Austin as if she were a Eugene O'Neill character would have been ludicrous. Joan played the lightweight material the only way it could have been played—anything more "serious" would have come off like overacting.

Crowther's reviews bothered Joan, primarily because she felt he never gave her enough credit for all the hard work she put into her portrayals. She would write him plaintive notes on her "baby blues" imploring him to tell her why he didn't like her. Bosley knew that Lawrence Quirk was friendly with Joan and told him that he never deigned to answer what he styled her "whining notes." Crowther felt that "stars should ignore criticism in print. When she whines she shows she has no class. Let her fans gush and rhapsodize. I am not a fan—I am an objective journalist." Joan also knew that Crowther had been an early mentor to Quirk, so she asked him why Crowther was always so "mean" to her. Quirk, who knew that Crowther objected to Joan's "movie-star ways" and acting style—he simply was not a fan of hers—tactfully told Joan that Crowther was "a man of rather rigid tastes."

Joan had one of her best roles in the highly popular suspense thriller *Sudden Fear* (1952), for which she received an Oscar nomination. In it she played playwright-heiress Myra Hudson, who objects to the casting of the talented leading man, Lester Blaine (Jack Palance) in her latest play, *Halfway to Heaven,* because he lacks conventional romantic good looks. Lester angrily tells her that she should study a painting of the famed lover, Casanova, who was not exactly a beauty either. Lester goes off in a huff, only to run into Myra again on a cross-country train trip. Myra finds herself responding to Lester's charms, and as they spend time together in San Francisco, she falls in love with him. The two marry and seem to enjoy an idyllic existence, but Lester has no love for Myra and is simply after her considerable fortune. Myra learns of his plot to kill her, and conspires to murder him instead and pin the blame on his lady friend, Irene (Gloria Graham), but the best laid plans of mice and men. . . .

Clark Gable was offered the male lead in *Sudden Fear* but turned it down. He and Joan had remained good friends over the years, but Gable didn't think the part was right for him. For one thing, at fifty-one he was too old for it. The man was supposed to be a young actor on the way up. Director David Miller knew he needed a very strong, indeed menacing, leading man or else Joan's powerful presence would overwhelm her counterpart and throw the movie off balance. When he went to dinner at Joan's, he brought along the picture *Panic in the Streets* so they could watch it in her private screening room. At first Joan thought he had the movie's star, Richard Widmark, in mind for her male lead, but he told her that wasn't the case. For the next two weeks Miller brought the same movie and insisted they "study" it; she didn't protest too vigorously the first week, but by the second week she had had enough of *Panic in the Streets* and demanded that Miller tell her what was going on. When

Miller told her that he wanted supporting actor Jack Palance to star with her, she became livid and threw him out of the house. She was used to handsome, sexy leading men, and in a real-life turn that mirrored the plot of *Sudden Fear*, she thought Palance was simply too ugly. In actuality, Palance was not a bad-looking man; he just wasn't a pretty-boy. Miller convinced Joan that Palance would be perfect because he had the raw masculinity and dangerous quality that would make the audience believe he really was a threat to the sturdy, self-reliant heroine. Joan reluctantly agreed and Palance was hired. It has been said that special wigs, make up appliances, and lighting were used to make Palance seem less Hun-like than usual in his early scenes, and that he reverted to his regular appearance as filming proceeded and his character became more menacing, but this does not ring entirely true: there are "unattractive" shots in the early sections and "attractive" shots of Palance late in the film.

In another case of life imitating art, Joan fell for Palance the way her character fell for his in the movie. Palance's machismo and confidence intrigued her, and she was anxious to find out what he was like in bed. Unfortunately, Palance had already zeroed in on supporting player Gloria Grahame, who played Irene, his character's lover. When Joan found out, she was even angrier than when Miller had suggested Palance be her leading man. Here she was stuck with him and he was "otherwise engaged." As for Grahame, didn't she know that the star always had dibs on the leading man? It didn't help that Grahame was frequently late for work, infuriating Joan and violating her sense of professionalism. The main problem between Joan and Palance wasn't the sex angle (or, rather, the lack thereof), but the fact that Palance, like other male leads before and after him, hated the way Joan showed up with an entourage each morning and even took the trouble to greet each crew member personally. Palance thought Joan was insincere about these greetings, but when Joan protested in her memoirs that she "*meant* those good mornings," she wasn't kidding. Joan has been accused of catering to the grips and cameramen and so on just so they would like her and make her look good, but she did truly respect her fellow professionals in the industry. Palance's main problem toward Joan was that she was a much bigger name than he was and he thought he was much more talented. A lot of Joan's male costars and supporting players simply didn't like strong women. "She's a woman and has to have her way in everything," Palance ranted to one reporter. He may have picked up one acting tip from Joan, however. A few years later it was reported that he was listening to music by Richard Strauss in his dressing room to psych himself up for a scene.

As previously noted, Joan had on occasion also used music to put her in the mood for certain sequences.

Sudden Fear did not have a very large budget and there was money for Joan's wardrobe, but not for Grahame's, which were bought off the rack, much to Grahame's dismay. When she protested, the costume lady— Joan's personal dress designer—angrily reminded Grahame that she wasn't the star. Some Grahame defenders insisted that Joan ordered Gloria's outfits to be altered so they would be less flattering on her, but there's no evidence of this.

So Joan was mad at Grahame and Palance and vice versa, which generated a great deal of tension on the set. Joan wasn't too thrilled with director Miller, either. She told him that Grahame was not to be allowed on the set unless she was in the scene that was being filmed. Grahame would mischievously sneak onto the set even when she wasn't needed and hide behind a wall or just outside a doorway, hoping Joan would spot her and become hysterical. When she did, shooting would stop until the offending party was removed. Joan and Palance didn't exchange words except when they were speaking dialogue to one another. Joan didn't allow her negative attitude toward her costars to affect her performance, however, although her dislike of Palance undoubtedly helped her in the second half of the film when Myra learns of her husband's perfidy. Mike Connors, also in the supporting cast, remembered that at times it was like a war zone. "There were days Joan looked so angry that I was afraid she was going to chuck something at Jack. She put all this intensity into her performance instead, thank goodness. She pretended Gloria didn't exist, and I just tried to stay out of her way. I think David Miller found it all a trial, but he stayed on keel in spite of it. Not the easiest way to make movies, but exhilarating, I guess."

Joan is excellent in *Sudden Fear,* which gives her ample opportunities to display the superb, expressive pantomiming that had been her trademark since the silent days. The best example of this is when Myra hears her husband and his lover plotting together (their voices recorded by her Dictaphone) and realizes that everything about her idyllic life with Lester is a complete fabrication. She is also splendid when Myra waits in a closet in Irene's apartment for Lester to arrive so she can shoot him, her face registering her confusion, determination, and disbelief over what she's prepared to do. Later on, when she spots herself in the living room mirror holding the gun, and is appalled by what she's planning, she seems to age twenty years in a few seconds. Joan also has a fine moment waking up in bed after her wedding night, looking at her new husband as if she were a young girl and he her prince. In real life, although she was quite capable of having torrid just-for-pleasure quickies, Joan always approached each romantic affair as if she were a young schoolgirl in love for the first time.

Despite their mutual enmity, Joan and Jack played very well together. This is especially true in a scene when Myra demonstrates her Dictaphone to Lester, and has him recite some lines from his play (the play Myra has fired him from), and then plays them back. There's a strange tension to the scene as Myra and Lester listen to the playback of Lester's voice, which is the only dialogue at that moment. In this and other scenes David Miller makes good use of the pause, such as when Joan accidentally smashes the record that has Lester and Irene plotting her demise on it and the camera stays fixed on her stricken face for several seconds as she stares down on the broken pieces, allowing the audience to absorb what has happened. Without the record, Joan has no proof for the police, so she must come up with the plan to stop the conspirators herself; the audience might not swallow this if she had the option of going to the authorities and be taken as something other than a hysterical, jealous female. (This is not to say, of course, that *Sudden Fear* is without its share of contrived and illogical moments.)

Joan had specifically requested Miller for the picture, as she had known him since his days as a film cutter at MGM. She may not have liked working with him all that much, but she was very pleased with his work. "Mentally he cuts as he shoots, and wasted angles and film are at a minimum," she wrote in her memoirs. Although making the picture had its pressures, sexual and otherwise, Joan never regretted it, not just for the obvious reason but because she genuinely believed it to be a good film and that she was very good in it. "One of my better efforts," she said. "Not humble, maybe, but it's the truth."

Miller contributed some fine touches to *Sudden Fear,* such as when Myra imagines how her plan will go forward as the shadow of a clock pendulum swings back and forth across her face; we see images of the assorted characters acting out what she's thinking superimposed over her features. There's a wonderful bit of business when Myra hides in the closet after losing the gun, and Lester plays with a wind-up dog which makes its way across the carpet to the edge of the closet door as Myra, fearing discovery when Lester picks up the toy, squirms inside. The last twenty minutes of the film, with Lester pursuing his terrified wife through the city streets, is so briskly directed and edited that it merits comparison with vintage Hitchcock. On the other hand, if Hitchcock had directed the film, we probably would have learned more about Lester's life and background (he's an interesting villain but not exactly three-dimensional), and Lester would have been played by a handsomer actor (Hitchcock always saw good-looking men as being a bit evil, and vice versa). The film also seems to miss the point that Myra, a woman with inherited wealth who embarks on a successful career to boot (an embarrassment of riches), is not exactly the most sympathetic of victims—not only as far as Lester is concerned, but for most of the audience as well.

Shortly after filming wrapped, a scandal-sheet columnist tried to get "dirt" on Joan from Grahame, who merely said Joan was "a true professional" and nothing more. According to Grahame, Joan sent her a note thanking her for her silence. But what exactly was she supposed to say: "Joan got mad at me because I was sleeping with Jack Palance"? Grahame kept silent more to protect herself than Joan. A couple of years later, Joan would have an affair with Gloria's ex-husband, Nicholas Ray, when he directed her in *Johnny Guitar.*

Joan lost the Oscar to Shirley Booth for *Come Back, Little Sheba.* Joan was terrific in *Sudden Fear,* but everyone, including Joan, agreed that Booth's was a once-in-a-lifetime performance deserving of recognition. Another actress who lost to Booth was Bette Davis, who had been nominated for her performance in *The Star,* which had an interesting genesis. The screenplay for *The Star* was written by Joan's old friend, writer Katherine Albert, and her husband Dale Eunson, whom Joan had known since the early days at MGM. Katherine ended her friendship with Joan when the latter encouraged Katherine's daughter Joan (named after Crawford) to marry her beloved, Kirby Weatherly, over her mother's disapproval. Joan even held the reception at her home. In revenge, Albert wrote a script about a Hollywood has-been, apparently inspired by Joan's life. The character of Margaret Elliott, the eponymous "star," is somewhat self-delusional, has to deal with parasitic relatives when she herself has money problems (a reference to Joan's financial situation after divorcing and paying off Phillip Terry, and to her relationship with Hal and Anna), and tries desperately to act younger than she actually is. Elliott goes about acting as if she still thinks she's in her prime, a top-drawer star with major box-office clout. Margaret Elliott was less the Joan Crawford of the early '50s as it was what Albert hoped Crawford would become. The part was never offered to Joan, but Bette Davis thought it had marvelous possibilities—she also thought it would be amusing to play a role that made fun of Joan. But Joan had the last laugh, as virtually everything in the script—right down to the greedy, no-account relatives—could be applied just as much to Davis as to Joan. The ending of *The Star* has Elliott turning down a chance to star in a film about a has-been actress much like herself for a new chance at love and marriage and a "normal" life with Sterling Hayden. Joan, of course, would never have turned down a good part, or even an indifferent one— she loved to work, loved every aspect of being a movie star, faded or otherwise. Davis wouldn't have turned it down either. Which is probably why they both made *What Ever Happened to Baby Jane?* instead of sitting home knitting or watching television like honest-to-goodness has-beens.

It was at the *Photoplay* awards dinner in 1953 at the Beverly Hills Hotel that Joan first saw Marilyn Monroe in the flesh. The giggling, silly, but supersexy Monroe was wearing a skintight gold lamé dress that exposed most of her ample bosom. Joan went on the attack, and her comments were quoted in the newspapers. "She should be told that the public likes provocative feminine personalities," Joan told columnist Bob Thomas, "but it also likes to know that underneath it all the actresses are ladies. . . ." It may seem hypocritical for Joan to have attacked Monroe for flaunting her sensuality, but Joan rightly saw herself—even when she was starting out—as being quite different from Monroe. Joan was sexy on the screen when it was appropriate for the part; she was sexy in private rooms with men who held out tempting offers in exchange for her body—indeed, she played that game as well as anyone. But Joan had never deliberately acted *in public* in a cheap or vulgar manner. The dances she did in clubs with Michael Cudahy bordered on virginal innocence compared with the common and pervasive antics of Marilyn Monroe. Joan was also shrewd in attacking Monroe, as she knew—given the public's intense new interest in her—that it would guarantee her plenty of press. Many years after Monroe's death, Joan said, "The girl had talent, and her death at such an early age was a tragedy, but my God she was just so totally *common*. I certainly come from humble beginnings, but I think it's everyone's duty to try to rise above those beginnings. With her cheap behavior, it was like Marilyn was trying to bring everyone down to her own level instead of rising up to everyone else's." When asked her opinion of Marilyn clones like Jayne Mansfield and Mamie Van Doren, Joan cursed, adding, "Those aren't even *actresses*. Those are boobs with mouths trying to get publicity. I got where I did through *hard work*. It isn't hard work to stick your chest out and make everybody stare at your tits. *Please!*"

Seeing herself as a Grand Lady (but certainly not a grand *old* lady) of Hollywood, Joan liked to play the voice of reason commenting on the younger generation and their foibles. Thus her famous comment when Joanne Woodward won an Academy Award in a homemade dress: "Joanne Woodward is setting the cause of Hollywood glamour back twenty years by making her own clothes," she stated with her trademark bluntness. This and other opinions helped give Joan a bitchy reputation, but she took being a star very seriously, regarded it as a great honor and a privilege, and honestly thought she had a right to point it out when she felt less grateful actresses had gone shamefully awry. At other times, her cutting remarks, picked up by eavesdropping columnists, were off-the-cuff comments made at parties where she'd been drinking. But Joan was rarely embarrassed when these appeared in the paper: she felt she was only speaking the truth.

Joan was the Queen Bee of Hollywood, and she wanted everyone to know it. Though she had lost her second chance for an Oscar, there was an unexpected bonus to all the attention that came with her nomination for *Sudden Fear*.

She suddenly found herself on her way back to MGM.

Bernard Wohl Collection

Chapter Thirteen

THE BITCH IS BACK

Joan had signed on for a major role in *From Here to Eternity,* even though director Fred Zinnemann didn't want to use her. Her chief defender in this project was Columbia Pictures studio boss Harry Cohn. But even Cohn turned against Joan when she made it known that she hated her wardrobe for *Eternity* and demanded that her personal designer, Sheila O'Brien, be assigned to the picture. After all, O'Brien knew best how Joan should look and how to achieve that look. This was too much for Cohn, who fired Joan and replaced her with Deborah Kerr. So Joan never got to writhe on the sand with Burt Lancaster in her arms and sea water washing over her. "I didn't want to admit it to myself then," Joan recalled, "but I think that whole experience warned me that I didn't have the clout that I'd had at MGM in those long-ago days."

Joan then got a call from MGM executive Benny Thau, who said he had a part that was just right for her. Would she be interested in seeing the script? She was, but she was more than a little surprised to be hearing from Thau, who had angered Joan years ago by being a Greer Garson supporter at the studio instead of being in the Crawford camp. She had always assumed that he had been one of the MGM executives who wanted her out in the early '40s. "I didn't know if he felt bad about what happened, if this was a peace offering, or what," Joan remembered, "but he seemed nice and genuine and I figured what harm could it do if I read the script." Joan liked what she read.

Joan returned to MGM after a ten-year absence to star in a Technicolor musical (her first full-length color film, in fact) in which she would sing—sort of—and dance. Joan was gratified that her dressing room was filled with flowers and fruit baskets and congratulatory notes from many of MGM's current stars. In *Torch Song* (1953), Joan played Jenny Stewart, a witchy, self-absorbed, domineering Broadway star who clashes with her new accompanist Tye Graham (Michael Wilding), who is blind. However, Graham has seen her on the stage before she became a star while he still had his sight, and he has always had a thing for her. He is able to bring out the warm, feminine, lonely side of Jenny hidden underneath her defensive exterior, and of course the two fall madly in love. This entertaining and unusual love story has some nice musical numbers, some bright and amusing dialogue, and a moving if unconvincing conclusion. Joan and Wilding are both excellent, with wonderful support from Joan's old friend and beloved co-worker Marjorie Rambeau as Joan's mother, and others. While *Torch Song* is undeniably superficial in some ways, it is so absorbing and well-played that the audience generally overlooks its improbabilities. An odd bit has Crawford listening to "herself" singing on a record (actually dubbed by India Adams) while she sings along in her natural voice. Most critics found *Torch Song* to be a real star turn. "Here is Joan Crawford all over the screen, in command, in love and in color, a real movie star in what amounts to a carefully produced one-woman show," wrote the critic for the *New York Herald Tribune*. "Miss Crawford's acting is sheer and colorful as a painted arrow, aimed straight at the sensibilities of her particular fans."

Gig Young was cast in *Torch Song* as Cliff Willard, a playboy who has his uses for Jenny, the type of parasitic male who has nearly turned her into an embittered man-hater. (Cliff refers to Jenny as "the distilled essence of affectedness.") Joan was quite attracted to Young and got into the habit of offering him a drink in her dressing room at the end of each day. One weekend evening in Palm Springs, Joan ran into Young, who was visiting with friends. At dinner with her, he poured out his heart over the recent death of a woman friend; Joan sympathized with his feelings of loss and offered some words of consolation. A bit later she asked him to come back to the cottage she had rented for the weekend. Whether Joan had it in mind to make a pass at Young or simply wanted company, Young reacted badly, thinking her suggestion was in bad taste considering what they'd just been discussing. Joan may have figured some life-affirming sex may have been just what the doctor ordered to get Young out of his funk, or perhaps she just wanted to talk some more. In any case, Young refused her invitation more emphatically than was tactful, telling her (falsely) that he had friends waiting for him elsewhere. Joan was not amused: she was more offended by his attitude and his blatant mendacity than by his refusal to accompany her back to the cottage. There were far more artful ways in which Young could have gotten out of it, she felt.

From then on, Joan was very cool to Young, no longer inviting him to her dressing room for cocktails. Some took this as a prime example of Joan's bitchy, unforgiving nature, but she was just as likely simply embarrassed; she may have also figured that there was no point in being overly friendly with a man who clearly had no interest in her. If he was going to assume her every move was a flagrant pass, then she was better off keeping her distance. Joan was otherwise perfectly cordial with him. Young later blamed Joan for having his scenes cut down to a bare minimum, but his part had never been that big to begin with. There's hardly a production in which some of the sequences featuring supporting players don't wind up on the cutting room floor.

Joan did not invite Michael Wilding to her dressing room for cocktails—or anything else—because he was married to Elizabeth Taylor at the time. Shooting *Rhapsody* practically next door, Taylor would scoot over to see Wilding whenever she had a break. By this time, the stories of Joan and costars like Clark Gable were legend—and legion—and Liz didn't want her husband succumbing to Joan's still considerable charms. One time, Taylor made the mistake of snubbing Joan, and Joan called her "a little bitch" under her breath. She wanted flacks to tell Taylor to be more respectful in the future, but no one ever did. There was one handsome cast member who caught Joan's eye, an actor named James Todd who played a gofer in one scene. Joan remarked, "If that boy doesn't go places there's no justice in this world. My, my, but he is good-looking."

Joan had wanted former choreographer Charles Walters to direct *Torch Song* because she'd liked his work on the Leslie Caron musical *Lili* and figured that he could certainly help out with her dance routines. It was after William Haines watched Joan rehearse a dance routine that he came out with his oft-quoted line, first reported—albeit sanitized—in Joan's memoirs: "Only God could get your legs up that high." In her cups, Joan delighted in giving her pals the real quote: "Only God or a good-looking man could get your legs up that high." At this point in Joan's life, Haines was the only one who could get away with comments like that. Joan and Walters, who also plays a chorus boy, dance well together, but it is clear that Joan isn't doing anything very elaborate or strenuous, and that Walters is the better dancer. Some have said that Joan sings the song "Two-Faced Woman" in blackface, but she was actually wearing tan makeup to transform herself into a woman of the tropics. In this number, Joan wears a mink stole over a gown with a satin waist and green chiffon skirt. Taking full advantage of the Technicolor process, the movie is full of pretty pastel colors and costumes.

Joan loved being back at MGM, where so many of the crew members remembered and admired her and where the production values where top-notch. She also knew that the part of Jenny was tailor-made for her particular talents. Her legs had come a long way since *Hollywood Revue of 1929*: "I really would have killed myself if I hadn't been good in that picture. I mean, it had 'Joan Crawford' written all over it. It was a good part for a woman who was no longer a spring chicken, if you know what I mean."

Many people have thought that Jenny Stewart was a thinly disguised Joan Crawford, but Joan was never that difficult or nastily temperamental. She knew that if you wanted to get the best effort out of your co-workers, the last thing you should do is antagonize them. It was mostly unprofessional behavior that got her dander up. However, like Jenny, Joan didn't suffer fools gladly, and she would occasionally get impatient with the incompetent; like Jenny, she would also volunteer compliments when merited and was never completely without a sense of humor. Where Jenny departs from Joan is that Jenny has no respect for people's feelings at all; her explosions come almost without provocation.

There are some moments in the film where Joan Crawford and Jenny Stewart almost merge. One takes place in a cab in which Jenny is arguing with her producer. He tells Jenny not to bother so much with her teenage fans, as they can't afford a ticket to her Broadway show. Jenny reminds him that they will be able to afford it in ten years. "None of us will be here ten years from now," the producer says, as a worried look crosses Jenny's face. Joan was always haunted by the thought of her career completely drying up and leaving her with nothing to do. The scene where Jenny's mother nags at her to pay for her sister's piano lessons is reminiscent of Joan's own parasitic relatives—indeed, Jenny's are more benign. In the scene in which Joan has an underling quickly throw together a party just because she's in the mood for one, it's hard not to notice that all of the guests are male; the real Joan adored surrounding herself with good-looking men too. Jenny tells Graham that "in this business you either hit first or get hit"—Joan's own philosophy, in blunter form. Later on, Graham observes that Jenny's "first loyalty is to your audience"—the same was essentially true of Joan—then warns her that someday she'll be a "cheap and vulgar has-been, and then it will be the bottle, but even liquor will lie to you." Joan did drink considerably in her later years, but it is debatable whether she ever became a true has-been. Like Bette Davis, Katharine Hepburn, and a few others, she had become too much of an American icon for that.

Joan is marvelous in *Torch Song*; it was a part she could really sink her teeth into. One of her best scenes has her expressively pantomiming as she looks around her room and out her window into the daylight, imagining what it must be like for Graham to live in endless darkness. For once in her life, Jenny Stewart is actually giving her full thoughts to another person—it's juicy stuff, and Joan made the most of it.

Esther Williams was on her way out at MGM when Joan was making her triumphant comeback. In her highly entertaining (if self-serving) memoir, Williams recalled Joan coming into her dressing room before shooting on *Torch Song* began and "begging" her to lend her her director, Charles Walters. This is rather unlikely, as this would have been a studio decision, and Williams didn't have much clout at MGM at the time—after all, Dore Schary was on the verge of pushing her out the door. It probably is true that, as a gag, Williams brought Joan a welcoming present of a nearly empty vodka bottle wrapped in toilet tissue. As Williams knew that Joan enjoyed her vodka, this was a rather insulting gesture, and Joan was right to dismiss it—and Williams herself—as "tacky." Williams claimed that Joan turned on her because the gift "was a chilling reminder that her bubble world wasn't real," but it is more likely Joan saw it, correctly or not, as a slap in the face from a short-lived star of limited talent to an actress who had been on top for decades. Certainly Williams had given some good light performances in both comic and romantic pictures, but she was no match for Joan in the dramatic department, as she knew perfectly well. Williams's assertion that she saw Joan on a darkened soundstage all alone and crying out, "Why have you left me? Why don't you come to my movies?" smacks of dubious invention. Christina Crawford's book did such a number on her mother that others may have felt that any tall tale or ludicrously imagined potshot against Joan had become acceptable. Williams was undoubtedly told by her publisher that her book had better be full of sensational material or it wouldn't sell. Joan, of course, was an obvious target. An unlikelier candidate was the late Jeff Chandler, who would costar with Joan in *Female on the Beach*. Williams claimed that Chandler was a closet transvestite. It is more likely that if Chandler dressed in drag at all, it was only to scare off the marriage-minded and essentially gullible Williams. It is also likely that Williams knew of the passionate affair between Joan and Chandler (before and during the filming of *Female on the Beach*) and never forgave either of them for it.

One story that Williams told about Joan is true. Being bisexual herself, Joan had no problem making passes at essentially gay men in the hopes that they too went both ways, and Charles Walters was no exception. Fortified with vodka, Joan showed up at his house one time (she slept at the studio most evenings during the making of *Torch Song*), wanting to spend the night with both Charles and his male lover. The two men took her in, gave her coffee, shared some laughs with her and let her sleep it off, after which they all had a happy breakfast together in the morning. On an earlier occasion, Joan opened her dressing gown, revealing her naked forty-eight-year-old splendor so that Walters could see what good shape she was in, and perhaps become intrigued by what he saw. He agreed that she was in great shape, but that was as far as it went.

Joan had gotten so much that she wanted for *Torch Song* that she didn't complain much when it was decided that India Adams would dub her singing. Despite some statements she made to the press for publicity purposes, Joan was no longer on the vocal kick she had been twenty years before, and she was insecure about her voice. She didn't mind casually singing along with a record of Adam's voice in the aforementioned scene, but she wasn't sure her vocalizing was good enough for the big production numbers. She was back at MGM and she wanted everything to go right.

It was around this time that director Joshua Logan realized that Joan would be perfect for Norman Krasna's Broadway show *Kind Sir*. He sent Joan the script; she told him that she loved the play and was interested in starring in it. According to Logan, Joan insisted on a special audition in which she would read an act or two so that she and Logan would both be assured that she had the proper projection for the theater. Logan thought that Joan's audition was absolutely wonderful, and wanted to sign her for the part that very moment. As Logan told the story, Joan then informed him that she had never been serious about appearing in *Kind Sir*, but simply wanted to know, as he put it, "whether or not I could do it, for my own satisfaction." She told him that she could never do a long-running play because she'd be "bored to death." Joan told a different story:

> I wasn't that crazy about the play, to tell the truth. I wasn't getting that many picture offers, and I thought going on the stage was a possibility. I figured I'd read for Logan and see what he thought. He was very flattering—too flattering. I was afraid I wouldn't get the kind of attention I needed from him if I really wanted to be *excellent*. He wanted a name on

the marquee. Sure, people might have come to see me, but then what? I didn't want to be just okay, or simply miscast. I just had too many doubts. Mr. Logan was one of those doubts.

This may be true, but one cannot discount the possibility that her chief reason for backing out was simple stage fright.

Director Nicholas Ray and Joan were supposed to make a film at Paramount called *Lisbon,* but Joan ultimately rejected what she felt was a weak script. Joan was more interested in doing the film adaptation of a novel entitled *Johnny Guitar.* She had bought the rights to the novel before it was even published, and offered it to Republic Studios with the stipulation that she star in it. It was the only film Joan ever did for Republic, which had churned out dozens of low-budget but often well-made serials in earlier decades. She probably would never have considered working for Republic were it not for the prestige they had accrued by releasing John Ford's *The Quiet Man,* with John Wayne and Maureen O'Hara, in 1952.

Johnny Guitar (1954) almost became the first film Joan did with Bette Davis, as she knew the other actress in the movie had to be a match for her, in both power and talent. She also thought her friend Barbara Stanwyck would work well. But now that Republic had Joan working for them, there was no way that they were going to shell out the money to hire either of those expensive powerhouses—Republic hadn't come *that* far from its origins. Joan then thought that Claire Trevor would be perfect in the role, but for one reason or another Trevor was never seriously considered. It was Nicholas Ray who brought in Mercedes McCambridge, figuring that she would supply the requisite fireworks to complement Joan's intensity. *Johnny Guitar* was the first Western featuring Joan since *Winners of the Wilderness* and *Law of the Range,* her silent films with Tim McCoy. While it has polarized her fans, it is one of her most fascinating movies, not so much for its alleged Freudian subtext but for the characters and the tension they generate, a tension marvelously sustained and exploited by director Nicholas Ray.

In *Johnny Guitar,* Joan plays Vienna, who has opened a saloon in Albuquerque, anticipating the town's expansion once the railroad is completed. This does not sit well with Emma (McCambridge), who prefers an open range for cattle to a town bustling with people she doesn't know and can't control. It doesn't help that Emma is after a guy known as the Dancin' Kid (Scott Brady), who has eyes only for Vienna. Because of her jealousy, Emma accuses Vienna and her employees of robbing a stagecoach and murdering her brother. Into this volatile situation comes Vienna's former lover and new employee, Johnny Guitar (Sterling Hayden), who has traded in his gun for the musical instrument. When the Dancin' Kid and his cronies rob Emma's bank, Emma accuses Vienna of being in on it, and tries to have her hanged. Vienna is rescued by Johnny Guitar, who also helps her to put an end to Emma's reign of terror.

Johnny Guitar begins with the eerie sight of a windstorm raging past a lonely structure in the desert with an overpowering mountain behind it. The windstorm is nothing compared with the emotional storm that's soon to follow. In the saloon, Eddie (Paul Fix) starts a roulette wheel spinning just as the door bursts open: in tramps Emma with her boys in tow, carrying her dead brother's body. The wheel continues to spin in counterpoint as Mercedes and Vienna—and their respective gangs—confront each other. The effectively constructed sequence is full of motion: the spinning wheel, the figures rushing in from outside, Vienna coming down the stairs, the quick intercutting between characters—it positively hums with tension. The tension begins to slacken about three-quarters through the movie, but it re-ignites for the suspenseful climactic shootout between the two combative women.

In *Johnny Guitar*, Joan had to run around and get dirty more than in her other films of that period. She was perfectly game, although there was a tense moment during a scene when her dress caught fire and it took her a bit too long to get it off. She wasn't hurt, however, and Ray and the crew acknowledged that she was a real trouper. Joan gives more evidence of what an accomplished, hard-working actress she is. More comfortable with outsize gestures than nuanced subtlety, Joan's performance in *Johnny Guitar* is striking and entirely appropriate. Indeed, subtlety was not exactly the character's strong point. With Vienna, Joan was allowed to let out her masculine side. Vienna is tough—considering the people around her, she needs to be—but never stereotypically "butch." In Republic's version of Technicolor, known as "Trucolor," Joan's hair emerges as a rather bright red.

As her archenemy, Mercedes McCambridge matches Joan's histrionics and power. Darting about arms akimbo like a rabid wolverine, McCambridge offers an absolutely mesmerizing performance. Nicholas Ray referred to her as "straight sulfuric acid!" The fact that the two actresses did not like each other off-camera only heightened their savage on-screen enmity.

Joan was still a very attractive woman, and in *Johnny Guitar* she was surrounded by enticing men. Sterling Hayden was an ideal leading man for her during this period—he was attractive and masculine, but not too young. He had, of course, been Bette Davis's leading man in *The Star* two years earlier, adding a bit of irony to the pairing. Joan and Hayden perform well together in a mock love scene between Vienna and Johnny which slowly turns into a real one. Scott Brady is less effective as the Dancin' Kid. Joan was more taken by young Ben Cooper as "Turkey" Ralston, who winds up getting hanged by Emma and her boys. Ernest Borgnine, Royal Dano, and John Carradine offered little sex appeal but did provide solid supporting performances.

There are two schools of thought about *Johnny Guitar*. Is it a dull, silly, ludicrous film with a miscast Joan playing a tough gal, a picture full of dramatic highs and lows that seem to have no rhyme or reason, and with a flop of an ending? Or is it a brilliant, symbolic, utterly original cinematic masterpiece? The truth is somewhere in between. *Johnny Guitar* ought be seen in one sitting, without commercial interruption, by a viewer willing to pay attention to it; otherwise it won't work. While it is true that the script could use more character development and backstory, much of what the viewer needs to know is contained in the rapid-fire dialogue. It is also true that *Johnny Guitar* is essentially a good B western, but it is uplifted by the two excellent lead performances and Ray's trenchant direction. *Johnny Guitar* is a western very much ahead of its time, one in which the women are the dominant characters and antagonists (and better actors than the two male leads), every bit as tough as the menfolk.

Johnny Guitar has been foolishly misunderstood by some as a battle between two "diesel dykes." First, this reading suggests that an exhibition of "masculine" strength in women is necessarily indicative of their sexual orientations, a narrow viewpoint to be sure. Second, there is nothing in the dialogue or even in the line readings to suggest any intimation of sexual interest between Emma and Vienna. Because of the forcefulness of McCambridge's portrayal (she did, apparently, play a stereotypical lesbian character, or what passed for one, in Orson Welles's *Touch of Evil* four years later), it is easy to see why some would isolate Vienna as the true object of her affection and not the Dancin' Kid, but the picture doesn't really bear this interpretation out, fascinating though it may be to consider.

The dialogue in *Johnny Guitar* is often perceptive, such as when Vienna complains (in one of Joan's favorite lines): "A man can lie, cheat, kill, but if he hangs on to his pride, he's still a man. But if a woman slips just once, she's a tramp." On the other hand, the picture's rare obtuse moments provide fuel for its detractors. When Johnny suggests that Vienna's white outfit will attract attention in the woods, she changes into a *bright red* one. When one of Emma's bullets smashes a hole in the window beside which Vienna is standing, Vienna never jumps out of range.

Joan had little fun making the picture, which was shot on location in Arizona (standing in for New Mexico). She admired Mercedes McCambridge's work ("I have to admit the little bitch gave a good performance," she told Larry Quirk), but she hated working with her. In her memoirs, Joan referred to McCambridge as a "rabble-rouser" who "hadn't worked in ten years." (In fact, McCambridge had won a supporting Oscar for *All the King's Men* only five years earlier.) McCambridge said: "I took no crap from her!" In short, the drama on the set of *Johnny Guitar* might have made for even a better movie than the picture itself.

There was bad blood between the two women from the start. Joan apparently had dated Fletcher Markle, the man McCambridge married, and McCambridge couldn't resist needling her that she had landed the guy Joan had been after. Joan had never had any interest in marrying Markle, but she did not take kindly to McCambridge's mocking attitude. McCambridge was also jealous that she was obliged to play second-fiddle to Joan when she, too, had won an Oscar, and she was determined to steal as much of *Johnny Guitar* away from Joan as she could. It rankled McCambridge that even with an Oscar she had never become a major star, as Joan had. McCambridge was furious when she found out Joan was having an affair with Nicholas Ray, figuring that the director would favor Joan at all times and that her plans to shunt Joan aside were thus doomed at the outset. Joan was also afraid that Ray was giving McCambridge "special direction" when she wasn't with her. "Joan Crawford is a movie queen," McCambridge told *Hollywood Reporter* columnist Mike Connolly after filming wrapped. "I had never met one before. I know now what I don't want to be." Joan's constant rebuttal: "I have four children. I don't need a fifth."

Joan used to gather members of the cast and crew for tea (or something stronger) in her dressing room, but McCambridge so irritated Joan that she eventually stopped inviting her and on at least one occasion ordered her out when she tried to crash an impromptu party Joan was having with some of the other actors. McCambridge's tactic was to tell Joan unpleasant comments that others had said about her, and then rush back and tell the rest what Joan's reaction had been. She would rush back and forth in this manner as long as negative comments were there to pass along. Then she would call the gossip columnists and relate it all to them as well. Before long, Joan and McCambridge weren't speaking, and the rest of the cast and crew had divided into two camps, pro-Joan and pro-Mercedes.

Sterling Hayden had no problem joining the pro-Mercedes camp. Joan did not like doing scenes with Hayden while his "mealy-mouthed" and very jealous wife Betty Ann watched them intently from the sidelines. McCambridge taunted Joan that Hayden's wife was "watching out for you." As tactfully as she could, Joan suggested that Betty Ann leave the set just for these particular scenes. Incensed, Hayden refused, so Joan had to demand that Betty Ann be ejected. Hayden later said that he would never work with Joan again, under any circumstances.

One person who remained loyal was John Carradine, who told a reporter, "Let's not be too critical. After all, she was the star of the picture." Carradine, a veteran performer whose always kept his ego in check, understood that with stardom came certain privileges—and a lot more responsibility than most people ever realized.

At first, Nicholas Ray encouraged the feud between Joan and McCambridge. He thought it helped the picture, just as the fact that Hayden and Brady were weaker actors than the two women helped the picture. "It really heightened the dramatic conflict," he said. "I thought it was heaven-sent that the two [women] genuinely couldn't stand one another because the hatred just radiated off the screen and made it that much more intense. But then I realized it had gone too far. I became afraid that all that anger would spill over and put an end to the picture. And no 'heightened reality' is worth that." After the night Joan and McCambridge had a major fight at the motel where the actors were staying, Ray realized that the situation had backfired. That night, an inebriated Joan grabbed as many of McCambridge's clothes as she could carry and started throwing them out onto the highway. (It has been reported that Joan threw McCambridge's costumes—the black outfit she wears throughout the movie—out of the wardrobe truck, but Joan often laughingly related that she'd thrown her costar's own clothing out of the motel room.)

A reporter who came to the set to interview Joan, finding her indisposed, instead spoke to some of the cast and crew. Annoyed because Joan had withdrawn access, he deliberately engineered an article intended to mock and denigrate her public image and portray her as a control freak. (The same thing would happen to other powerful women in the film industry, for example Barbra Streisand, many years later.) Members of the pro-Mercedes camp were quoted verbatim, but members of Joan's camp found that their comments had been distorted or taken out of context. The writer also interviewed some of Joan's previous coworkers who had been verbal in their dislike of her. Taking his cue from Joan's well-known interest in elegance and cleanliness, he quoted an unnamed former maid of Joan's who said she quit when she learned that Joan—horrors!—expected her to take off her shoes when she walked in the house so as not to get dirt on the rug. What would seem a perfectly sensible request of a domestic working in a house with expensive carpeting was used as evidence of Joan's alleged nastiness. Hearing unkind things said about her by the likes of Hayden's wife or Jack Palance was one thing, but Joan was astonished to discover even former silent star Theda Bara—who had not made a movie since 1926—attacking her in print. If she hadn't understood long before, she now sadly grasped that many people hated her not because of anything she did, but simply because of her remarkable success in what is perhaps the world's most brutal profession. Some of her peers could appreciate Joan's drive (because it was also part of their own temperament), but has-beens and also-rans could only sleep better at night if people like Joan were exposed for the "monsters" they obviously had to be to achieve such success. Then they could tell themselves that they hadn't made it because they had been too nice.

It wasn't just her costars' comments about her that kept Joan in the papers. In February of 1955, Joan went to a party for *Photoplay* magazine, now published by Irving Manheimer and edited by Ann Higginbotham. She made her entrance at the Bel-Air Hotel wearing a floor-length silver mink. As *Hollywood Reporter* columnist Mike Connolly put it, "she took it off and BOINNGGG! her dress came too." Former dates such as George Nader and Rock Hudson rushed forward to shield Joan's exposed décolletage, while Jane Wyman and Barbara Rush got Joan back and zipped into her dress. Joan had been in such a hurry that she had forgotten to "hook herself up." Connolly deemed it "the season's most spectacular entrance." Mortified at the time, in retrospect Joan later found the whole incident hilarious: "At least I exposed my breasts on accident," she said, "not on purpose, like Marilyn."

For her next assignment, Joan sweet-talked Universal Studios president Milton Rackmil, with whom years earlier she'd had a brief fling, into giving her an advantageous deal for her first and only picture for the studio. Joan was teamed with Jeff Chandler in *Female on the Beach*, which was based on a novel by Robert Hill called *The Besieged Heart*. In it, Joan plays Lynn Markham, who moves into a beach house formerly owned by Eloise Crandall (Judith Evelyn), who fell to her death from the balcony. Chandler plays Drummond Hall, the former tenant's gigolo, who feels free to use his keys and wander around the place even though Eloise no longer lives there and Lynn is already settling in. Cecil Kellaway and Natalie Schafer are hilarious as an older married couple who serve as Drummond's procurers. Now that Eloise is no longer among the living, the couple encourages Drummond to make a play for Lynn. She finds the dead woman's diary and decides she isn't having any of it. Drummond persists, and eventually they fall in love. They get married and it all ends happily—the older couple are sent on their way—but not before Lynn begins to suspect that he not only did away with Eloise but plans to do the same to her. The real killer, however, turns out to be Amy Rawlinson (Jan Sterling), the real-estate agent who rented Lynn the property. It seems she was once Drummond's girlfriend and has no intention of sharing him with anyone.

Larger-than-life as always, Joan is quite good in the film; a highlight has her reacting with increasing anxiety after a temporary break-up with Jeff, as she waits for him to phone her. When he finally does, Joan expertly gets across the character's desperate relief and joy at finally giving in to the passion that's been building inside her for weeks. She plays Lynn as a very hard and callous woman; you sense she's been hurt once too often and isn't about to let it happen again. For instance, when Drummond asks her, "How do you like your coffee?" Lynn snaps, "Alone!" Joan had a particularly good supporting cast in this, with both Evelyn and Sterling registering as Drummond's cast-off lovers, and Kellaway and Schaefer having the time of their lives as the old reprobates down the beach. Jeff Chandler gives an uncompromising performance as an unapologetic male hustler, more proof of this underrated actor's versatility. He is especially unnerving in the sequences when Lynn and Drummond first meet: his blithe entrances into her new house would give anyone the jitters.

The movie is vivid and entertaining, but every single one of the characters is relatively unpleasant—even Lynn. No one ever seems even mildly dismayed by Eloise's death. *Female on the Beach* comes awfully close to being an extremely good picture, but it's done in by the B-movie treatment and a half-baked screenplay. Much of it plays like a black comedy theater piece (there are some very funny lines in the first half) played unwittingly as straight melodrama. Even Joan thought that "the parts are better than the whole." She thought that the script lacked credibility, but it was certainly a juicy part for her. Joan was intelligent enough to see that in many of her films, the writers were more interested in constructing "moments" for the actors than in maintaining believability or even coherence. Still, most screenwriters did this not out of any lack of talent but rather because they knew that most stars were more interested in those big scenes than in anything else.

Joan had had a passionate affair with Chandler a few years earlier, when he was one of several contract players she interviewed for her production company. Things became very serious between the two for a while, and Chandler moved out of the home he shared with his wife and into his own apartment, where Joan was a frequent visitor. When the columnists noticed which recently separated man was accompanying Joan to so many premieres and other events, they put two and two together and the private affair became public. Joan took this as a sign that she should end the dalliance. Jerry Asher said of the affair:

> She was very fond of Jeff and very attracted to him. But she wasn't in love with him. He was in love with her, however, and he took it hard. But then, he also was concerned with how the break-up would affect his career. Joan did not dump him as a friend or colleague. She had promised him they'd work together someday, and in *Female on the Beach* they did. Joan was instrumental in getting him signed for the male lead. Of course, she had her underlying motives. Her strong attraction to Jeff never wavered.

Joan made moves on Chandler during filming. Not wanting to be hurt again, Chandler was smart enough to handle her with the proper combination of charm and muscle—at first. Then they resumed their purely sexual relationship for the duration of filming. Joan would frequently remain in her dressing room after everyone else had left. Chandler would return to the studio and join her in the dressing room, often staying all night. Reminiscing about *Female on the Beach* many years afterward, Natalie Schafer said, "I don't doubt it!" when asked if Chandler and Joan had resumed their relationship. "They had, umm, very good chemistry. Let's just say they were really convincing together—no matter where they were."

Joan also thought Chandler quite talented. "He was a damn good actor, better than anyone gave him credit for," she said. Chandler's sex appeal was not lost on Joan. "He's so masculine and good-looking but not in the stereotypical way. He was not some cookie-cutter beach boy." Joan had demanded that Chandler be her leading man, and fulfilling her promise to him was the least of it. He was also the top Universal Pictures star at that time. The name of Tony Curtis had been bandied about, but Joan had always found him too vulgar. Drunk, she may have found him appealing; sober, he was déclassé and "second-rate in the looks department." She had once had a small crush on Curtis, but when she invited him to dinner he made the mistake of bringing his wife, Janet Leigh, and that was the end of that. (Joan took it well—according to Leigh, Crawford just paid more attention to Curtis than to her—understandably—but was otherwise perfectly civil. Others who weren't there insisted that Joan rudely "ignored" Leigh, which simply wasn't the case.) Rackmil had other plans for Chandler, whose films did not need Joan to register at the box office, and tried to interest Joan in Curtis. She would have none of it; she rejected Tony as being too young for the part. Since the role was that of a gigolo who preyed upon older women, that did not seem to matter to Rackmil, but he understood that Joan was concerned about how old she would appear next to such a young costar. At the time, Chandler had attractive, prematurely graying hair, and didn't look that much younger than Joan.

In 1973, twelve years after Chandler's death from a botched operation, Joan still had nothing but praise for him: "I love him. He was such a good person, a really nice guy. In the picture he was playing a sleaze, an opportunist, but when his character seems to redeem himself at the end, he makes the transition convincing. He even got across the feeling that all along the man he was playing hadn't been such a bad guy."

Queen Bee was the first of several pictures she would do for Columbia. Joan had one of her best roles as neurotic Eva Phillips, and it is yet another of her movies that improves with each viewing. Along with *Harriet Craig,* it is the role that is most identified with Joan's image, but it is after all a role and not to be confused with the real Joan Crawford. Some aspects of Joan's personality did make their way into her characterization, however. The movie was based on a novel by Edna Lee; Ranald MacDougall, who had contributed to the script for *Mildred Pierce,* wrote the adaptation and also wanted to direct it. Joan agreed to do the film as long as MacDougall got the assignment.

In *Queen Bee,* Eva Phillips lords over a household in the South that consists of her alcoholic husband Avery (Barry Sullivan), who has a slightly scarred face and is nicknamed "Beauty"; her sister-in-law Carol (Betsy Palmer); her two small children with Avery; and a new arrival, her cousin

Jennifer (Lucy Marlow). Judson (John Ireland), who supervises Avery's mills, once had an affair with Eva but now wants to marry Carol. Eva and Avery's marriage has been tainted ever since Avery left another woman at the altar to run off with Eva, who had been pursuing him relentlessly. Eva's little boy, Ted (Tim Hovey), has a persistent nightmare of a car racing toward a mountain. "When they reach the mountain, they'll die," he tells Jennifer. When Carol commits suicide after learning of Eva's relationship with Judson, Avery says good-bye to his children, foolishly determined to kill himself and Eva in a car crash. But Judson realizes what he's up to and does the deed himself. Ted wakes up crying, "It happened! It happened! I know how it ends!" His nightmare has finally reached its expected conclusion with the fiery demise of his mother. Avery and cousin Jennifer, who have been since become close, seem destined for a happier union than Avery had with Eva.

Fay Wray was cast as Sue McKinnon, the confused middle-aged woman who was supposed to have married Avery on that fateful day long ago. When Joan learned that the star of *King Kong* and many other classic movies would be playing the small role in *Queen Bee,* she sent her a note that read: "Welcome. . . . We need you." Wray was very impressed with Joan. "I had the opportunity to see how she continued to challenge each of life's moments as she lived them: self-critical, compulsively clean, washing her hands often and applying lotion from elbows to fingertips, using every free moment between scenes to answer fan mail, never relaxing." Decades later, Betsy Palmer, stilted and obvious as Carol, came to a sort of prominence as the deranged Mrs. Pamela Voorhees, the multiple murderess of the first installment of the *Friday the 13th* series of horror movies.

Joan gives one of her best performances in *Queen Bee.* While there are those who would wrongly dismiss her acting style as Old Style Glamorous Movie Star thesping, Joan constantly gives us glimpses of the human being underneath the external beast. Calling on the resentments and disappointments of her own early life, she has some of her most powerful moments expressing Eva's bitterness as she tells her cousin how Avery's friends and family always treated her like an outsider. "You don't know the things they've made me do trying to protect myself," she says. Eva also has a powerful reaction to the news of Carol's suicide, expressing self-disgust by smearing cold cream all over her image in the mirror, and then collapsing into tears. Joan is amusing in a scene in which Eva gets out of going to a party given by a hypochondriac acquaintance by lying that she has a virus. (Joan would sometimes do this in real life to get out of what promised to be a tedious situation.) Flirting with her son's ordinary-looking psychiatrist, Eva needs the same constant reaffirmation of her attractiveness that Joan herself often did. "I don't ever want people to have bad thoughts about me," Eva says. Joan outacts everyone in the picture; Palmer and Sullivan and Marlowe have their moments, but all are decidedly uneven.

Joan looks strikingly attractive in *Queen Bee,* with a kind of helmet hairdo that gives her an appropriately evil mien. She is also glamorously appointed in *Queen Bee,* at one point turning up in a low-cut black satin gown with plunging décolletage, a long train, and a long black above-the-elbow glove on her left arm. A beautiful portrait of a younger Eva (obviously a picture of Joan herself) hangs in the living room of the Phillips household.

As Southern dramas go, *Queen Bee* is hardly comparable to the best of Tennessee Williams, but it remains a rather good movie with a satisfying conclusion. The only real problem with it is that despite Eva's bitchy, controlling qualities, she seems to love her children, and vice versa. A sadistic nurse named Miss Breen brutalizes the children, but, unlike Avery, Eva seems unaware of this. Is murdering a child's mother ever a solution? Ted's obvious horror and dismay (effectively carried off by Tim Hovey) over what happened to his parent is heartbreaking.

Joan thought that "in my death scene I was getting precisely what I deserve." She recalled to some interviewers that it was difficult to make the picture because she came to despise the character so much, finding her "a downer." Indeed, Joan called Eva "a thoroughly selfish bitch." On another occasion, Joan said that she admired her own work and thought that *Queen Bee* deserved a better reputation. "No, it's not Eugene O'Neill. I suppose there are contrived moments, silly spots. But I have no apologies. It was a study of a woman who makes everyone around her miserable because of her own unhappiness, and on that level it works. I think Randy [MacDougall] did a fine job." When asked if she may have unwittingly intimidated the cast, none of whom really play up to her level, she said: "I think you have to remember that Eva was a very intimidating person, always on the edge, and people tiptoed around her because they didn't want an explosion. I think the actors were more than adequate in getting that across, and it may have affected their performances. But it worked somehow, don't you think? Maybe some of them could have *delivered* a little more, a little bit more energy, but no one was really *bad,* were they?"

Around the time of *Queen Bee,* Joan made a public-service short for a charity called the Jimmy Fund, which collects money for children with cancer. She is shown at the top of the stairs in her home, saying good-night to her unseen children. She then addresses the audience, asking them to give generously to the fund and explaining its function. This short was shown in movie theaters. When Joan was through speaking, the lights would come up and ushers would pass canisters into which patrons could put their change. (The Jimmy Fund continues the same fundraising technique to this day.) Besides doing this featurette, Joan also donated quite generously to the Jimmy Fund. It is safe to say that Eva Phillips probably would not have done the same.

Joan was about to enter a mostly disappointing phase of her motion picture career, but something unexpected was to happen that would take some of the sting out of it. A new man was coming into her life.

And he would bring a new sense of purpose for Joan.

Bernard Wohl Collection

Chapter Fourteen

THE QUEEN OF PEPSI-COLA

Alfred Steele, who would become Joan's fourth husband, was the person most responsible for turning Pepsi-Cola from a small soda company into Coca-Cola's chief competition. This was partly because he had worked for Coca-Cola for so many years and absorbed a number of trade secrets before jumping ship to Pepsi with another executive and friend named Mitchell Cox. Steele was stimulated by the challenge of taking the rival cola company and turning it into a genuine challenge to Coca-Cola's supremacy. Within a year he was made chairman of the board at Pepsi-Cola, whose profits had increased about 300 percent since his original appointment. Alfred Steele was a man who took no prisoners in his determination to take himself—and Pepsi-Cola—to the top.

Joan had known Alfred and his second wife Lillian socially for several years when she heard that the two were getting divorced. The first time she encountered him newly single was at a dinner party at the home of Joseph Cotten. According to Cotten, "[Joan and I] felt more cozy than we actually were" because of this, although Cotten was under the misapprehension that Joan and Alfred were meeting for the first time. Actually, this was the first time that Alfred began to wonder whether the still-attractive movie star might not be as unattainable as supposed, and the first time that Joan began to see the possibilities in a relationship with Alfred.

Although he was a little overweight and not handsome, Alfred Steele was an attractive, outgoing man with a build that recalled his college football career. Unlike Joan's three previous husbands, Alfred Steele was very solid—both physically and emotionally. Furthermore, there was something about him that reminded Joan of herself. Alfred had no patience with dithering, unambitious people who didn't know what they wanted out of life and didn't have the strength or determination to go after anything. Joan responded to Alfred's inner drive and intensity. She kind of liked it when he announced to her after a couple of dates that one of these days she was going to marry him and that was that. By that time the thought of becoming Mrs. Alfred Steele had become rather appealing to her.

Alfred Steele was not a vain, self-centered, hypersensitive actor, as her first three husbands were. Sheltered from life's vicissitudes by money and privilege and his famous father's connections, Douglas Fairbanks Jr. had been too weak and insubstantial. Franchot Tone had more substance, but ultimately proved another weakling when he allowed his career and marital disappointments to lead him to drink and abusive behavior. Phillip Terry had been much too mild-mannered. Alfred Steele was, on the other hand, a real man to Joan, not just a pretty face who would resent her fame and feel emotionally impotent and physically emasculated because of it. As Jerry Asher put it: "Al Steele was another strong bull like Joan, and the two butted horns, but privately enjoyed it. I think she was really in love with Al, and felt for the first time like she was sharing someone's life, going through life *with* someone, which is what she'd always wanted. That's why she threw herself into her activities with Pepsi-Cola. She wanted to be at Al's side, his partner in life *and* business."

There were other reasons for the marriage as well. Joan had no intention of retiring from the screen, but she knew that her career at this point was in a slump from which it might never recover. Working with Alfred for Pepsi gave her a new purpose; she also figured that the exposure it gave her in the media would not only keep her in the public eye, but also convince movie executives that she still had a large, appreciative fan base. If movie roles didn't materialize, Joan would still have a "public," in the form of millions of Pepsi-Cola drinkers.

Joan also figured that Alfred would be a strong influence on her two "problem" children, Christina and Christopher, especially the latter. Christopher at this time had taken to running away on a regular basis. Joan felt that a strong father figure might be able to do what she could not: reach the unhappy and difficult young man. There are those who feel that Christopher, then in his early teens, resented going to boarding schools and the like, but it was his surly attitude and antisocial behavior that made such banishment unavoidable. A different kind of parent, with a less demanding career and less determined nature, might have found the way into Christopher's heart and soul, but there is reason to believe that few people could have broken through the rebellious, destructive, defensive shell the boy had erected around himself. To Joan's credit, she understood that bonding with Christopher was quite beyond her, so she made appointments for him with a child psychiatrist. To her way of thinking, Joan had given the boy everything—a loving parent, a beautiful home, every advantage—but he behaved more like her brother Hal than a child of privilege. Joan tried to maintain a happy medium of love and sensible discipline that would neither spoil nor provoke her children, but in this she only succeeded with the twins, Cathy and Cindy, who would enjoy a warm relationship with Alfred Steele. As Christopher and Christina got older, both would mock their mother's movies and make fun of her performances, just because she wouldn't give in to their every demand. Jerry Asher always defended Joan when it came to her relationship with her children. "With all the distractions, pressures and emotional problems Joan was and is undergoing all the time," he said, "I think she's done the best she could for those kids." Asher did not live to see the publication of *Mommie Dearest,* which would have appalled and saddened him greatly, but he did witness the behavior of Christina and Christopher toward their mother on some occasions. "I hate to say this, but I think those two are just not very nice people. Cindy and Cathy are lovely, they have their heads on straight, but the other two— let's just say Joan didn't get the pick of the litter with those two."

Joan and Alfred picked out a wedding date in late May of 1955, but as the guest list expanded (Joan had half of Hollywood to invite, and Alfred had his many business associates) and the plans for the reception became more and more elaborate, Alfred suddenly suggested that they elope to Las Vegas. He was already wary about what this marriage—and Joan—might wind up costing him. He was already paying plenty in alimony and child support, and he knew movie stars had expensive tastes, and that Joan was no longer earning what she had in her heyday.

In her memoirs, Joan made it seem as if the elopement were perfectly all right with her, but privately she admitted that it was like a punch in the stomach. "I can't tell you how much time I spent figuring out who to invite and where to seat everyone and exactly where it would be and how we'd handle everything, and then all out of the blue he pulls *this.* I almost canceled the engagement right then and there." What prevented her from doing so was that she really did want to marry Alfred, and she didn't want to give him a chance to change his mind. "I thought he was getting cold feet. I wouldn't have blamed him. He'd had two unsuccessful marriages already and I'd had three. But I honestly had fun with Al and I was so lonely. I told myself: 'Have the big party afterwards but land him now while you can.' So we flew to Las Vegas."

At two o'clock in the morning on May 10, 1955, Joan married Alfred Steele in a suite at the Flamingo Hotel before a municipal judge. It was over two weeks before they could sail to Capri on their honeymoon, as those plans had already been made and could not be altered. During the voyage, Joan noticed another side of Alfred's personality that she had never glimpsed while he was courting her. She discovered that Alfred could be as stubborn and intractable as she was, by-products of the drive and determination that Joan had found so attractive in him, and so similar to her own temperament. Determined not to make this marriage another failure, both for her own sake and for the sake of her children, Joan may have given in more than she normally would have. Yet she was still strong-willed Joan Crawford and she would not roll over for anyone. They were in their fifties and both had become set in their ways, but as they argued they realized that there would have to be some sort of give and take, compromises both could live with, if their marriage was to work. They both wanted it to work—both had fantasies to fulfill. Joan had at last found a middle-aged Mr. Right, and Alfred had found a queen to rule by his side. But were either of them truly capable of such an adjustment? Enjoying their honeymoon to the fullest, they returned to civilization rested and ready to tackle the world as Mr. and Mrs. Alfred Steele. Joan reported to Columbia for work on *Autumn Leaves*. Despite her happy outlook and her public statements, she was nagged by doubts about the marriage and the tenacious Mr. Steele. As always, she found consolation in her work.

One of her favorite movies, *Autumn Leaves* (1956) was Joan's first movie with director Robert Aldrich. In this she played Millie, a middle-aged and unmarried freelance typist who meets a younger man, Burt (Cliff Robertson), in a restaurant after a concert. Reluctantly, Millie begins dating Burt, but when the relationship becomes more serious she worries about the age difference. He overrides her objections, and the two are married. She then learns that Burt has serious emotional problems, which have been exacerbated by his seeing his former wife Virginia (Vera Miles) and his father (Lorne Greene) in bed together. After becoming violent toward Millie, Burt is institutionalized. The doctor warns Millie that when Burt recovers he may no longer need her as he did before, that his attitude toward her may change altogether. Happily, after Burt is released, he realizes how much he still loves and needs Millie, and the two are reunited.

Joan's performance in *Autumn Leaves* is generally very good. She used her apprehension about her age and fading looks, as well as those about her marriage to Alfred Steele, to bolster the shy unease of her character, which is apparent in her early scenes with Robertson. Her wonderful expressiveness comes into play when, in close up, Millie silently thinks about what she's learned about her husband and what it means for their future together. There are a few times, however, when she is somewhat mannered and masculine in her approach, and seems too strong to be effectively vulnerable. That forcefulness is very appropriate in the scene in which Millie tells off Burt's sleazy ex-wife and even sleazier father. On the other hand, when she is attacked by Burt (he throws a typewriter at her as she cowers on the floor), she has no trouble conveying her character's abject fear and pathos. In some ways, the movie plays like a rehearsal for *What Ever Happened to Baby Jane?* Robert Aldrich was able to get Joan to shed some of that steely outer shell and show the frightened, insecure woman underneath. This is certainly true in the final scene, Joan's finest moment in *Autumn Leaves* and one of the finest in her career, in which Millie stands looking helplessly at Burt, convinced that he no longer wants her but determined to set him free if necessary, talking rapidly to keep from bursting into tears, so vulnerable and desperate and needy that it's almost uncomfortable to watch. It is a very moving conclusion.

As Burt, Cliff Robertson gave one of his best performances. Having played an emotionally disturbed woman herself (in the second *Possessed*), Joan gave Robertson pointers on how to approach the part. Even in the early scenes Robertson communicates Burt's mental instability and immaturity without overdoing it. There are rumors that Joan wanted Marlon Brando to be her leading man in *Autumn Leaves* (and a number of other pictures), but Joan was no great admirer of Brando's acting style—or of his looks. "There's something flat and dead about his eyes," Joan once remarked. "Brando doesn't really have the handsomeness of a Clark Gable or a Cary Grant. They were well-groomed and intelligent looking. Brando looks like he changes his underwear about every two weeks." Vera Miles is very good and looks delectable as Virginia, and Lorne Greene is quite credible in a role far removed from the loving father of *Bonanza*.

Although never considered a "cinematic" director along the lines of Hitchcock, Aldrich adds some nice touches to the proceedings. As Millie sits in the concert hall listening to Chopin, a flashback shows the lover who left her because she was devoted to her sick father. Aldrich dims the lights all around Millie, isolating her in a sea of darkness and loneliness—a simple move, but effective. Later, after Millie has decided not to see Burt anymore, she sits on a rock at the shore, the off-kilter angle suggesting how difficult a decision it was, and suggesting her indecision about the whole situation. Sometimes *Autumn Leaves* has a detached and unreal quality to it, but at other times it is very stark and believable.

Autumn Leaves is a film favorite for those who love not wisely but too well, who enter into neurotic, dependent relationships that sometimes work out in spite of the psychological complications and melodramatic angst. For some people, life is just like the movies. Joan, of course, loved *Autumn Leaves,* terming it the "best older woman/younger man movie ever made." She admired Cliff Robertson and Vera Miles, and liked working with them. "Everything clicked on *Autumn Leaves.* The cast was perfect, the script was good, and I think Bob [Aldrich] handled everything well. I really think Cliff did a stupendous job; another actor might have been spitting out his lines and chewing the scenery, but he avoided that trap. I think the movie on a whole was a lot better than some of the romantic movies I did in the past. It did all right at the box office, but somehow it just never became better known. It was eclipsed by the picture I did with Bette Davis."

Joan and Alfred decided to settle down in New York, but in order to do so they had to find a worthy domicile for the Pepsi King and his Queen. Alfred's bachelor pad on Sutton Place was out of the question because it wasn't big enough. So Alfred bought the top two floors at 70th Street and Fifth Avenue overlooking Central Park and converted them into a duplex penthouse with several spacious rooms. After several weeks of noisy renovations while the couple stayed in a hotel—the top two floors were virtually gutted—a neighbor downstairs felt her nerves coming unglued and filed a three-hundred-thousand-dollar lawsuit against the Steeles. She was later made to understand how necessary the renovations were to the Steeles' plans and dropped the lawsuit. "If that bitch thinks I'm inviting her up here for tea, she's got another think coming," said Joan. All visitors to the penthouse had to take their shoes off before they entered. This was seen by some as another example of Joan's need for control, but it was a perfectly sensible precaution to protect the beautiful and expensive white rugs. Joan frequently joked about it: "These things get dirty so easily. I hope you put on clean socks today." William Haines, of course, decorated the apartment from top to bottom.

Alfred charged the reconstruction costs to Pepsi-Cola on the rationale that the exquisite apartment would be used to entertain business associates and hence would enhance both Pepsi's image and its coffers.

So he was a bit stunned when the board of directors made it clear that they considered the money to be a loan—at six percent interest. Given his other expenses, Alfred had to take out loans from the bank as well as from Joan to pay back the money. He managed to return every penny— to Pepsi, if not to Joan. It galled him, however, especially as Pepsi had never done as well as it did during his tenure, and was then doing better than ever, with its new inroads into foreign markets often outstripping the efforts of its rival Coke. Some board members blamed Alfred's movie-star wife for his preoccupation with his new apartment, a perception that did not sit well with Joan. As soon as Alfred realized that they would have to pay for everything in the duplex, he cursed himself for having done everything on such a grand scale. Crawford mythology has it that it was Joan's idea to create such a sensational apartment and fill it with expensive rugs and furniture, but Alfred had his own image to cultivate, and he wanted—and loved—the place every bit as much as Joan did.

Joan won over several Pepsi executives and board members with her tireless efforts for their company. She attended conventions, learned everything she could about the business, entertained business associates on little notice, played hostess at conferences, and in general played up Pepsi-Cola wherever she went. Her high profile, however, would eventually earn her the enmity of at least one executive in the Pepsi-Cola Company.

It was around this time that Lawrence Quirk did his first piece on Joan, for the December 1956 issue of *Films in Review*. Quirk knew that, like Bosley Crowther, *Films in Review* editor Henry Hart was no fan of Joan's. Hart had once said that "Bette Davis is an *artist*; Joan Crawford is a *trouper*," which Quirk felt ignored Joan's work in pictures like *Mildred Pierce* and the 1947 *Possessed*. He knew that Hart wouldn't spare Joan in his editing of Quirk's piece on her. Quirk wanted to say something respectful yet accurate about Joan in the subhead, but Hart wasn't having any of it. While he was right that Quirk needed to be objective, apparently that didn't apply to the subhead Hart imposed on the article: "For 32 years she has made people want to see her in films rarely worth looking at." Although it qualified as a backhanded compliment, it was hardly accurate, as by 1956 Joan had made *Mildred Pierce, Possessed, Grand Hotel, Rain, The Women, A Woman's Face, Johnny Guitar,* all of which had become classics. Hart said, "Crawford may get angry with the evaluations of her work that Bos Crowther and I give her, but she respects us for our independence."

Hart insisted that Quirk recast the article, interjecting observations on Joan's "ruthlessness." Louella Parsons was quoted to the effect that Joan had done kind things for people down on her luck, but that she, Louella, always thought that Joan's greatest achievement was "Joan Crawford." And so forth. The article concluded on the note that if Joan, after years of upward climbing and conflict ever found herself without something to struggle over, she might not know what to do with herself. Since Quirk was friendly with Joan and found her very cooperative in answering questions for the article, he wondered what her reaction might be. "To hell with what she thinks," Hart snapped. "She's getting a big publicity break with this story and she should be damned grateful." He added that her career was on the downslide and any publicity she got would be good for her.

Quirk sent the issue of *Films in Review* to Joan, explaining as tactfully as possible that Hart wanted his articles to be objective and "distanced." Joan responded that she had been up against many commentators and critics like Hart over the years and always took their comments in stride; she told Quirk not to give it a second thought. Quirk was pretty sure that Joan still didn't like Hart's approach, and wouldn't have blamed her if she threw the magazine clear across the room.

In 1957, Joan flew into London with Alfred to make *The Story of Esther Costello*. Their arrival made the papers—Joan was still considered a major Hollywood star and was still news—and there were photos of the big limousine carrying Joan and Alfred, followed by three white vans from the Pepsi-Cola Company. The couple checked into the Dorchester hotel, where they were ensconced in the Oliver Messel suite. A welcome party was held in Joan's honor at the ritzy Les Ambassadeurs restaurant. Among the attendees were Noël Coward, Laurence Olivier, Vivien Leigh, Marlene Dietrich, and Rita Hayworth. Joan was seated in a throne-like chair in one of the restaurant's banquet rooms. Throughout the evening distinguished guests came by to say hello.

The Story of Esther Costello was being produced by Romulus Films, which was run by two brothers, John and James Woolf. James Woolf was a good friend with another Joan—Joan Collins, who was named after Crawford—whom he invited to the party. Collins also knew *Esther Costello*'s director, David Miller, as she had recently worked for him on *The Opposite Sex*, an inferior musical remake of *The Women*. A theatrical agent named Gordon White was Collins's date. At one point, James Woolf took Collins over to meet the older star. Collins remembered Joan as "a middle-aged, regal, but not terribly attractive, woman in a sea-green silk dress embroidered with sequins in the fashionable 'short in front and long in back' style. With eyebrows as thick and dark as Groucho's, lipstick and matching nail varnish obviously 'Jungle Red,' and black hair done in a curiously old fashioned '40s style, which was echoed in her ankle-strapped, platform-soled stilettos, she was a formidable sight." When Collins offered her hand, Joan gave Collins the once-over and ignored her, speaking only to Woolf. Joan always felt that just because a woman was highly sexed didn't mean that she had to dress the part. Her disdain for sex symbols like Collins, Marilyn Monroe and others had less to do with jealousy than with her distaste, especially as she grew older, for vulgarity. She simply found Collins's low-cut dress offensive. "I get so sick of these young actresses who think they have to let their boobs hang out all over the place to get attention," she said on more than one occasion. Joan was furious that Collins had used a party for *her* as a place to "exhibit her goods." She was probably also aware that Collins had played her role, Crystal Allen, in *The Opposite Sex* (1956). Perhaps in the back of her mind Joan wanted Miller on *Esther Costello* to remind him what a *real* star was. Collins was a good enough actress on her own terms, but no one thought she would be anything like the next Joan Crawford. *The Opposite Sex* was promptly forgotten, and although Collins has been a showbiz survivor for many years, her career was never on the level of that of her namesake. Joan's opinion of *The Opposite Sex*, a box-office flop, was as follows: "It's ridiculous. Norma [Shearer] and I might not ever have been bosom buddies, but we *towered* compared to those pygmies in the remake!"

In *The Story of Esther Costello*, Joan played the wealthy Margaret Landi, who reluctantly becomes ward to a teenage girl named Esther Costello (Heather Sears), who has been psychosomatically deaf, dumb and blind since she was caught in the explosion that killed her mother, traumatizing her. Under the care of understanding doctors, Esther makes great progress, thanks in part to Margaret's constant help and support. Margaret is reunited with her estranged husband Carlo (Rossano Brazzi), who convinces her to start an Esther Costello foundation to help disabled children. (For some reason, the Esther Costello doll shown in the movie resembles Barbara Stanwyck more than Sears.) Unfortunately, Carlo and sleazy promoter Frank Wenzel (Ron Randall) skim most of the profits. Carlo finally goes too far when he rapes Esther, the shock of which undoes the earlier trauma and "cures" her. Margaret kills Carlo and herself, and Esther is left to carry on with a reporter named Harry (Lee Patterson), who has fallen in love with her.

Joan Collins's opinion notwithstanding, Joan had become quite a handsome mature woman by the time of *Esther Costello*; wearing gowns by Jean Louis, she looks wonderful in the picture. Her performance as Margaret Landi is, for the most part, excellent. Unfortunately, when the film becomes artificial at the end, she does as well. When Margaret dispassionately decides to kill her husband and herself late in the movie, the tone shifts from drama to melodrama, and Joan's performance makes the same shift. She has a superb reaction when Margaret finds Carlo's cufflink in Esther's bed and realizes what has happened, but she is too perfunctory in the scenes that follow, acting like an imperturbable femme fatale deciding to ice her faithless lover when she should be enraged and heartbroken over his actions. Instead, Margaret Landi suddenly becomes Mildred Pierce.

As Joan had long since proven that she could portray anger and heartbreak with aplomb, one might surmise that Miller, who had also directed *Sudden Fear,* had suggested an approach that smacked more of that film than *Esther Costello*. But it was really the other way around: Joan actually chose to ignore her director's advice, in spite of the fact that Miller had once guided her to an Oscar nomination. She told one interviewer that she played the role "in my own pitch, the way I thought it should be played, and I was right." Joan and Miller ultimately had violent confrontations over her interpretation. It wasn't just that Joan wanted to come off the way she did in her younger, more glamorous days—although that was certainly part of it—she also wanted to recreate the effects of triumphs like *Mildred Pierce,* while Miller kept reminding her that *Esther Costello* was an altogether different kind of picture, and Margaret a different kind of role. Joan felt that a melodramatic scene should be played like melodrama (even if the movie was a drama), which explained her approach to roles in movies like *The Damned Don't Cry* and *This Woman is Dangerous*. She didn't see this as artificial acting, as Bosley Crowther and others did; she saw it as part of a grand and larger-than-life tradition of movie acting, one that in certain kinds of sequences her fans expected from her. She saw nothing wrong about her performance, and was highly disappointed that she wasn't nominated for an Oscar. She regarded *Esther Costello* as her last worthwhile movie.

The Story of Esther Costello does come close to being a fine picture. The early scenes in Ireland depicting Esther's grim daily existence are photographed in a naturalistic, gritty, low-budget manner that becomes incrementally glamorous as Esther becomes more famous. The picture's look at charitable foundations and their casual exploitation of the disabled is surprisingly unsentimental. There is also an outstanding sequence in which Esther is "presented" to a huge throng of sycophants in a gargantuan art deco amphitheater (that might have been designed to Cecil B. Demille's specifications). There are also sequences that are quite touching, such as one in which a nervous girl receives a diploma from Esther and collapses into her arms in tears. Esther's recovery of her vision and hearing is marvelously demonstrated, as images emerge from an out-of-focus cloud and odd sounds like a passing airplane suddenly intrude. The script exhibits an intelligent cynicism, in that Margaret actually becomes jealous of Esther's emerging sensuality and its effect on Carlo (a bizarre variation on *Mildred Pierce*). *Esther Costello* is one of those movies that is so good in parts you can't help but wish it was better overall.

Whatever its good points, the movie is ultimately done in by its ludicrous finale. Esther has already been traumatized by the violent death of her own mother; is it really wise for Margaret to kill herself and Carlo in a car crash when Esther has come to see Margaret as a surrogate mother? One senses that Harry is not going to find it easy to deal with Esther and her emotional instability. The deaths of Carlo and Margaret were not filmed, perhaps because the sequence is too similar to the end of *Queen Bee*. Then there is the rather tasteless suggestion that the trauma of rape cures Esther, when in reality it probably would have undone whatever progress had been achieved.

The publication of *Mommie Dearest* ensured that immature viewers of the film would never take *Esther Costello* seriously. Some contemporary audiences see scenes of Margaret genuinely bonding with Esther as perversely hypocritical, and the moment when Margaret slaps Esther during a temper tantrum often elicits howls of laughter. The expressive face of Heather Sears as Esther makes an impression without a single word of dialogue; later, when she speaks, she is less effective. In one scene, Sears radiates some of Joan's imperiousness as she tries to find out how Harry feels about her.

Joan later wrote, "What made [the film] a delight . . . was working with Heather Sears. This twenty-one-year-old girl gave a memorable performance. . . . It was a reward to work with one so young who knew so much about character and acting." On the set, Joan was also gracious to former silent film star Bessie Love, who had one brief scene as a customer at Carlo's art gallery. Joan was always kind to Hollywood survivors like Love and Fay Wray, whose careers didn't share Joan's durability.

Joan still had an eye for good-looking men and she surrounded herself with handsome fellows in *Esther Costello*. Joan was crazy about leading man Rossano Brazzi and, under the influence of vodka, would later talk about him in very lascivious tones. "Absolutely one of the most gorgeous creatures God put on this earth," she raved, "I wanted to strip him down the minute I set eyes on him"—but she would never admit that she'd had an intimate relationship with the man. "Yes, there were a lot of good-looking guys on that set," Joan recalled. "Lee Patterson was a doll and I thought Ron Randall had a certain mulish charm about him. Did you notice he talked just like Humphrey Bogart? Look, you never know how the hell a picture is going to turn out, so you might as well have a lot of attractive actors around to make it more bearable. I think that picture had more than most."

Many critics have seen *The Story of Esther Costello* as a partial rip-off of *The Miracle Worker*. In fact, the two films have entirely different storylines and themes, and *The Miracle Worker* was not filmed until five years later, after a successful Broadway run. While *The Miracle Worker* was originally presented on television as part of the "Playhouse 90" series the same year *Esther Costello* was released, the latter film was based on a novel entitled *The Golden Virgin* by Nicholas Monsarrat and was not influenced by the Helen Keller story.

Joan and Alfred were vacationing in Bermuda when they learned that Joan's mother, Anna, had passed away after a series of strokes at the age of 74. Joan and her husband flew home for the funeral, where Joan found herself more affected by her mother's death than she would ever have thought possible. Joan had tried on several occasions to cultivate a warmer relationship with Anna, but whenever the two got together Anna would castigate Joan for how "little" she did for her mother—of course, by this time Joan was completely supporting her mother and paying for her medical care. Still, Joan cried at her grave site. "I think I cried more for the utter waste, for what might have been between us, than anything else," Joan recalled. "My mother wanted what I could do for her, but I don't think she ever really wanted to be part of my life. I know everyone thought it was the other way around, but I honestly *tried*." Soon another death would devastate Joan far more than the death of her mother had.

Alfred had been feeling tired and out of sorts for some time when he died April 19, 1959, from a heart attack. The general consensus was that he ate, drank, and smoked too much and had too little regard for his health. Joan's fourth marriage had not even lasted four years. Some said that Joan did not grieve for Alfred, but nothing could be further from the truth. "It was the most solid of my four marriages," she said, and she meant it. True, Alfred may not have brought out the wild, passionate, sensual side of her nature as Clark Gable had, perhaps he was not in that sense her one great love, but she would have happily spent the rest of her life with him. Joan was not being cold when she made funeral arrangements and went on with her life in the weeks after Alfred's death, she was simply dealing with her pain in a way that was natural to her—many people find relief from grief in constant activity. She did her crying at home alone, or with the twins, who had also been close to Alfred. Realizing that she could be a continued asset to the company and recognizing her efforts on their behalf, Pepsi-Cola put her on its board of directors and eventually made her their worldwide ambassador.

In part to help her get over her grief over Alfred's death, and also because she needed the money, Joan took a small role in the adaptation of Rona Jaffe's *The Best of Everything* (1959). It also helped that old friend Jerry Wald would again be her producer. And Jean Negulesco of *Humoresque* would direct! The novel, which is about secretaries and lady editors and their relationships with assorted males, was sort of the *Valley of the Dolls* of its time, only not as sexy and far less entertaining. Today, the movie version feels very dated in its attitude toward career women. Perhaps because of her mental state, Joan gives perhaps the most uneven performance of her career, as Amanda Farrow, a tough editor.

On the one hand, Joan generally plays (sometimes overplays) with real style and panache, forcefully occupying the movie, even when she's not on-screen. When Amanda learns that Caroline Bender (Hope Lange) has been reading manuscripts and tells her, "You young secretaries think you can breeze in here and become editors overnight," it's almost as if it's Joan directing her words to the young contract players in the cast. Perhaps Joan's best moment comes when Amanda confronts Gregg Adams (Suzy Parker), warning her that her lover, David (Louis Jourdan), will not marry her. "Those who can love, do," responds Gregg. "Those who can't, preach."

On the other hand, when Amanda has a conversation with her married lover on the telephone, there's no sense that anyone is actually on the other end of the line. There is virtually no other instance in her career in which Joan is as transparent as in this scene. In Joan's earlier days, when she was the star, Negulesco would never have let her get away with this, insisting on multiple takes until it was just right. In a later scene, when she returns to work after a failed marriage, she is much too theatrical and completely out of sync with Lange and the other performers. This was what Bosley Crowther had always been harping about, that affectedness that he saw even when it wasn't there. Joan's acting is perfectly fine in the rest of the movie, and she herself always thought that she had shown "all those young bitches" in the cast a thing or two about acting.

Joan often got impatient with the hesitant and apprehensive approach of some of the young women who were starring in the movie. Joan got into a spat with Hope Lange (who, in spite of her inexperience, is quite good in the lead role), and she expected the director to side with The Great Crawford. Negulesco bitterly disappointed her by siding with Lange. Joan realized that her days of being deferred to were probably over, at least on big productions like this, in which she had only a small part. Some of her scenes were dropped from the final cut, including one that she felt would have explained and humanized her character. If a certain script hadn't come her way, *The Best of Everything* might well have been Joan's last picture.

It would be an understatement to say that Pepsi-Cola got annoyed with Joan when Louella Parsons' interview with her around the time of filming was published, with the headline "Joan Crawford Flat Broke." Joan had told Parsons that Alfred had expected the company to reimburse them for the money they spent on their apartment in New York, and that when it hadn't, she'd been left in greatly reduced circumstances. She complained that everything her husband had left her went to pay off back taxes and other debts. The powers-that-be at Pepsi informed her that the story not only made the company look bad, but could also have a negative effect on Pepsi stock. Joan issued a press release recanting much of the interview and putting her financial situation in a much better light. Parsons was not amused.

Joan's financial problems would be over when she found herself in one of the biggest hits of her career. But she would have preferred her money woes to a massive headache named Bette Davis.

Bernard Wohl Collection

Chapter Fifteen
TEEN IDOL

Bette Davis once said of working with Joan on *What Ever Happened to Baby Jane?*:

> We were polite to each other—all the social amenities, "Good morning, Joan" and "Good morning, Bette" crap—and thank God we weren't playing roles where we had to like each other! But people forget that our big scenes were alone—just the camera was on me or her. No actresses on earth are as different as we are, all the way down the line. Yet what we do works. It's so strange, this acting business. It comes from inside. She was always so damn proper. She sent thank you notes for thank you notes! I screamed when I found out she signed autographs: "Bless you, Joan Crawford!"

It was Joan's idea to team up with Davis in the film adaptation of Henry Farrell's novel *What Ever Happened to Baby Jane?* She approached Davis backstage when the latter was starring on Broadway in Tennessee Williams's play *The Night of the Iguana. Baby Jane* is about two sisters, both show-business casualties, who live together in a mansion in Hollywood. Jane Hudson (Davis) was once a child star known as "Baby Jane" Hudson, but she failed to make the transition to adult stardom, while her sister Blanche (Joan) became a major movie star. Apparently Jane once ran Blanche over with a car out of jealousy and has cared for her crippled sister ever since. Jane has been exhibiting signs of mental disturbance for years, but two new factors push her over the edge. Her sister's movies are being shown again on television, eliciting fan mail that only reminds her of her envy and failure; and she has learned that Blanche intends to sell the house, take the maid Elvira (Maidie Norman) with her as a companion, and put Jane in a home where she can be looked after. Jane's first actions are relatively benign; planning to revive her career against all odds, she hires a musical accompanist, Edwin Flagg (Victor Buono, who later played "King Tut" on the TV series *Batman*). Eventually, however, she imprisons Blanche in her room and torments her, murders Elvira when she tries to free Blanche, and finally takes Blanche and flees to the beach, where Jane descends into complete delusion. Before she dies and Jane is taken away by the police, Blanche confesses that she became crippled because she was trying to run over Jane, who had been horrible to her at a party that night, and not the other way around. (The movie also implies that Blanche was motivated by a desire to end Jane's moribund career, which was acting as a drag on Blanche's aspirations.)

What Ever Happened to Baby Jane? is an effective enough comic horror movie that gave the two actresses juicy roles. Its examination of the dark side of celebrity is endlessly fascinating, and the picture gets high marks for entertainment value. But while *Baby Jane* is a better picture than the horror films Joan would do later, it isn't *that* much better than, say, *Strait-Jacket,* because its script and characterizations are equally superficial. With its understandable emphasis on grotesque situations, the two women, despite their excellent performances, emerge more as caricatures than as real and sympathetic human beings. One watches without feeling a trace of true pity. Another problem is that Robert Aldrich, who later became an efficient director of "guy films" like *The Dirty Dozen* and *The Longest Yard,* was not exactly a master of suspense, either then or afterward. He fails to achieve the tension crosscutting might have generated on the two occasions that Jane leaves the house only to return at inopportune moments. (Granted, Jane's hammer murder of the maid is very well handled.) And while *Baby Jane* can comfortably be classified as a black comedy, certain sequences, such as the one in which Edwin Flagg rides around in Blanche's wheelchair, border on the burlesque. It doesn't help that Frank DeVol's musical score is merely serviceable—and sometimes less than serviceable. Jane's reaction to Blanche's climactic revelation—"You mean all this time we could have been friends?"—is surely not meant to be taken literally; had Jane realized that Blanche had been trying to run *her* over on that fateful evening, she probably would have started her campaign of terror many years earlier or simply left Blanche alone to atrophy and had nothing to do with her.

Yet Aldrich does add some interesting touches to the movie, such as the way he keeps a light on a portrait of the young Blanche hanging over the very bed where she lies gagged and bound. The casting of Gina Gillespie as young Blanche is inspired, as the girl radiates Joan's own intensity. The opening shot of the movie shows another young girl, neither Blanche nor Jane, crying as a jack-in-the-box, also with tears on its cheeks, pops out and frightens her, perhaps signaling that the story to come is scary and macabre but nothing to take too seriously.

Whatever reservations she may have had about the story, Joan took her role very seriously, and it shows. Her carefully planned movements make her a believable cripple, and her pantomiming is superb throughout. There is a particularly wonderful bit as she sits in her wheelchair, helpless and hopeless, after Davis throws at her a crumpled note Blanche had thrown out the window in hopes of rescue. Her face beautifully registers her despair and frustration at having her hopes dashed so cruelly. She then wheels herself over to the table where her sister has placed her supper. Tormented by thoughts of what Jane might be serving her now (Jane has already given her a dead pet canary for supper), she can't even find the courage to lift up the cover over the plate. Joan is also excellent during the long sequence in which she struggles to get out of her wheelchair and make her way down the stairs to the first floor, where the telephone is. She calls a doctor and again struggles, this time to make him understand how sick Jane has become and how much danger she is in. There is also a certain poignancy in watching Joan as she watches her much younger self on television (the scenes are from *Sadie McKee*). She wears a touching expression as she reads the first of the fan mail discarded by Jane but retrieved from the trash by maid Elvira. Bette Davis has the showier role and is wonderful, but Joan matches her the whole way in the quieter part. It was easy for her to be tense, nervous and apprehensive on-screen because that was pretty much the way she felt the entire time she was making the movie. It is baffling that screenwriter Lukas Heller complained that "Crawford never reacted to anything, she sat in her wheelchair or her bed and waited for her close-ups," when that is patently untrue. Perhaps Heller didn't realize that no actress on earth could have made any of his paper-thin characters seem three-dimensional.

A line of dialogue given to Jane matches Davis's feelings about Joan's career many decades before: "They didn't even want to show my films," Jane says. "They were too busy giving a big build-up to that crap you were turning out." Davis fancied herself an *artiste* appearing in (or wanting to appear in) "serious" films, while Joan was a mere entertainer churning out divertissements. Whatever the two women thought of each other, they made a good team. For sheer histrionics they are almost matched by

Buono's Edwin Flagg and his slightly daffy Cockney mother, played by Anna Lee.

Another *Baby Jane* performance of note is that of Maidie Norman, who plays Elvira. Norman had first appeared with Joan in *Torch Song*, in which she played her efficient and understanding secretary with consummate understatement. Her Elvira is a more fundamental creature, a sympathetic soul who won't put up with any of Baby Jane's nonsense and dies horribly for her trouble; Norman makes the most of her scenes. B.D. Merrill, the teenage daughter of Bette Davis and Gary Merrill, played the part of the daughter of the neighbor, Mrs. Bates. She married a man named Jeremy Hyman and betrayed her mother in much the same way that Christina did Joan. From her amateurish performance and unexciting looks, it is easy to see why B.D. never got very far in show business. Christina was hurt, confused, and enraged that Joan didn't secure the part for her (another nail in Joan's coffin), but if Davis was willing to indulge her untalented youngster, Joan certainly wasn't. Besides, at twenty-three Christina was probably too old for the part. Joan never pressured her directors or producers to cast Christina in any of her movies because she felt that she was too inexperienced and that she should make it on her own—just as she herself had.

While it would perhaps be overstating the case to say that Joan and Bette Davis had a lifelong feud, it must be said that they were never good friends. First there was the fact that Joan had married Franchot Tone, whom Davis had fallen in love with during the filming of *Dangerous*. Then it was also true that Joan was already a star in major productions when Davis was just doing small roles in forgettable movies. Joan blamed Katherine Albert for *The Star* (in which the public did not recognize the protagonist as Joan anyway) more than she did Davis. In truth, they did not have much contact with each other until they made *Baby Jane*. If they did have a feud, it began with this picture. Up until the time of *Baby Jane*, and for much of the time afterward, Joan and Davis had to deal with their own lives—difficult children, unhappy marriages, careers on the wane, all of the small tasks and burdens that go with a career in show business—and spent little of their time thinking of the other, still less time scheming against one another. "There is no feud," Davis told *Hollywood Reporter* columnist Mike Connolly. "We wouldn't have one. A man and a woman, yes, but never two women—they'd be too clever for that."

For all of their similarities, however, Joan and Davis mixed like oil and water. Joan could be "one of the guys" just as much as Davis, but it had to be when she was in the mood, with people she liked. If she didn't feel right, she might give off a "grand dame" vibe. The same was true of Bette Davis, frankly, but Davis at least fancied herself a more down-to-earth sort of person. On *Baby Jane,* they were both eager to protect their primary investment—themselves. When you consider what both of them had gone through, the battles won and lost, the anxious need to work and stay on top, it is no wonder that neither of them wanted to give an inch. Joan always felt that Aldrich and the publicity department hoped that the two would feud in much the way they had hoped that she and Norma would feud during *The Women*—because it would be good for business. Joan and Davis didn't exactly feud while making *Baby Jane,* but there were occasional flare-ups. Now and then Davis might make a crack under her breath, or Joan would lift her head high as if she had to be ever so patient with her cranky and difficult costar.

So much fiction has sprung up over their relationship during filming of *Baby Jane* that it is time to put some rumors to rest. Davis would often claim in subsequent interviews that she had contempt for Joan because Joan gave herself the glamour treatment as Blanche, but if she did so, it certainly isn't evidenced by her scenes in the picture. Joan's classic bone structure and lack of grotesque makeup such as Davis used in her characterization of Jane makes her look a lot better than Davis, but she *never* looks glamorous or wears heavy makeup. Besides, in movies like *Strange Cargo* Joan had already proved she was willing to go with the scrubbed look if it was in the picture's best interests. Then there is the tale that Davis hauled off and really let Joan have it in the scene in which Jane kicks Blanche all over the floor. This sequence was cleverly edited to make it appear as if Davis's foot was actually striking Joan's body, but in reality there are no shots showing actual contact. When Davis lashes out, the camera is usual focused on her angry facial expression; Joan was nowhere near Davis when these shots were filmed. Finally, there is the delicious canard that Joan hid weights on her body so that Davis would have a hard time lifting her off the bed when she takes her out of the house for their trip to the beach. "*Weights!*" Joan laughed when asked about this story, "And have Bette tell everyone I was as heavy as an elephant! Absolutely not. I may not have made it as easy for her to lift me out of the bed as I could have, at least at first, but when you're a pro you get over any animosity you may feel and help your fellow player out. It simply didn't happen." It has also been widely reported that Joan told Davis's daughter B.D. Hyman to stay away from her twins so as not to expose them to negative influences, but as the source for this story is Hyman's suspect and ludicrous *My Mother's Keeper,* its veracity is certainly questionable. If anything, Joan may have been impatient with Hyman's complete lack of acting talent, which may be why Hyman made up the story in the first place.

Victor Buono remembered that Davis had been quite rude to him during filming (she later apologized for this), while Joan had been just the opposite. Buono recalled:

> In the scene when I discover Joan tied up in bed and have to react to seeing her there, Joan had already filmed her part and was about to go home when she found out that my close-ups were being done that afternoon and not the following day. She went back to makeup to get that gaunt, haunted look, put the clothes back on, and get back in the bed, so that I could see *her* there and have the proper reaction. It wasn't just for the good of the picture; it was to do *me* a favor. I was nobody and she was "Joan Crawford," and yet she did that for me when no one would have blamed her or criticized her if she'd just gone home as she was supposed to have done. She was a trouper, a real professional, and I thought she was marvelous in the picture.

Clearly this does not square with the image of Joan as a selfish, pampered star only interested in her perks at the expense of others.

The two women's intense dislike of each other actually began after *Baby Jane* came out and was a tremendous, unexpected hit. As the budget had not been large to begin with, it earned back its costs almost immediately and went on to make millions of dollars in profit. Joan found herself in very good financial shape, the best since Alfred's death. But she was not thrilled when the Oscar nominations were announced and Davis was nominated and she was not. This did bring out Joan's competitive, "ruthless" side, but there was another reason for the events that followed. Now that she found herself starring in a hit movie that had galvanized the country's attention, she felt like she was once again being invited to the most exciting party in the world, and she wanted to go on feeling like a treasured guest. Bette's Oscar nomination effectively cut her out of the loop, until the Oscar ceremonies themselves helped restore some balance between the two, at least in terms of the attention lavished on each.

Nobody knows whether Joan actively campaigned against Davis (one tends to suspect it was Davis's paranoia that fueled the story), but she did offer to accept the award on behalf of any Best Actress nominee who could not be in attendance. The now legendary sequence of events had Joan "graciously" holding court backstage at the Oscars. Davis was in a good, conciliatory mood—after all, she had been nominated and Joan had not—and the two were quite friendly for much of the evening. But then the winner was announced and Davis went almost literally into shock. Everyone was certain that Davis would walk off with the award but then it went to Anne Bancroft for *The Miracle Worker* instead. Joan brushed past Davis, went on stage, and accepted the Oscar for Bancroft. Now it was Joan who was in the limelight and Davis who was suddenly ejected from the fabulous party.

Did Joan revel over this development? Of course she did, as she admitted many times over the years. Joan was only human. Davis had made it clear on more than one occasion that she thought she was much more talented than Joan, who understandably resented such remarks bitterly. To have her rival humbled was sweet indeed. Joan never denied that she thought Davis had talent and was a great star, but she also felt that Davis was in no position to condescend to her, and she was right about that.

Although Joan had given somewhat mannered performances in some early and mid-career assignments, in her later years she was actually a much more "natural" performer than Davis. Joan's post–*Baby Jane* performances betray none of the affected posturing and vocal tics that bedeviled Davis in her final films. Splitting all of her sentences into three distinct parts and assuming dreadful high-pitched voices and prima-donna attitudes, Davis generally descended to the level of the script while Joan tended to tower over her material.

A cartoon in *The New Yorker* magazine had the last word on the Bette and Joan combo. It shows two women looking up at a movie theater marquee presenting *What Ever Happened to Baby Jane?* "I like Bette Davis," one woman says to her friend. "And I like Joan Crawford. But I don't think I'd like Bette Davis and Joan Crawford *together.*"

Still, with the grosses of *Baby Jane* still ringing in the actresses' ears, and the realization that this cheap horror picture had won them a whole new generation of fans and made them *stars* again, Joan and Bette would decide to try it all over again.

Joan made the unfortunate decision to take a supporting part in Hall Barlett's production of *The Caretakers* (Bartlett also directed and cowrote this mess) because she liked Bartlett and some of his previous film work. She thought the part of Lucretia might be juicy, and she found the subject matter intriguing. The script went through many changes both before and during filming, which may explain the shoddy results, or it may be that, anxious to work, Joan never examined the initial screenplay carefully enough.

In *The Caretakers* (1963), Joan played Lucretia Terry, head nurse at the Canterbury mental hospital. Her main adversary is Dr. Donovan McCloud (Robert Stack), who runs a "borderline" therapy group in an attempt to reach patients Lucretia thinks are too dangerous and should be isolated from the rest. Said patients include Marion (Janis Paige), whose "illness" appears to be nymphomania; Lorna (Polly Bergen), who has suffered a nervous breakdown after the death of her son in a car accident that took place while she was driving; and Edna (Barbara Barrie), who for some reason refuses to speak to anyone.

Unfortunately, the sensationalistic, exploitative and dated approach to the material (there's no mention of drug therapy for the patients, for instance) dilutes the drama and poignancy of the story. A lot of *The Caretakers* plays like improvisational theater in a high-school drama club. The movie is pretty dull until Joan shows up half an hour into the proceedings. In fact, *The Caretakers* only comes alive when she's on screen. (Mirroring this, the crew applauded when Joan showed up on the set.) Highly artificial and full of dime-store psychology, the movie only succeeds in making the viewer believe that Lucretia is probably on the right track—especially after Barbara Barrie sets the curtains on fire. The movie is a far cry from *Possessed*.

The Caretakers was shot by talented cinematographer Lucien Ballard, but Joan, billed fourth (after Stack, Bergen, and, as another nurse, Diane McBain), looks a bit haggard; her hairstyle, too youthful despite its silvered effect, only underlines her aged appearance. But Joan plays with her usual fire and passion, especially when Lucretia confronts Dr. McCloud, who she feels is hopelessly naive about their deeply disturbed charges. She's very commanding in these scenes, but never overplays to the point where she becomes some kind of dragon lady; rather, she comes off as a woman who is powerfully committed to her beliefs. Handsome Dr. Denning (Van Williams) rightly observes that Lucretia is the toughest kind of opponent because she "honestly believes she's right." Whatever the ravages of time and alcohol had done to her face, Crawford's figure was still smashing, as she demonstrates in the scene in which she puts on black leotards and gives her nurses lessons in judo.

In the original script, Joan was supposed to go stark raving mad after being rejected by her lover—which would have been another idiotic moment in a picture filled with same. She was then to wind up as one of kindly Dr. McCloud's patients instead of being locked up in a ward. Joan insisted that the sequence was shot and was (mercifully) dropped from the final cut. (Joan would get to do a mad scene in her next picture anyway.) Bartlett told her that several scenes were dropped because they only cheapened her character. "Every woman who's rejected by the man she loves looks cheap," she replied.

Joan was delighted to be working with Herbert Marshall, who had a supporting role as Dr. Harrington. Like Joan, Marshall was a Hollywood veteran who understood the importance of professionalism. Marshall, who had a wooden leg, was rather feeble at this time in his life, and was drinking heavily as well, so he is always seen seated behind a desk. Despite the fatigue he registers, he plays very well with Joan and retains his excellent delivery, always with that impish twinkle in his eye. When Dr. Harrington and Lucretia discuss Dr. McCloud and his methods, with Dr. Harrington remarking that Dr. McCloud in some ways reminds him of his younger self, the magic of these two old pros working together almost fools the viewer into thinking that he's seeing a good movie. Realizing how sick Marshall was, and in part identifying with this fallen giant of Old Hollywood, Joan insisted that Bartlett film his close-ups before hers in their scenes together so that he could leave as quickly as possible.

When she wasn't chatting with Marshall, Joan was eyeing Van Williams, whom she found "delectable." She said of Williams, "In the old studio star system that boy would have been given quite a build-up." Williams would later star in the short-lived TV series *The Green Hornet*. Joan also had quite a crush on Robert Stack, who did not reciprocate her feelings. She was less charitable in her opinions of Janis Paige ("well-cast") and Diane McBain, both the kind of pretty, rising starlet that she found threatening and generally not very professional. She had little to do with Polly Bergen, who'd already been in many movies and, as a protégée of Alfred Steele, had appeared in ads for Pepsi. During a break in shooting, Joan took Bartlett via limo to the famous Pickfair, where he was introduced to certain members of Hollywood's old guard, including Mary Pickford. Pickford greeted Joan warmly.

It was around the time of the release of *The Caretakers* that Joan learned that her brother Hal had died of complications to appendicitis. After two failed marriages, Hal had lived with his mother for many years. It is unknown whether Joan supported him for a while after their mother died, but she probably sent him money from time to time. If she did, it was more out of pity than out of love. She could never forgive Hal's attempts to extort money from her, his threats to talk to reporters about her early promiscuous years or her relationship to Harry Cassin. Hal had become a drunk, which made him even more impossible to deal with. Joan cut off all contact with him. Eventually Hal got a job as night clerk at a hotel and joined Alcoholics Anonymous. Joan did not attend his funeral. "My brother died for me a long, long time before 1963," she remembered. She admitted to many interviewers that Hal had been so mean to her in childhood and throughout her life that she literally hated him. "Hal thought because he was a man he was better than any woman, yet he lived off and used women—and other men—all of his life. He never appreciated anything I ever tried to do for him. I don't think anyone was ever more vicious to me than he was."

Joan Blondell was to have been the star of *Strait-Jacket*—it is certainly interesting to contemplate Blondell in the part of the axe murderess—but she had an accident before filming began, and director-producer William Castle needed someone else in a hurry. Castle was well-known for the cheap but often inventive horror films that he dashed out with alarming regularity. It stuck in his craw that Alfred Hitchcock had invaded his territory and made a cheap black-and-white horror film, *Psycho*, to huge publicity and acclaim. From then on, Castle made it his business to try to outdo *Psycho* with an even more attention-getting picture. His first attempt was a nifty *Psycho* imitation entitled *Homicidal*, which was no work of art but had its moments. Now he hired Robert Bloch, who had authored the novel on which *Psycho* was based, to write a script for a new shocker entitled *Strait-Jacket*. If knifings in the shower got the public's attention, Castle figured, juicy ax murders ought to make him a million. The ad copy screamed: "Warning! *Strait-Jacket* Realistically Depicts Ax Murders!"

In the '50s, Castle's major motion-picture star had been Vincent Price, at the beginning of his horror cycle, which he completed with Roger Corman and increasingly less-established filmmakers. For Castle, Price had starred in such popular, amusing and well-received (by teens, anyway) thrillers as *House on Haunted Hill* and *The Tingler*. Now Castle had an even bigger and more prestigious star, Joan Crawford, and he had no intention of letting her go. Joan agreed to do *Strait-Jacket* because of her $50,000 fee and because Castle agreed to the rest of her demands. Castle came on to her like a sycophant, and guaranteed that she'd get the full star treatment—if not a lot of glamour.

In *Strait-Jacket* (1964), Joan was cast as Lucy Harbin, a hot tamale who comes home late one night to find her hunky husband in bed with a local tramp. Outraged, Lucy picks up an ax and chops the two to bits, as her little daughter looks on. Twenty years later, Lucy is released from a mental institution and arrives at the home of her brother Bill (Leif Ericson) and his wife Emily (Rochelle Hudson), where Lucy's daughter Carol (Diane Baker) has been living. Lucy has some problems adjusting to her new life, and Dr. Anderson (Mitchell Cox), who is tending to Lucy's well-being, suggests he accompany her back to the sanitarium. Shortly afterward, he is attacked by an ax-wielding assailant. The chop-chop routine continues on blackmailing hired hand Leo Krause (George Kennedy), and the father of Carol's fiancé.

It turns out that Carol has committed these new murders, in the hopes that her mother will be blamed, because she knows that the parents of her fiancé will never let them get married. Although the entirely different tone and overall approach help to disguise the fact, the basic premise of the film is taken from *The ABC Murders,* by Agatha Christie. In that classic novel, the killer murders a series of people to try to create the illusion of a maniac on the loose so that the murder of his intended victim will not point back to him. The most imaginative part of *Strait-Jacket* comes at the very end of the film—the lady in the Columbia logo is missing her head!

While it isn't necessarily "great" acting, Joan gives a very compelling and commanding performance in *Straight-Jacket*, never descending to the level of the material. Wisely eschewing the glamour treatment except when the script calls for it, she gives a very convincing portrait of a woman who's been out of society—and in a very bad place—for a long time. When she enters her brother's home and is about to see her daughter for the first time in twenty years, she conveys all of the apprehension, guilt, need, hope, and regret that anybody would feel in such a situation. She is also splendid in the sequence in which she and her daughter wait for the girl's boyfriend to arrive, moving adeptly from anxiety and insecurity over meeting him to the sloppy way she puts the make on the young man once he finally shows up. Another good moment occurs when she watches Leo butcher a fowl while she holds an ax, trembling and screaming as the horrible memories rush through her. Her performance is also shrewd enough never to give away her ultimate guilt or innocence to the audience. There is also quite a transformation from the younger, cheap Lucy we see at the opening to the aged, gray, somber woman she becomes twenty years later.

Strait-Jacket is undeniably schlocky, but it is also quite entertaining and effective; while no means on the level of Joan's greatest pictures, it actually seems to improve with age. The murder of Leo, as he stares at the headless body of Dr. Anderson stuffed into the meat locker, is superbly handled for maximum suspense, probably because it was filmed just as Bloch wrote it. The picture cries out for a musical score that doesn't sink so many scenes, and the conclusion is unfortunately pat and perfunctory. Diane Baker's sweetness nicely hides her devious, psychotic nature; Joan thought a lot of the actress, who had also been in *The Best of Everything* and would later appear with her in *Fatal Confinement,* a television production. Joan was also taken with the good looks of John Anthony Hayes, who played her daughter's fiancé Michael. When someone commented, not disparagingly, that he did his acting with his lips, Joan murmured, "Yes, and such sexy lips, too." For a lark and some added publicity, Pepsi-Cola vice president (and good friend of the late Alfred Steele) Mitchell Cox played Dr. Anderson with amateurish sincerity. The bust that Carol has sculpted of Lucy was actually done by artist Yucca Salamunich on the set of *A Woman's Face* in 1941.

Joan went the extra mile to do publicity for the film—literally: she toured several cities in the United States and Canada over two weeks for personal appearances in theaters of the Loew's movie-theater chain. Dorothy Kilgallen would sit with her on the stage and interview her. Joan had no shame for her performance in the film, which she knew was vivid and vital and as true-to-life as the movie deserved, but she also recognized that the audience was not exactly seeing her at her best. *Strait-Jacket* was not *Mildred Pierce,* after all. She fortified herself with vodka and went out to face the fans, gratified to see that there were so many and that they were of all different ages. Of course, many of the teens only came to see somebody being beheaded (as the advertisements promised) and couldn't have cared less about Joan. Still, even they got a casual thrill out of seeing the picture's formidable star in person.

Joan was treated like a queen every step of the way, down to the brand of vodka and other spirits awaiting her in each hotel suite, and the limousine waiting to pick her up at each airport. Some ridiculed Joan when these extensive lists made their way into the hands of the press, but her demands were no different from those of many other stars of the period, and indeed less extreme than the demands of many of the highly overpaid stars of today.

Joan had proven many times over that she could handle just about anything that was thrown at her. But her next film assignment would prove too much of a challenge, even for her.

Bernard Wohl Collection

Chapter Sixteen

WAR OF NERVES

Bette Davis did not want Joan as her costar in *What Ever Happened to Cousin Charlotte?* That was the title of Robert Aldrich's follow up to *Baby Jane* for the same studio, and Joan pretty much felt the same way. Still, despite her reservations about working with Davis, she didn't want to be left out of the party and the possible profits it might accrue. She knew that *Baby Jane* had done a lot to keep her in the public eye and to attract a younger generation of fans, and *Cousin Charlotte* might be even more successful. Davis tried to cut Joan out by recommending Ann Sheridan for the part of "Cousin Miriam," but Aldrich informed her that the studio wanted Joan; indeed her participation was essential for major financing. Davis reluctantly accepted Joan as her costar; Aldrich had no trouble talking Joan into taking the part. When Davis told one reporter that she looked forward to working with Joan, that compared to a lot of newcomers with big names she was "a *real* pro, serious about her acting, always on time, always *prepared,*" she was being honest, albeit selectively so. In her public statements, she was concentrating strictly on her positive feelings about Joan. She was also exaggerating quite a bit with her remarks about how much she "liked" working with Joan.

Joan felt cut out of the loop almost from the beginning. Davis was Aldrich's supposed partner in the production, but Joan was not. Joan feared, wrongly, that Davis and Aldrich were sleeping together. Due to an alleged miscommunication, when she arrived in Baton Rouge for location filming, there was no one there from the production to greet her. And Davis was doing her best to make Joan as uncomfortable as possible every minute of every day.

Joan also wasn't crazy about the script, which had been revised by *Baby Jane* screenwriter Lukas Heller, who Joan also thought was intimate with Davis. In truth, Davis was angered when Henry Farrell, the original screenwriter (and author of the *Baby Jane* novel) was summarily replaced with Heller without her knowledge or permission, due to conflicts with Aldrich. Farrell's screenplay was undoubtedly better than the hodgepodge concocted by Heller, who later cravenly blamed Aldrich for the new script's resemblances to *Diabolique* instead of his own inadequacies as a screenwriter. It is safe to say that the rare excellent dialogue in which Miriam and Charlotte explain their backgrounds and motivations was scripted by Henry Farrell.

If Joan had had more faith in the script, she might have ignored the unpleasantness of her costar. She knew a war with Davis would help neither the film nor anyone's career, and she did her best to make peace with her, but Davis sneered at her overtures. Davis had never forgiven Joan for her machinations at the Academy Awards and had decided to ignore her as much as possible and make Joan's time on the set miserable. During pre-production, Davis had assured Aldrich that she would do her best to get along with Joan for the good of the picture, that she would focus only on the positive (hence her complimentary remarks to interviewers regarding Joan's professionalism), but once she was actually confronted with Joan in the flesh, she simply wasn't able to stick to her word. Most observers agree that by this time, the feud was entirely one-sided, with Davis as sole instigator.

Davis threw parties in her cottage to which she invited everyone but Joan. Joan would greet Davis warmly, but Davis would hardly deign to reply. As happened on the set of *Johnny Guitar,* the cast and crew were soon divided into camps, and the pro-Joan camp certainly seemed smaller than the pro-Bette camp. Joan had known and been friends with many of the crew members for years, but that was no longer the case. She had always befriended crew members, but when she saw Davis playing up to them (in efforts to turn them against Joan), she decided to keep her distance. Many felt that Joan acted as if she were still the Great Star of Hollywood's Golden Age, which was not at all intended to offend anyone or to declare superiority over anyone; it was simply the role to which Joan was accustomed and which made her feel secure. Nevertheless, it offended certain parties, especially those who had never been privy to the studio system, and it had always offended Davis, whose own massive ego wouldn't allow her to admit that she liked being the star every bit as much as Joan did. Davis also did not like the fact that Joan was four years older than her but still looked younger and much more attractive. (Davis made sure that everyone, including members of the press and distinguished visitors to the set, knew that Joan was really 60 years old, rather than the 56 she admitted to.) She would also stand next to director Aldrich while he was filming Joan's scenes and make loud, negative comments.

Alone in her bungalow or with a few loyal friends or attendants, Joan sipped at her vodka and Pepsi and fumed. "There is just no dealing with that woman," she told Larry Quirk, visiting the set to report on the production, by this time retitled *Hush . . . Hush, Sweet Charlotte.* Joan confided that she knew Davis was angry because of the Oscar business, but added that "she acted like *Baby Jane* was a one-woman show after they nominated her! What was I supposed to do, let her hog all the glory, act like I hadn't even been in the movie. *She* got the nomination. I didn't begrudge her that, but it would have been nice if she'd been a little gracious in interviews and given me a little credit. I would have done it for her. I've tried to be conciliatory but it just isn't working." She would also get upset after a few drinks because her denial would weaken and she would realize that the script for *Charlotte* wasn't really much better than the one for *Strait-Jacket.* Joan was always acutely aware in those days that the films she was making were far beneath the achievements of her heyday, but there were times when she could not bring herself to admit it—either to herself or anyone else. She was always looking for quality dramatic scripts, but they weren't being offered to her. She and Davis both liked to think of *Baby Jane* and its follow-up as true dramatic pictures and not mere horror films, but deep down, both knew better. These pictures had better production values and bigger budgets than their subsequent films, that was the only difference.

In *Hush . . . Hush, Sweet Charlotte,* Bette Davis was again playing a person with alleged homicidal tendencies who turns out to be innocent of the original crime. Just as Jane Hudson had not really run over her sister Blanche, Charlotte did not take a meat cleaver and chop off the head and hand of her lover John (Bruce Dern). The main difference is that whereas Jane does eventually become sadistic and homicidal, Charlotte remains a victim until the end of the movie, when she drops a heavy planter on her tormentors. The victim in *Baby Jane* (although the original perpetrator of the crime), Joan was to become the victimizer in *Charlotte,* plotting with her ex-lover Dr. Drew Bayliss (Joseph Cotten) to drive Charlotte crazy and get control of her money. Still, Joan ruefully observed that Davis's Charlotte was once again the showier role.

For this and other reasons, Joan was one 60-year-old woman who felt that it wasn't worth putting up with Davis just to make an inferior picture. This may have been a mistake on her part, but it was an understandable and possibly necessary mistake. Joan might have stuck it out, but on the last day of location shooting the crew packed everything up and went back to the motel, leaving Joan stranded as she rested in a trailer. She had to call for someone to come pick her up. This may have been another "miscommunication," but Joan was convinced that Davis was behind it, and furthermore that Davis was manipulating Aldrich behind the scenes. "She's practically directing the picture for him right in front of me," she complained, "so God knows what else she's up to behind my back. I might wind up on the cutting-room floor." Davis had already succeeded in getting cuts that eliminated some of Joan's dialogue, as well as that of Joseph Cotten.

Cotten was sympathetic to Joan, and tried not to get drawn into either camp. "Bette is determined to make her mark on this picture," he said on location, "and Joan is determined to do the same and not be, how shall I put it, gobbled up by Bette, but for heaven's sake, don't quote me." Off the record, he admitted that Davis was being quite hard on Joan and he sensed that Joan was reaching the boiling point. "I think that's what Bette wants, and frankly it's foolish of her." Years afterward, he confessed that he thought that Davis chewed the scenery with a vengeance, overacting and trying to steal the picture, and that Joan didn't know how to deal with it. In his memoirs (published while Davis was still alive), he wrote that "Joan was finding her refinement of style difficult to weave into the strong and colorful pattern of raw emotions," but off the record he said that, unlike Davis, Joan wanted to approach her role with some dignity and "not completely give away the fact that she was a villainess, which was supposed to come as some surprise." (Joan's character of Miriam does not commit the cleaver murder of the prologue; it is committed by the victim's wife, played by Mary Astor. Cousin Miriam is still a blackmailer and conspirator, and does later murder the maid Velma, played by Agnes Moorehead.)

Cotten confessed that he found some sequences of Davis screeching and gibbering and descending into madness embarrassing to witness: "It was not a 'dignified' exhibition, as Joan would put it, and although Joan realized in some ways that Bette had to play it that way, she was also a little appalled." Joan may not have seen the more extreme of these sequences, as they were filmed after she left the picture, but she thought that Davis was overacting and pulling down the tone of the picture even in its quieter moments. According to Cotten, who was kind to *Charlotte* in his memoirs but less charitable in private interviews, "I think we all wanted it to be a different picture than it was, especially Joan. She felt Bette wasn't trying enough to lift the script up to their level instead of simply playing down to it. She never came right out and said it to me but I could see it on her face. Joan wanted it to be a 'quality' picture. I think the movie works well enough for what it is, but it's no *Gone with the Wind* or anything resembling a true 'quality' project."

Joan could see it happening all over again. Bette would chew the scenery, steal the picture, get nominated for or even win an Oscar for what Joan felt was shameless overacting, while her more restrained, more appropriate work would go unrecognized. She called her lawyer to see if she could get out of the picture, but he told her that she could be sued for breach of contract and possibly face financial ruin. So Joan arrived in Los Angeles after departing Baton Rouge and immediately checked into Cedars of Lebanon Hospital (later Cedars Sinai) so she could think over her options in peace. She was not feeling well, but her troubles were fundamentally psychosomatic in origin. Various ailments were reported to Aldrich and the studio: a high fever, fatigue, a respiratory ailment, dysentery, dyspepsia, and other vague syndromes and symptoms. Eventually she developed a cough, then a cold, finally "a rare form of pneumonia," as Hedda Hopper put it in her column. In the meantime, she instructed her lawyer to turn down an offer by the studio to buy her out, and turned her attentions to the screenplay. She was going to turn it into another *Mildred Pierce* if it was the last thing she did. She passed on some of the suggestions to Aldrich, who passed them on to Davis, who made it clear she wasn't interested. In truth, while Joan's request for deeper characterization and motivation—unlikely to come from Lukas Heller—was laudatory, other suggestions, such as another big ballroom scene (when there already was one in the prologue), were ill-advised.

It has erroneously been intimated that, before production began on *Hush . . . Hush, Sweet Charlotte,* Davis told Aldrich that she wanted to shoot all of her scenes with Joan with a stand-in instead of Joan. Joan could do the same (she is said to have suggested) and their shots could be spliced together to make it appear that they were actually in the same scene talking to one another. Davis, who was after all a professional, may have joked about this, but she would never have seriously suggested it. She would have known that neither Aldrich nor any other director would have gone for such a plan, and that not only would it have limited both actors and the shooting options for each scene, but it would ultimately have compromised the artistic integrity of the film itself. What actually happened is that Bette shot some scenes with a stand-in while Joan was in the hospital. This is a common practice when circumstances make it unavoidable.

When Joan felt better and was furthermore assured that she had paid Davis and Aldrich back a bit for their treatment of her, she returned to the production—but only for a while. She said she was too weak to work for more than two hours a day. Relations between her and Aldrich deteriorated to the point that they began communicating through a third party. Aldrich reportedly hired private detectives to follow Joan when she was supposed to be resting at home, to see if she was as weak as she claimed. Convinced that Joan was faking, he insisted on a medical examination. Oddly enough, for insurance purposes it would have been to the picture's advantage if Joan's illness turned out to be legitimate. The doctor for the insurance company said that Joan had a slight fever but was otherwise well enough to report to work. Joan protested that she got tired "so easily, I must be sick." Davis was outraged by the whole situation. Another exam was scheduled, this time by a specialist. Joan felt panicky; she was sure that Aldrich and Davis were "out to get her." Before the specialist could confirm or deny the insurance doctor's diagnosis, Joan rushed back to Cedars of Lebanon by ambulance.

Larry Quirk went to visit Joan at Cedars of Lebanon, where he found her giving a classic Joan Crawford performance. She was made up and beautifully coiffed, but her expression was taut and conflicted. It was almost impossible to calm her down, and eventually she began snapping at the nurses. She was upset because she was convinced that everyone was holding back news of her condition, and also because of the goings-on behind the scenes on the set of Hush . . . Hush, Sweet Charlotte. She wanted to know what Davis was up to and what was happening on the set. "Nothing is going on," Larry told her. "The production has been suspended while you recuperate." That seemed to relax her for a while, until she took a series of X-rays out of a drawer and held them up to the light, turning them this way and that. "I can't figure them out," she said. "I know there's something wrong, and they won't tell me and I have to do it all myself!"

She frowned when she saw a nurse she disliked enter the room, but when she noticed the good-looking young doctor accompanying the nurse, Joan's mood and manner changed abruptly. Joan primped herself as the doctor told her how much he had admired her performances. He told her it would be good if she took her sedative and that she should get back into bed. Joan complied—so charmed by and smitten with the doctor that she took his orders without complaint—and in no time nodded off. "Keep me posted," she yawned as Quirk left the room. The general consensus was that Joan was hoping the picture would be shut down for good, letting her off the hook and stymieing Bette's plans to make money and get another Oscar.

By the time Quirk next visited Joan at Cedars of Lebanon, she had learned that she had been replaced on *Hush . . . Hush, Sweet Charlotte* by Olivia de Havilland. De Havilland had been talked into the part after Loretta Young, Vivian Leigh, Barbara Stanwyck, and Katharine Hepburn had all either been vetoed by Davis or rejected Aldrich's offers. Joan was furious that she had heard the news over the radio instead of from Aldrich or somebody else connected with the production. Joan blamed Aldrich almost exclusively. "He didn't even have the balls to come and tell me to my face or even over the phone!" she screamed repeatedly. "I had to hear it over the radio!" Aldrich may have made the final decision to fire her, but it was probably Davis who leaked it to the press before Aldrich had time to relay the news to Joan. In truth, Joan was as relieved to be free of Davis and the picture as she was angry with Aldrich. Once again Joan calmed down and began to purr when the good-looking doctor came in to check up on her. She had apparently already taken her tranquilizer, because she was getting very sleepy by the time the doctor left. She asked Quirk for a good-bye kiss and murmured, "Isn't Doctor Robert handsome? Don't you think he'd be perfect for the movies?" When vodka wasn't available, Joan always found a handsome face soothing.

Years later, Aldrich claimed he was "disappointed" that Joan hadn't finished the picture despite the added tension her presence had created. "I can't think of a picture that took more out of me," he recalled. He admitted that most of the tension was actually caused by Davis, not Joan, and thought that Joan would have done a lot for the picture, and vice versa. Aldrich thought he had made a genuinely great movie. While this is not true (although *Hush . . . Hush, Sweet Charlotte* is certainly well-produced and entertaining), it must be said that the picture cries out for Joan Crawford, who would have added immeasurably to its impact and power. While de Havilland is fine as Cousin Miriam (a kind of deranged Miss Melanie from *Gone With the Wind*), the part was tailored for Joan and her special delivery and persona. Watching the film today, one can imagine Joan snapping out Miriam's bitterness toward Charlotte as she recalls how she was always treated like the poor relation by Charlotte's family; one can imagine her imparting an extra dimension to the sequence in which Miriam and Charlotte drive off to get rid of Dr. Bayliss's body, and Miriam winds up slapping Charlotte on the drive home. De Havilland confronting Agnes Moorehead's maid Velma and knocking her down the stairs with a chair is menacing enough, but

Crawford's formidable, threatening presence might have made the sequence crackle with fury and tension. But it was not to be.

Although there were predictions that being replaced on *Hush . . . Hush, Sweet Charlotte* would make Joan forever uninsurable, this was not the case. The official version was that she had simply become ill, been regrettably replaced, and then had a complete recovery. Of course, insiders aware of the situation with Bette Davis doubted if she had ever been ill at all; these "insiders" amounted to everybody who counted in Hollywood. Soon she was back doing a picture for the comparatively amiable William Castle.

William McGivern's script for *I Saw What You Did* (1965) was based on a novel by Ursula Curtiss. Originally there had been no intention to cast Joan in the film, as the part was rather small. When it was decided that a name actress was needed to bolster the grosses, there was some talk of signing Barbara Stanwyck, who had appeared in Castle's *The Night Walker* the year before, but she was busy with her TV series *Big Valley*. Joan was shown the script, told how much money she'd be getting ($50,000 for four days' work) along with top billing, and decided to do the picture. It wouldn't be much work, it would keep her name in the public eye, and the script seemed much less schlocky than others she'd been offered.

It was a smart decision; the picture made money and was one of Castle's best-received movies. However, some associates, such as George Cukor, felt that Joan was always rationalizing about her film choices. "You couldn't tell her the scripts were bad, she just wouldn't listen," said Cukor. "She told everyone they were quality scripts, but it was like she was really just trying to convince herself." It is more likely that Joan was simply trying to put up as game a front as she could while she hoped for the best. She had always been able to tell crap from class. *I Saw What You Did* was somewhere in the middle.

In fact, the picture has a splendid premise. Two callow schoolgirls get into trouble by calling up strangers on the telephone and saying such things as "I Saw what you did—I know who you are." One man on the other end of the line, Steve Marak (John Ireland), has just finished murdering his wife and is understandably a bit perturbed by the call. He manages to track down the one of the girls but is shot by police before he can murder her. Joan plays a neighbor, Amy Nelson, who has a hankering for Marak, who dispatches her as well when she informs him he has to become her lover or else she will go to the police. "You married a selfish, empty-headed little tramp—but now we can make something wonderful," Amy tells him. "It's a simple choice. Life with me or no life at all." Ireland pulls her to him in what he pretends is a romantic hug and then stabs her in the belly.

Joan has a wonderful death scene, as Amy slowly climbs down Marak's body with a disbelieving look on her face, throws her head back in anguish, falls all the way to the floor, sighs "Steven," then flips her head to the side, stone dead. It's dramatic and convincing—and even a little poignant—even though her character is not very sympathetic. As usual Joan nipped at the vodka during breaks in filming and seems a bit drunk—which works in any case—when she finds the girl who made the phone call hanging around Marak's house, and attacks her. Andi Garrett, the young actress who was "introduced" in the film, was positively terrified by Joan's verisimilitude when Joan was required to pull Garrett's hair and drag her back to her automobile.

Joan's performance is quite good and professional and it gives the picture a certain solidity. Photographer Joseph Biroc was unable to prevent her from appearing haggard, however. Her hair is also piled too high, a style that was never flattering for Joan. While *I Saw What You Did* captures the innocence and emerging sexuality of young girls and has some taut moments, the climax is too flaccid and prolonged to be effective. It remains a very good idea crying out for better treatment, which it did not get in the abysmal 1988 television remake.

William Castle finally got to do his own version of Hitchcock's *Psycho* shower murder in this picture, although he uses only about ten shots instead of the dozens that Hitchcock used. Instead of the killer sneaking up on someone taking a shower, Marak stands in the shower and pulls his wife in with him, then butchers her and smashes her body through the glass door. It's effective and clever, but not exactly on Hitchcock's level.

Christina wasn't happy that she wasn't cast in the picture—at twenty-five she was simply too old to play a teenager—and she remained bitter that she never got a major role in any of Mommie's movies.

In 1965 Joan realized that she had no choice but to sell the penthouse apartment in which she'd lived with Alfred. There simply weren't enough parts for her in the movies or on television, and the $3000 monthly maintenance fee was simply more than she could manage. The wealthy woman who bought the penthouse from her brought along a decorator one afternoon and went through the apartment, all the while talking loudly about how *this* must be changed, and *that* had to go; she so irritated Joan that she could barely keep her temper in check. Joan got a chance for some minor revenge when the woman complained of being chilly while standing in Joan's opulent bedroom. Holding her head up high, Joan pushed open one of the closets so that the woman could see her many expensive furs. Joan pulled out a silver fox coat, wrapped it around the woman before she could protest, and said, "*There!* That ought to keep you warm!"

Joan rented an apartment in the Imperial House on 69th and Lexington, and hired top interior designer Carleton Varney to decorate the new place. While most people would certainly have no problem moving to an Upper East Side apartment consisting of nine rooms with four baths and two terraces, to Joan it was the crushing end of an era. Moving from the penthouse to a smaller apartment indicated that she had also fallen from the heights of stardom, and its perks. One afternoon before she moved in, she went by limousine to check out the new apartment and collapsed before she could make it to the elevators. Varney and Christina had to carry her back to the limo and take her to the penthouse, where she finally calmed down and did her best to accept that the move was necessary, whether she liked it or not.

Some of the belongings that wouldn't fit in the smaller apartment were auctioned off at Sotheby's (they brought in much less money than she was hoping for), while others were sent to the Archdiocese (mostly furnishings), the Fashion Institute of Technology (her costume jewelry) and Brandeis University. Incredibly, the latter institution had established a Joan Crawford School of Dance!

To take her mind off of the move and what she saw as her fall from grace, Joan occupied herself with writing another memoir, *My Way of Life*. She also did her best to comfort Christina, whose marriage to producer Harvey Medlinsky had ended in divorce. (He was also unable to do much for her acting career.) While Joan was searching for a new apartment and dealing with the stress and trauma of such a major life change, she was also doing her best to find Christina a new place to live. In the meantime, Christina stayed in the tony Mayflower House on Central Park West; Joan footed the bill. Christina eventually wound up back in California, staying in a small place Joan owned on Fountain Avenue.

At age 63, Joan was a "special guest star" on the highly popular tongue-in-cheek spy program *The Man from U.N.C.L.E.* in 1967. In the two-part episode "The Five Daughters Affair" (released theatrically overseas as *The Karate Killers*), the agents of U.N.C.L.E. try to secure a formula for extracting gold from seawater before their evil counterparts at THRUSH do. The scientist who invented the formula has five daughters, all of whom figure in the plot to varying degrees, as well as a widow named Amanda True, played by Joan. Instead of employing Joan in a sharply written role as a deadly THRUSH mastermind, the show has her killed off and written out in the first act. When her husband has a heart attack, Amanda assumes it's because of her affair with THRUSH agent "Randolph" (Herbert Lom, the only actor with whom Joan has any scenes, aside from a couple of extras). Randolph tells her that he actually put poison in her husband's pills. "You murdered him!" Amanda screams, lunging at Randolph with a knife, which he then uses on her. Joan looks terrible lying dead on the living room floor behind the curtain where U.N.C.L.E. agent Illya Kuryakin (David McCallum) finds her. Joan gives a very commanding, stylish, and showy performance (if perhaps a bit superficial), indicating that she would have made a wonderful THRUSH villainess, given half a chance. In a way it is just as well that Joan was underused, as "The Five Daughters Affair" was not one of the program's more memorable episodes.

Diane Baker again found herself playing Joan Crawford's daughter in a television pilot, *Royal Bay,* which was later released on video under the title *Fatal Confinement* (it is also listed in some sources as *Della*). In a modern-day variation on *Bonanza,* Charles Bickford played ship builder and city council member Hugh Stafford in the town of Royal Bay. The premise of the show was that he would provide guidance for his four sons, one of whom which would be featured in each episode. The pilot episode focused on his lawyer son Barney (Paul Burke). (The other brothers, seen briefly, included psychologist Richard Carlson.) The plot of the pilot was about a wealthy recluse, Della Chappell (Joan) and her daughter, who never leave their estate and whose lives are interrupted by Barney, who wants Della to sell some valuable land to an industrial client of his. In addition to fighting over the land, which Della does not wish to sell, Barney finds himself in a contest of wills over Della's lovely daughter Jenny (Diane Baker), who is falling in love with him. Barney assumes that Della is a clinging, neurotic mother who won't let her daughter grow up, leave the house, and find love, but in fact Jenny has a rare skin affliction, which makes her ultrasensitive to sunlight. Going out in the daylight could result in her death, which, in a way, it does, when she pursues Barney in her car and drives over a cliff.

Joan gives a good performance in *Fatal Confinement.* Like Joan herself, Della Chappell likes it when people stand up to her, and she is one tough cookie when circumstances demand it. Joan is graying but attractive, although in her close-ups, it seems like the lens were covered with gauze. She has a nice bit of pantomime at the end when she faces life alone in her massive house, then opens the blinds and lets in all the sunlight. She and Paul Burke play against each other very well. Like his character, Burke never gave an inch where Joan was concerned and gave a vital, dynamic, *loud* performance that was in every way a match for Joan's. Offscreen, Joan found Burke very attractive and liked the way he played up to her. "Paul Burke is my idea of an appealing man," she said. "Very masculine, very sure of himself, very confident in his attractiveness. He certainly got the juices flowing." Although she was referring to his acting style, she admitted a moment later that his sex appeal also affected her. "What a fine strutting animal you are," she tells him in anger at one point. "That's all you'll ever be and all you'll ever understand."

There is a sequence in *Fatal Confinement* that will elicit snickers from people who believe that *Mommie Dearest* is totally accurate. When Jenny accuses her mother of wanting Barney for herself, Della smacks her in the face, and then hits her again for good measure. After Jenny's death, Della says, "I loved my daughter. Sometimes she hated me and blamed me. I expected that. Sometimes I had to fight her—brutally. Her life didn't destroy me—and not this [either]." Although Joan is seen to good advantage in *Fatal Confinement,* she had understandable reservations about the script. It's the kind of dopey story in which so much turmoil could have been avoided if only someone had told Barney earlier about Jenny's peculiar affliction (a real-life disease known as xeroderma pigmentosum; the September 16, 2001 edition of *The New York Times Magazine* featured a major story on the disease titled "Midnight's Children," by Lawrence Osborne). Admittedly, Jenny's condition may have prevented her from enjoying a totally normal life, but why couldn't she have gone out at night and slept till five—as many heiresses do?

But *Fatal Confinement* would seem like *Mildred Pierce* compared to Joan's final two theatrical films, which would give millions of people—and especially Joan—the horrors.

J.C. Archives, Inc.

Chapter Seventeen

SECRET STORMS

In 1968, Lawrence J. Quirk came out with his book *The Films of Joan Crawford,* which provided synopses for all of Joan's movies, sample reviews, a mini-biography, and lots of exclusive photographs. Joan was enthusiastic about the project from the outset, saying that Quirk knew more about her films than anyone. She got MGM to lend him stills of her pictures from their New York photo archive. This saved Quirk a great deal of money, as it would have been expensive to track down and pay for the hundreds of stills needed. Of course, Joan wasn't being entirely selfless, as the book came out during a low point in her career and provided a great deal of publicity for her. On the other hand, other authors of books about movie stars (even such generally non-controversial books like *The Films of . . .* series) were often threatened with lawsuits by their subjects.

When the book came out in the fall of 1968, Joan offered to sign copies at bookstores. A minor contretemps between Joan and Quirk broke out when Joan arranged for Quirk to appear on the Ronnie Barrett TV Show in Chicago; unfortunately the same day she alone would be autographing copies of his book at a leading New York bookseller. Quirk also had to pay for his own transportation to Chicago. Still, Quirk eventually realized that Joan, always with one eye on her career, saw his book as a lifeline, a new connection to the fans who had never forgotten her, and he understood and forgave. To be fair, Joan always made it clear that Quirk was the one and only author of the book.

Then it came time for Joan to appear on *The Merv Griffin Show,* again to hawk the book. Naturally, the publisher was pleased that Joan was doing so much to promote *The Films of Joan Crawford* and had put her stamp of approval on it. In another attempt to do something for her daughter's career, Joan asked if Christina could appear on the show with her. Joan continually tried to help Christina, both up front and behind the scenes, but nothing was ever enough. After some minutes talking about Christina's career, Joan did her duty and held up the book for the cameras. When Griffin joked about the name "Quirk," Joan, in her best chiding manner, reminded the talk-show host that Quirk was a distinguished name in film journalism, Quirk's uncle being James R. Quirk, who ran *Photoplay* in the golden days before it deteriorated into a cheap fan magazine.

It was shortly after this that Christina became ill and her mother temporarily replaced her on *The Secret Storm,* the soap opera on which Christina had a part. Of course, Joan was too old for the part, but she played it with her customary authority. From her hospital bed, Christina seethed, convinced that her mother was holding them both up to ridicule instead of doing her a favor. Joan was afraid that Christina would be replaced by whatever young actress they got to fill in for her, but knew the producers couldn't resist having Joan play the part, just as she also knew they would never let someone her age play it continuously. Indeed, Joan thought she was saving her daughter from losing the role. Of course, Joan undeniably also enjoyed being in the spotlight again. Most of Joan's friends found the entire episode a little bit sad—in that whatever Joan did, it just made Christina madder—and, unfortunately, somewhat hilarious. While it may have been true that Joan fortified herself with some vodka before taping her scenes, it was not true that she was obviously drunk on camera. Many people thought she was being as unrealistic as Bette Davis had been in the scene in *The Star* (the film inspired by Crawford) when she auditions for an older character part by foolishly playing it as if she were many years younger. Actually, Joan did not overdo the girlishness.

When the film version of Mart Crowley's play about a homosexual birthday party, *The Boys in the Band,* was released in 1970, the birthday boy, Harold, played by Leonard Frey, holds up a copy of *The Films of Joan Crawford* in a scene where he is dawdling near a desk. Joan was a bit amused by the reference: "I can't imagine why that book was used." Quirk ran into Leonard Frey at Joe Allen's restaurant on 46th Street in Manhattan, and asked Frey why director William Friedkin hadn't used Bette Davis or Judy Garland instead of Joan, as it was well-known that they were cult figures among some members of the gay community. According to Frey, it was his idea to hold up *The Films of Joan Crawford.* "Joan's so *intense* and *abandoned* when she's mad about some man in her movies," Frey explained. "I just thought she suited the histrionics of the characters in *The Boys in the Band* better."

Laughing, Quirk recited some ad copy for some of Joan's films: "Nobody can hold a candle to Joan Crawford when Joan is carrying the torch," and "Disillusioned, sick with men, does Joan dare love once more?"

There!" Frey smiled. "You see what I mean?"

It wasn't as easy to explain to Joan, but Quirk gave it a try. He told her that much of the garish atmosphere and heavy emoting in *Boys in the Band* recalled her own style on certain occasions and the mood of a number of her more highly charged films. Joan didn't mind having gay fans and was perfectly friendly to gays (quotes allegedly made by Joan in which she makes pejorative references to homosexuals reflect the interviewer's bias more than any on the part of Joan), but she didn't like the idea that some of her movies might now be considered "camp" to younger audiences. Quirk tactfully explained that it was the wonderful theatricality of many of her performances that excited the younger generation and those gays who loved her movies, worshipped old-style Hollywood glamour, and identified with the suffering over men that she endured in film after film. Joan replied, "I'm just glad the exposure will help the book."

Joan had many gay friends, including, of course, William Haines, and certain gay men had been instrumental in shaping her style and career and in offering encouragement. She loved to repeat her celebrated remark that, given their decades-long attachment, Haines and his companion Jimmy Shields had the best marriage in Hollywood. (Jimmy later emphasized this when he committed suicide after Haines's death, leaving a note to the effect that life wasn't any fun without Billy.) But Joan still seemed to be—or pretended to be—somewhat nonplussed by the idea that she might be a homosexual icon. Perhaps she was afraid some fans would see her as gay or feared exposure of her lesbian adventures in her younger days. During dinner at Joan's apartment in 1973, Joan again asked Quirk if he could explain why some members of the gay community identified with her.

Quirk pointed out that her gay fans identified with her on- and offscreen struggles for career success, love and happiness, and with her romantic and sexual encounters with a variety of men. Joan smiled wryly when Quirk mentioned that gays tended to see her—at least on-screen—as sexually active to the point of nymphomania. Joan literally hooted with laughter when Quirk told her that a gay acquaintance had remarked that when Joan ogled a man, she gave him a blow job with her eyes. Joan always had a very ribald sense of humor.

"Look, Joan," Quirk told her.

"Let's take the plot of a typical picture of your thirties period—how about *Sadie McKee*? You're the servant's daughter who wants to go off to the Big Town and find adventure. She's in love with a handsome heel who takes her to New York and soon deserts her for a lady who can further his fortunes. She then ends up with a rich older man because she's cynical and disillusioned and figures hustling an older guy who can give her advantages beats the hurtful vulnerabilities of loving a handsome rascal her own age who will drop her when he tires of her. And, of course, there's the hunky aristocrat hovering around all through the picture with whom, it is implied, she will find "True Love" after all.

Now, some gays leave small towns for the freedom of the big city, get away from all the narrowness and prejudices of the self-righteous benighted, just as Sadie and many of the other women you played wanted to get away from the gossiping small-town housewives who called her "slut" behind her back. Then there are the guys gay men fall in love with who are sometimes no good, and the older guys they outright hustle or live with for quick cash or long-range security, all the while hoping, as Sadie did, that eventually "Mr. Right" will show up for the long haul. You see the similarities? Of course, many of your female fans identified with you for the same reasons.

Joan wasn't entirely convinced. She reminded Larry that she played heterosexual characters with which the general public could more easily identify. Quirk pointed out that while the characters she played may have been heterosexual, they were often outsiders from the wrong side of the tracks. "They were looked down upon by girls from the middle class, girls who laughed at the cheap clothing and perfume"—as Joan had herself been laughed at by the girls of her youth. "Outsiderism takes many forms, but it does help create a kind of identification. That's what gays are identifying with, in many of your movies. Being out of the mainstream but fighting for happiness in spite of it."

Despite her friendship with William Haines and his long-time partner, Joan wondered if gays were generally as romantic as all that. "A lot of them seem to prefer one-night stands or movie-house quickies," she noted, this being during the very early days of Gay Liberation, when it was widely believed that homosexuals were after sex alone and couldn't actually fall in love. Joan may have thought that the long-term relationship of Haines and Shields was atypical. "There are gays like that," Quirk told her, "but remember: Many people, male and female alike of any persuasion, seek sexual episodes as consolation for a romantic disappointment, or because they can't find the right partner and are lonely because of it. But then another person comes along and there they are pursuing love again, and maybe just settling for sex."

This got to Joan; she understood. "Yes," she said thoughtfully. "I can see the parallels in my movie plots clearly now."

"Think of all the kids," Quirk told Joan, "who come to big towns like New York to get away from small-town prejudices and meanness. They get off at Grand Central or the Port Authority Bus Terminal. They are raw, fearful, roughly defensive, just like the vulnerable girls in your earlier movies. They weather the come-ons of predatory older men, they bond in mutually supportive friendships with others like them—just as your girls did—they meet Mr. Right, they love him and lose him, and so on."

Joan agreed that many of her films had a gay-identification element to them, but more importantly, Quirk noted, they reflected the universal verities of the human condition.

By this time, things had dried up for Joan in Hollywood, and she was seen as a bad risk, because there were very few people who weren't aware of her drinking. She looked elsewhere for work, and found it across the ocean. *Berserk* (1968) was the first of two English horror pictures Joan made for producer Herman Cohen, who was originally from Detroit. *Berserk* had the same basic premise as the earlier *Strait-Jacket*: Joan is suspected of a series of gruesome murders, which have actually been committed by her psychotic daughter. This time, the setting is the circus owned by Monica Rivers, one of Joan's most unpleasant characterizations. Monica is a nasty, callous bitch who seems not to care about the grisly murders going on under her big top because each new butchering brings in lots of new customers. (This same idea was used before in *Circus of Horrors* (1960) and *Circus of Fear* (1967)—in fact, *Berserk*'s original title was *Circus of Blood*.) Buxom Diana Dors is turned into sausage when the buzzsaw in her act malfunctions. In the film's most memorably nasty moment, Michael Gough has a rivet driven into the back of his head and out through his forehead. In a truly impossible bit of business, the broken end of a rope somehow encircles and wraps itself around the neck of a trapeze artist. And so on. The colorful acts and tents of the real-life Billy Smart Circus (including an intelligent-poodle act that nearly steals the picture) stood in for the Rivers Circus.

Joan seems a bit over-rehearsed in the picture. She delivers her lines with her usual forcefulness, but it isn't terribly natural. Director Jim O'Connolly's work is competent but so routine and uninspired that it's unlikely he offered Joan much help. The film is too deliberately paced to offer that many real thrills, but in its own way is quite entertaining.

Judy Geeson played the daughter who commits murder to get her mother's attention. This was another role Christina coveted. She was the right age, and the part would not have been terribly taxing. When asked privately why she didn't fight to get Christina the role of her daughter, Joan gave different answers, depending on her mood. "This kind of picture is not a good debut for a young actress," she said at one point. Another time she confided that "Christina is not ready to have such responsibility. To costar with 'Joan Crawford'? Isn't that a lot of pressure to put on the girl, on any young performer?" She went on record with one interviewer, claiming that Christina "was much too old to play the part." It was clear that Joan did not think that Christina was ready to appear in a Joan Crawford movie, or indeed a lesser one either.

In later years, Joan had little to say about the picture or her costars. She thought Judy Geeson "pretty, but she doesn't have the stuff to make it for the long haul." For her part, Geeson was impressed by Joan. "She's fabulous, she—concentrates on her part with fantastic intensity and professionalism," Geeson gushed. While Joan had reservations about Ty Hardin's acting abilities, she raved about his manly good looks. Hardin plays a young roustabout hustler who sleeps with Monica (offscreen). No reference is made to Joan's age in the movie, except when Geeson tells her that she's too old to be dating Hardin. In her cups, Joan would talk about how much she enjoyed her love scenes with the hunk. A famous shot of Joan and a bare-chested Hardin in the circus owner's trailer has become a hot collector's item for Crawford fans.

Joan at first had mixed emotions about working with Diana Dors. Before filming began, she confided that she thought Dors, who'd become quite portly by this point, was "a cow. She's absolutely disgusting." Once touted as the British answer to Marilyn Monroe, Dors had big, pouty lips as well as mammary glands of major proportions, which were undoubtedly responsible for her start in pictures. This was enough to earn her Joan's enmity. But as filming progressed, Joan noticed that Dors was not a bad actress at all, that she stood up to her in their few scenes together with vivid authority, and that, offscreen, she was respectful but not frightened of Joan. Dors had also come from humble origins and built herself up from nothing. Compared to some of the emerging female film stars of the '70s, who seemed positively pornographic, blatantly exhibiting naked breasts (something Dors would refuse to do throughout her career), Dors seemed almost old-fashioned and ladylike. For these reasons, Dors earned Joan's respect, and the two became friends.

Dors was in the middle of a financial and marital crisis with second husband Richard Dawson, later the host of *Family Feud*. While Dawson was off in America with their boys, Dors moved into a rented house in Berkshire, but had departed by the time filming began on *Berserk*. Wild parties had done so much damage to the property that the owner filed suit and won. A credit agency sent no fewer than four men to the Shepperton studios, as well as to the location tent, but Dors managed to evade them every time. Joan found out about these difficulties once when Dors ran off in the middle of coffee and conversation; Joan simply figured, "It must have been a man who'd got her into so much trouble." She also pitied Dors because her looks were fading and her career was in the doldrums, as Joan's was. Five years later, when Dors was hospitalized with a near-fatal case of meningitis, Joan sent flowers and called to give her personal good wishes. When Dors died of cancer in 1984, she cut one of her three children out of her will—not unlike Joan.

Dors eventually found relative happiness with her third husband, Alan Lake, but a remark she made between her second and third marriages could have applied equally well to Joan at this point in her life: "It's highly unlikely I'll ever have a truly successful love affair. The fact that I'm in show business, which loads the dice against you anyway, and the fact that I've led a pretty hectic life, and that I'm a victim of my own image—oh, and all sorts of other neurotic things—make it almost impossible to think about ever having a successful, happy love life. It's just one of those hard, cold facts you have to face sooner or later. And it makes the future look pretty bleak." On that point, Joan would have readily agreed.

During filming, producer Cohen laid down the law to Joan—with extreme tact. He wanted her to curb her drinking habits as much as possible. He told her that she would have to wait until at least lunchtime before she started imbibing. And she had to ask his permission first. Joan countered that sipping a little vodka from time to time during the day to keep her "peppy" made her neither a lush nor unemployable, but she agreed to Cohen's terms. He was single and not bad-looking, and Joan hoped that he would make a good escort in London, if not a romantic or sexual partner. Cohen managed to find time to take her to dinner or to the theater on more than one occasion. Often she would wake him up in the middle of the night for a boozy discussion about the script. She later insisted, "He just wouldn't listen to any of my ideas to make it a better picture. I did have a lot of experience in making good pictures, didn't I?" For his part, it was reported that Cohen was simply trying to get the picture out, on time and under budget, so he could make a profit. There was no time for such niceties as "script revisions."

While *Berserk* got very mixed reviews, most critics agreed that Joan acquitted herself nicely and still had "star" written all over her—and great legs! Wearing a handsome ringmaster's uniform designed by none other than Edith Head, Joan displayed what one critic called "luscious to the pelvis gams."

Just as the American crew on *The Caretakers* had cheered her arrival on the set, so too did the British crew on *Berserk,* which was filmed primarily at the Shepperton studios. On occasion, she would make breakfast for some of the crew members who arrived especially early. She threw a whole party for the crew when filming wrapped. It was as if she were making the sequel to *Mildred Pierce* at Warner Brothers, rather than a cheap grade-C horror flick at Shepperton Studios, London. But that's what made her a star. No matter where she was, she was always a star.

This was even the case in her last picture, also produced by Cohen, which is easily the worst film Joan ever made, the lamentable *Trog* (1970). In *Trog,* Joan plays an anthropologist who captures a "missing link," or prehistoric troglodyte, and takes it to her laboratory for study. The creature eventually breaks free from confinement and goes on a rampage in the nearby town. You have to see Joan screaming "Trog!" at the misbehaving ape-man to believe it. Stock footage from the 1955 documentary *Animal World* recreates the prehistoric world of dinosaurs that Trog remembers. (The script for *Trog* is so poorly researched that, as in many other films, it has humanoids and dinosaurs existing at the same time.) Joan's power to delude herself had to be on overdrive during filming, as even she must have known that *Trog* was light-years away from *Possessed* and *Humoresque.* But Joan wanted to keep in front of the cameras. She wanted to work and she needed the money, so she went to England, where the work was. One might have thought that Cohen, or anyone connected with the film, realizing they had a fine actress and a glittering (if tarnished) major Hollywood name on their hands, might have ordered a rewrite—or even a new script—so that they would have something halfway worthy of their star. But it was not to be.

Still, Joan gives a good performance. Her authoritative manner and commanding presence are fully evident; she never condescends to the material but tries to lift it up by playing the part of the anthropologist with absolute conviction. Her trained manner of speaking and professional approach are in sharp contrast to the other actors and the rest of the production in general. She didn't look young in the picture, but she looked quite good. Her skin was taped back to remove wrinkles, the tape hidden beneath her hairdo.

The budget for *Trog* was so low that Joan had to supply her own wardrobe for the film and she showed up with seemingly more luggage than the rest of the cast combined. When the location shifted from the studio to the country areas where Trog hides out in a cave, there was no trailer for Joan to relax in, so she had to make her costume changes in a car. This was a sad comedown from her movie-queen days in Hollywood, but Joan took it like the trouper she was. It was easy to do because the cast and crew liked and respected her. As was her way, she was friendly with everyone, right down to the lowliest grip. While the camera crew set up the shots, Joan would sit in the car and be pampered by many concerned with the production, still in awe of her famous face. Anything she wanted she got immediately—coffee, a cigarette, nips of vodka to "keep away the chill of the English countryside." Sure, *Trog* was crap, but she was still the queen of the lot.

A problem developed when director Freddie Francis (who had won Oscars as cinematographer for *Sons and Lovers* in 1960 and *Glory* in 1989) decided to shoot much of the film in extremely long takes, which had the unfortunate effect of making a dull script even duller. He said he did this to prevent the producer from making too many changes in the editing room, but it was really to keep costs down. Because of these long takes, Joan had trouble remembering her lines. The drinking may have been a factor, but it was mostly that she was not used to such slapdash filmmaking.

Francis, for his part, thought that Joan "was sort of past it. For the first time in my life I had to resort to using idiot boards." Nevertheless he and Joan got along very well, mostly because Francis never made the mistake of trying to direct a woman who knew more about the movie business than he did. "I became very friendly with Joan," he recalled. "She adored my two young kids and my wife, and until she died we never stopped hearing from her." As for the picture, even Francis felt "it was a terrible film. Hardly Steven Spielberg, was it?"

Speaking of Spielberg, Joan was the star of his first directorial effort, a segment of an anthology telefilm entitled *Night Gallery* (1969), which Joan did between the two Herman Cohen films. Spielberg had been given the assignment by Sid Sheinberg, the head of production of Universal's television division. The TV movie was a pilot for a projected series written and hosted by *The Twilight Zone*'s Rod Serling. Serling would stand in front of a painting in a gallery, and the camera would zoom into the painting to tell the story behind it. In Joan's segment, she played a wealthy blind woman in Manhattan named Claudia Menlo who pays a desperate man $9000 for his eyes, the same amount he owes a murderous loan shark. An operation will allow Claudia to see for several hours. After the surgery, she regains her sight but the city is in the middle of a blackout—so she can't see anything. Screaming out in abject rage and frustration, she stumbles out of a window in her penthouse and falls to her death (more intimated than shown due to a low budget and Spielberg's inexperience).

"It's not like Joan Crawford was too happy with the idea of this kid directing her," remembered Spielberg, who was 22 years old at the time—but could have passed for 16. Learning that Joan had been cast, he got a copy of *The Films of Joan Crawford* and read it from cover to cover. (Actually, considering Spielberg's well-known distaste for reading, he probably skimmed the book and studied the pictures.) He agreed to meet with Joan to talk over the script, which she found problematic. When Joan saw him, she immediately got on the phone and tried to get him fired. She had experienced a lot of debasement since her days as a star, but she would not be directed by a completely inexperienced "child." She thought it was the final insult. Sheinberg, Serling and others calmed her down and convinced her that Spielberg had genuine talent, which he would prove if she would give him a chance. Anyway, Serling was in charge and he wanted to use Spielberg.

Joan was bolstered a bit by the fact that Barry Sullivan from *Queen Bee* would be in the TV movie with her; at least he was a professional of long standing. Because of the pressure of getting the film done in only a few days, Joan at first had trouble with her lines and used cue cards, but after a couple of days she dispensed with them. She was anxious to do a good job in something that would be seen by many millions more people than *Berserk* or *Trog* ever would.

Spielberg certainly had chutzpah, and he seemed to know what he was doing. Before long, Joan began to admire the young man in spite of herself. He had the intensity and drive that she recognized; he would become a famous film director or be damned. That kind of ambition was something Joan understood, and she placed herself in his hands. For the most part, the two got along well together, with few on-set disagreements. Spielberg's work on the film, while it shows promise, hardly suggested the spectacular future awaiting him, but it got him on his start, with Joan's sterling help. She would watch his progress in Hollywood, on occasion sending him congratulatory missives.

Around this time Christina, who months before had been dropped by *The Secret Storm*, received word from Joan, who wanted her daughter to leave the Fountain Avenue apartment and fend for herself. Communications had broken down between the two women, and Joan was sick of Christina living off her and showing no gratitude or respect. "I do whatever I can for her," Joan sighed. "I've wracked my brain thinking of ways to help her. But is it *good* for her if I just let her live off me for the rest of my life?" Joan felt that Christina should accept that movie stardom might not be in the cards for her, that she might not even be able to make a living at it for any great length of time. Joan knew what most actors' lives were like; she herself was having a (comparatively) tough time of it during this period. Joan knew that an actor could get an assignment like *Secret Storm* and then be out of work for months or years when the assignment was over. Her compassion for Christina—who, as Joan put it, "simply would not listen"—was being replaced by anger, frustration, and impatience. In short, Joan was exasperated. She felt it imperative that Christina find another means of support, something to tide her over, to be a backup in case her plans came to nothing. Joan also stated more than once that she thought Christina wanted stardom but wasn't willing to work for it. It was only about being famous, not about being good at something. Try as she might, Joan came to realize that Christina was not very serious about her career. "I think she could be very happy just living off all that I've worked for all my life," Joan said. To a hard worker like Joan, such an idea was abominable. The idea of Christina partying, living rent-free, sleeping late, moping and whining— on Joan's dollar—when Christina was over twenty-one and should be making her own way in the world, was intolerable to her mother, as it would be to most parents.

Christina was informed that she would no longer be on Joan's dole. She had to get out, get a job, make a living, support herself, be her own woman—as Joan had been.

This was the beginning of the end of their relationship.

Christina would have her revenge.

Reel Stills Collection

Chapter Eighteen
END OF AN ICON

Around 1972, Joan learned that the Imperial House was going co-op. For less than $100,000 she bought a two-bedroom apartment in the same building and moved from the nine-bedroom apartment she had happily occupied for several years. This move was not as traumatic as the one seven years earlier, as she would not be leaving the neighborhood or even the building, and for both economic and health reasons she was ready to simplify her life. She was surprised when, some months later, *Architectural Digest* expressed interest in photographing the "tiny" apartment, but her name still had a certain cachet that appealed to the publication's snobbish readers—not to mention its editors. A photographer named Richard Champion was originally assigned to take the pictures, but for one reason or another he couldn't make it on the appointed day; a woman named Bettina Cirone showed up instead. It has been erroneously reported that Joan was rude to Cirone because she was annoyed at Champion's not showing up and took it out on his replacement, but she was really reacting to Cirone's altogether negative aura and distinctly unpleasant personality. Joan didn't expect people to genuflect when they met her, but she did expect the respect and politeness that would be anyone's due in one's home. To say that Cirone was not a "people person"—at least as evidenced by her encounter with Joan—would be putting it mildly. Joan was always amazed at people she found totally devoid of graciousness—or even just basic politeness. "How do they expect to get along in life?" she would wonder. What some people found affected about Joan was often just good manners.

The last five years of her life, Joan realized that for all intents and purposes her career was finished and her life as a Hollywood movie star was over. Lawrence Quirk sat in her apartment one afternoon as she attempted to enlist a Columbia Pictures executive into finding her "a strong picture." (Joan still received scripts for low-budget horror films, but she made a decision to refuse them outright. "I don't need the money that much," she said, "and why do what I know I wouldn't enjoy?") It was obvious that the executive, who liked Joan personally but thought that she was "through," was merely embarrassed by her efforts. It was difficult for her to deal with this and to get older at the same time, just as it is difficult for anyone to get older and realize that one's way of life is in the past. When you have reached the heights—and Joan had reached very high indeed—you only have that much farther to fall.

Her situation was worsened when she learned that Pepsi-Cola was dumping her as their spokesperson when she hit 65 (she was actually 69). For this she blamed "Fang," her nickname—borrowed from Phyllis Diller—for PepsiCo (as the Pepsi-Cola Company was now known) executive Donald Kendall. Mitchell Cox, who'd appeared with Joan in *Strait-Jacket,* invited her to be guest of honor at their convention in San Francisco, but she refused. She and Kendall had never liked each other, primarily because Kendall disliked the way the press gravitated toward her instead of to him; in turn, Joan resented his resentment.

A bright spot during this period was her appearance at Town Hall as part of the "Legendary Ladies" series put together by Don Koll and others. About 1500 fans gathered to honor Joan and watch clips from her movies. She had a little stage fright, and asked that instead of having questions called out from the audience they be read from slips of paper collected from the crowd earlier in the evening. She was also consulted as to which clips would be used.

Don Koll, who worked with Joan on putting together the clips, found her rather difficult. "She could be very nice, sweet, and charming," Koll recalled, "as long as you didn't cross her. She didn't take suggestions lightly or easily." Koll wanted to present clips from her silent period, but Joan would have none of it. "I think she wanted to give the impression she was a *modern* person," says Koll. "'Who gives a fuck about silent films?' she would say. 'Who cares about Harry Langdon?'" Joan got impatient with Koll when he tried to correct her on certain facts about her career. "Joan wanted the clips to begin with *Dancing Lady,*" Koll remembers. "She said that she gave Fred Astaire his start. I reminded her that Astaire had quite a career on Broadway before doing the film. 'I *meant* I gave him his start in *pictures,*' she snapped. She also seemed to think that she had made two films with Spencer Tracy, when it was only one, *Mannequin,*" which she deemed "terrible." Says Koll, "It's possible that there had been plans to team her and Tracy in a second picture, and that's what confused her." In general Koll felt that Joan's fans knew more about her career, at least certain details of it, than she did, which is typical of aging stars who have made dozens of sometimes forgettable movies.

Koll says that Joan could also be very helpful, however. "The rights to *Sudden Fear* had reverted to the author's estate," he recalls. "There was only one known print, in the Library of Congress. Joan made a couple of calls and got us the final reel from the film." Of course Joan would have wanted scenes from her third Oscar-nominated film to be shown on the big night, but she made things a lot easier for Koll by helping out. Don Koll is not the only person to report that Joan could be prickly in her dealings in her later years with people she did not know well. Part of it was that she was wary of everyone she came into contact with because so many were trying to use her—not true in the case of Koll, who indeed was trying to help her—and she sometimes overreacted. (In this way she was known to alienate people who might otherwise have become friends.) It is also true that she had decidedly mixed emotions about appearing at Town Hall in the first place.

Jean Arthur and Ginger Rogers had been first and second choice to join the first three "legendary ladies"—Bette Davis, Myrna Loy and Sylvia Sidney—on stage in separate appearances, but when they turned it down Joan was asked, and she reluctantly agreed. She turned out to be a bigger draw than Arthur and Rogers combined would have been. For a time she felt like a real movie star again, and she reveled in the applause and attention. But after the night was over, she of course had to face reality once again.

Actor-turned-writer Tom Tryon was one of the men Joan liked to use as a "walker," or escort, in her later years. Although she tried to put the moves on Tryon more than once, she didn't get anywhere with him—not because she was too old (although that did prove to be a problem where other men were concerned), but because Tryon was already involved with a certain E. Calvin Culver, better known as gay porn star Casey Donovan. By this time Tryon, who had starred in such films as the entertaining *I Married a Monster from Outer Space* and *The Cardinal*, had become a successful writer of fiction. His first book, a thriller called *The Other,* was turned into a movie, and another thriller, *Harvest Home,* became a television mini-series called *The Dark Secret of Harvest Home,* starring Bette Davis. People had been after Joan to write another, even franker memoir, now that so many people who might have been hurt had passed on, and Tryon was afraid that Joan would want him to co-author the book with her, or at least help her with the manuscript. Tryon did not need to be ghosting celebrity biographies at this point in his career, and in any case wondered if Joan was any more willing to be honest than she had been in the past. (In truth, Joan's autobiographies were surprisingly frank, evading the truth more in what they omitted than in what they included.) He got in touch with Joan's friend and *Films of Joan Crawford* author Lawrence Quirk and asked him his opinion. Quirk assured Tryon that Joan did not really expect him to write the book with her, and that, despite her personal frankness on many matters, Joan would have trouble revealing everything in print.

Tryon kept digging for information—not just about Joan, but also about many stars of the golden age. In 1986, some years after Joan's death, Tryon came out with *All That Glitters,* a collection of interlocked showbiz novellas that was a kind of sequel to the similar *Crowned Heads.* Narrated by an actor-turned-writer loosely based on Tryon himself, the plot dealt with a Hollywood agent of shady reputation and his involvement with five major female movie stars. One of these women was called "Claire Regrett," and was clearly based on Joan Crawford. Claire was married to a Douglas Fairbanks Jr. type (among several other husbands), wrote dozens of notes to her acquaintances, came from humble origins but had haughty pretensions, was supposed to have appeared in a blue movie—and on and on. But Claire Regrett had no children, adopted or otherwise. It is another character named Belinda who has a bitchy daughter who keeps threatening to write a tell-all about her mother until she's blown to bits by her grandmother—a literary equivalent of Mary Pickford!

The five women in *All That Glitters* are composed of bits and pieces of famous movie stars—Crawford, Garland, Taylor, and others—until it becomes hard to figure out where one ends and another begins. Claire Regrett is first presented as an utter monster and untalented actress who virtually blackmails the narrator into working on her memoirs with her, then tearily confesses that she made a gangster in love with her "fix" the Academy Awards so that she would win the Oscar. As should be obvious, Claire Regrett was only Joan Crawford in Tom Tryon's lurid imagination. Joan's talent was real and her Oscar was well-earned; while she could be a very determined lady, she was hardly a blackmailer. A more believable picture of Joan emerges in the sympathetic pages that end the novella, when Claire realizes she is dying and tries to view the world, and everyone in it, as something other than her mortal enemies. Friends and fans of Joan could recognize pieces of her in Tryon's portrait, but the author only used Joan and the other thinly-disguised stars as a framework for some grotesque showbiz horror stories. No one should ever consider "Claire Regrett" to be an accurate representation of Joan Crawford.

A prime user, Tryon had hoped to use some of Joan's contacts for his own purposes, and was annoyed when for various reasons (Joan's shrewdness, for one), it didn't work out. Some of the passages about Claire Regrett are even more caricatured and exaggerated than anything in *Mommie Dearest*. But in the end his conscience got the better of him and he made Regrett more human and more understandable, and even pays homage to her as a truly great star. As a work of literature, however, *All That Glitters* was aptly named. Taking his cue from old Hollywood legends, Tryon fashioned an elegant beach read that was more dishy than edifying about stardom.

To ease her loneliness and torment, Joan continued to nip at her beloved vodka during the afternoons and evenings, and on rare occasions it affected her adversely. Some would have classified Joan as an alcoholic, but when she realized she was ill she gave it up cold turkey, which a genuine addict would have found difficult indeed. Most of her friends would have agreed that she used alcohol for various purposes, but that it rarely impaired her. Except on the rare embarrassing occasion, Joan was always perfectly able to function. Whenever she went out she brought along a flask of 100 proof vodka. Unfortunately, Joan's drinking undoubtedly contributed to the cancer that originated in her liver.

Joan kept her apartment neat and clean and orderly, as she did all of her homes, with the ubiquitous plastic slipcovers much in evidence. She would laugh about it and say, "I'm Harriet Craig—but I can't help it!" Her preoccupation with cleanliness has been portrayed as pathological, with the implication that everyone who prefers to live in spotless homes is mentally disturbed. As is true with many people, Joan simply hated messiness. As Carleton Varney put it, "she was no psychopath about dirt."

Joan loved to watch her movies when they were broadcast late at night on TV. She loved to bestow presents on people, sometimes quite casual acquaintances, as if she were buying their friendship. In addition to several true friends, she was surrounded by people who wanted to use her, as many aging movie stars are. People were always giving her scripts to read; they were usually amateurish junk. "God, even my interior decorator has a role he wants me to play!" she once lamented. Sadly, there was little possibility of her getting financing for any of these projects—even had she wanted to do them.

Joan continued to hold parties and have lunches in her apartment, and she saw the twins on a regular basis. Cathy was now an artist in Pennsylvania; Joan was proud of her, as she was of her sister Cindy. Joan had very little contact with Christina, and virtually none with Christopher. Among the few friends who would lunch with her was Lawrence Quirk, who on occasion brought along fans, writers, or film historians to meet her. One afternoon Larry brought a fan named Mike Ritzer who had a speech problem so severe that most people who met him assumed that he was mildly retarded, which was far from the case. Joan was kind and understanding to Ritzer, who had trouble making himself understood but otherwise was, interestingly, not in awe of Joan. "That man is not retarded," Joan told Larry afterwards. "He just needs speech therapy and a little patience." Larry found it interesting that a woman labeled "self-absorbed" by so many had taken the trouble to listen intently to the man's stumbling, fragmentary sentences—which tried the patience of so many others—and to respond to him as she would have anybody else.

Joan saw Myrna Loy for the last time over lunch at '21.' Joan hinted that she was ill but did not let on how serious it was—it's possible that at this point she may not have known herself. When Myrna complained about age spots on her arms, Joan told her of a lotion she used and offered to give her the prescription. Joan laughed, "The only thing better is horse pee!"

After she had passed the age of seventy, Joan told Larry Quirk that she just didn't bother getting mad at people anymore; it seemed too pointless and futile. But she still harbored a few grudges. She complained frequently about her *Autumn Leaves* costar Cliff Robertson, for instance, who repeatedly ignored her letters and never returned her phone calls. After Joan's death, Robertson (among others) got his share of publicity by pompously and hypocritically droning on about Joan at her funeral.

Joan alienated many people because of her drinking, her late-night phone calls, and her temperament, which by 1976 seemed to be out of control. This was seen simply as a movie star being bitchy or demanding, but it was also true that Joan had simply taken on the cranky personality that many old people who are not physically healthy develop. She wasn't a bitch or a monster, she was just an elderly woman annoyed by the demands of users and non-friends and hiding a terrible secret from almost everyone who knew her. She had serious health problems and she was in a lot of pain. When it was confirmed that what she feared was true—that she had cancer—she told virtually no one. She decided to refuse treatment because she was a Christian Scientist (suicide, assisted or otherwise, was out of the question for the same reason), but she allowed a registered nurse of the same religious background to come in and help her. She did not want the tabloids keeping a death watch on her; most of all she did not want to become an object of pity. Joan was going to do it *her* way—the lonely way, perhaps, the hard way, but for her the way of dignity and self-respect. She had started with nothing so long ago in Oklahoma, turned herself into a figure famous and admired all over the world, and at the age of seventy-three would face death with her own unique valor.

In terrible pain and frightened of the void awaiting her, Joan withdrew from life and her friends, with the exception of a woman named Darinka Papich and a Christian Scientist named Mrs. Campbell. Her loyal maid of many years, lovingly called "Mamacita," had gone home to Germany because of a family crisis. Occasionally she still called people on the telephone, but she was sober and comparatively alert, and she kept more reasonable hours. She could no longer move her legs or lower body. She gave her Shih Tzu dogs away, and parceled out some of her keepsakes. On Mother's Day a couple of days before her death, Joan heard from Cathy and Cindy. Christina sent flowers, possibly with money from Joan, but did not call. Christopher was as silent as the tomb awaiting Joan.

On May 10, 1977, the phenomenon that was Joan Crawford breathed her last.

There would never be another like her.

J.C. Archives, Inc.

Chapter Nineteen

SERPENT'S TOOTH

"For reasons that are well known to them."

With these words did Joan Crawford cut her first two adopted children, Christina and Christopher, out of her will. Their mother had just been buried next to her last husband, Alfred Steele, in Westchester. Now at the Drake Hotel on the Upper East Side of Manhattan, Christina and her brother were getting the bad news. Cathy and Cindy were to receive about $80,000 apiece, and another million was to be divided among several charities.

Christina immediately raced into action. She hired an aggressive lawyer who tried several strategies to contest her mother's will. First he contacted several of Joan's acquaintances and asked if they would testify in court that at the time of her death Joan was either certifiably insane or hopelessly alcoholic. Next he sued the assorted charities that had been mentioned in the will. The estate lawyers gave Christina a settlement of approximately $55,000, but after paying off her own lawyers and splitting the rest with her brother, she got little more than ten thousand, a far cry from what she'd been hoping for.

But she had apparently always had an alternate plan for making money off of her mother.

Hollywood can be tough on children. Whether the child is adopted or not, it isn't easy to live in the shadow of a famous parent and carve out one's own identity. Furthermore, there are many stories of the questionable legitimacy of some Hollywood children. If certain stories are to be believed, Barbara Stanwyck adopted a boy who just seemed to fade out of her life when he reached adulthood—discarded, almost as if he were a chair or a table Stanwyck no longer found appealing. Hedy Lamarr told her son that he was adopted, and it wasn't until after her death that it came out that he had actually been her natural-born son. Loretta Young spent a lifetime concealing from her daughter the fact that she was the love child of Young and Clark Gable. But even if there is no question that the child is legitimate, it can be very difficult. Paul Newman's look-alike son was in such competition with, and felt so abandoned by, his father that he committed suicide at an early age. Jennifer Jones's daughter threw herself off the top of a building.

The rigors of pursuing a full-time profession in one of the most difficult fields in the world do not always go well with raising children. But some children of famous parents never forgive those parents for not, in turn, making them equally famous.

The first thing that an objective reader of *Mommie Dearest* will notice is that much of the book simply does not ring true. Just as a judge will assume a person who is caught in one lie may therefore be lying about a great deal else, one cannot dismiss the inaccuracies and phony moments of the book, and what these frequent lapses signify. Christina remembers conversations and incidents that she was much too young to recall in such detail, and has her mother unhappy and raging at the fates, lashing out in drunken anger, during periods when Joan was one of the two or three biggest stars in Hollywood. What comes across most vividly is that Christina completely fails to understand or appreciate her mother, is unwilling (then or ever) to see Joan's side of things, and has cast herself forever in the role of victim—whether she deserves the distinction or not. Her self-absorption is all over every page, a self-absorption that may well have contributed to the ultimate breakdown in her relationship with her mother.

Then there is the matter of the twins.

Cathy and Cynthia Crawford have always flatly denied that *Mommie Dearest* was in any way a truthful document. These girls were not the troublemakers Christina and Christopher were, and they had no reason to resent or hate their mother. And no reason to cover up for her, either. It might be argued that perhaps they objected to *Mommie Dearest* not because it was untrue, but because it aired dirty laundry. But if the book were true, once it was published, the twins would have been more likely to ignore it rather than speak out against it loudly and publicly, thereby garnering more publicity for it. They spoke out against *Mommie Dearest* because they knew it to be full of falsehoods; they could not in good conscience allow their mother to be victimized in so repellent and irresponsible a fashion. Since according to United States law the dead cannot be libeled or slandered, the twins couldn't sue Christina on their mother's behalf. Suing on their own behalf, however, was something else again.

"I think Christina was jealous," Cindy said. "She wanted to be the one person she couldn't be—Mother. I think she'll use Joan until she can't get any more out of it. Then she'll dump her." Cathy made it clear that while Joan may have disciplined them, there were neither beatings nor any nonsense about wire coat hangers. "I think Christina must have been in another household," she said.

Mommie Dearest had credibility not because it rang true, but for an entirely "negative" reason. Just as in a sexual dispute between a man and a woman, the woman is always given the benefit of the doubt, so, too, in a sexual or otherwise controversial dispute between an adult and a child, the child is also often given the benefit of the doubt. Nowadays, when children talk about physical or sexual abuse (sometimes the product of an overactive imagination), they are taken very seriously, with the result that some innocent people have been arrested for vile offenses that they never committed. In the case of *Mommie Dearest,* no one wanted to believe that anyone would tell such terrible lies about her own mother. And it seemed equally terrible to let Joan off the hook—in the event that the stories were true.

Even if one were to credit the stories in *Mommie Dearest* and believe that Christina was sincere in telling them, there are reasons to take the manuscript with a grain of salt. Unlike most children, Christina Crawford grew up with a famous movie star for a parent. For children who have a celebrity for a parent, it can be hard to understand or appreciate what life is like for a child who has "normal" parents—parents who aren't celebrities. Even Christina's playmates had famous, or at least very wealthy, parents, and their lives were completely different from those of most children. There was no way for Christina to know this, to know that in many ways her mother was not as different from an ordinary parent of that time as she had imagined.

Nowadays, disciplining children has become virtually a thing of the past. The term "tough love" has been invented to describe the kind of parenting that was once the norm, not the exception. If a parent recognizes that their child is spoiled and difficult, too dependent on the parents, too disrespectful of the parents, the decision to take firm action is now called "tough love"—when once it simply would have been considered common sense. Today, corporal punishment is frowned upon; indeed, some parents have even been reported to the authorities because they spanked their children. But it was not always this way.

Christina did not and could not know that during the time she was growing up, it was the norm and not the exception for children to be sent to bed without supper if they refused to eat what was on their plate. It was the norm and not the exception for disobedient children to be spanked. They were expected to be seen and not heard, to stay silent until addressed, to behave in front of visitors, and to keep their good clothes clean. If they spoke back to a parent, especially if they used foul language, their mouths would be washed out with soap. To punish a child, a parent might take away a treasured toy. The situations Christina found herself in were hardly unique or unusual. Christina didn't realize that disputes between mothers and daughters were commonplace and that the sons and daughters of wealthy families were frequently sent off to boarding school, especially if the children were unruly, disrespectful, inclined to be "wild," and resistant to any kind of reasonable discipline, much of which applied to Christina and her brother Christopher. To discipline a child who refused to obey a parent was in no way considered child abuse. Many of the readers of *Mommie Dearest* in the 1970s, when many of these practices had fallen out of favor and were even considered abusive, didn't understand this any more than Christina did. Then again, perhaps Christina understood it better than she ever let on.

Regarding *Mommie Dearest,* Christina told one interviewer: "I wrote the book as a personal journal. I didn't even realize it was ever going to be published. I thought that a few close friends and family members would read it and that would be it. You know, like the way you'd share a diary with your close friends." Isn't it interesting, then, that the book wound up being published by a top New York City publishing firm, William Morrow? Did Christina just happen to "share her diary" with an impersonal editorial director?

In truth, Christina had been smarting ever since Joan wrote frankly about the difficulties of their relationship in her memoir *A Portrait of Joan.* Joan only did this because Christina complained about her mother in a 1960 *Redbook* article called "The Revolt of Joan Crawford's Daughter." Even back then, Christina was hoping to embarrass and humiliate her mother and get attention for herself, and she was livid when the magazine gave Joan a copy of the piece before publication and asked for her comments, which were then included in the article. Joan's comments in *A Portrait of Joan* are very telling: "I am only filled with sorrow and compassion for my daughter because she's paying too much for whatever it is she wants. I certainly understand ambition, but you can't afford to throw away people, especially the people you love—and you can't afford to use them." She also disputed many of her daughter's claims, such as that she never let Christina know her birth date or her real parents' names, that she insisted she change her stage name and move out of the penthouse, and that they were even having a feud. "It takes two to feud and I'm not one of them. I wish only the best for Tina."

Christina did not feel the same way about her mother.

Joan did everything she could to help Christina in her acting career, to no avail. The trouble was that Christina wanted to be another Joan Crawford, when there was and could only be one Joan Crawford. Christina didn't have the looks, the talent, the charisma, that certain something that equals star quality. Christina had spent her formative years longing for the day when she could step out of her mother's shadow and get the attention that her mother got, for the day when she would no longer be ignored by all the people who clamored around her famous parent. When she was stymied in her ambitions—obviously through no fault of Joan's—Christina turned on her mother. In a reflective mood, Joan told a friend: "I worry about what's going to happen to the girl. I know she wants to be me, and she just can't be."

At the same time, Joan became exasperated with the handouts she was constantly obliged to give Christina. In truth, she did not think her daughter had the talent or drive to succeed in show business—not that she would crush her dreams and tell her that—and she feared the prospect of having to support her for the rest of her life, should Christina not accept her limitations and forge a career in another field, perhaps on the fringes of the movie business. Joan wanted her daughter to be fulfilled and happy. She was once asked if perhaps she should encourage Christina to get involved in the production side of the motion-picture or television industry, but Joan shook her head sadly and said, "It's stardom for Christina, or nothing, I'm afraid. She's going to be so disappointed. She's got my determination, in a way—but . . ." Then she shook her head again. Joan was also annoyed that Christina expected the world—or rather, her mother—to simply hand her a living when Joan had had to struggle years for everything she'd acquired. Unlike Joan, Christina had been brought up in an atmosphere of luxury. Unlike Joan, Christina had a mother who was already in the business and could show her the ropes. Unlike Joan, Christina accrued contacts every time she met one of her mother's show-business friends. But still Christina wasn't grateful.

During one teary late-night phone conversation, Joan confided to Larry Quirk that she was afraid Christina was going to write a book, a terrible book, about her after she was dead, if not before. It had gotten back to her that Christina was asking friends of Joan's for "dirt" on her mother. For instance, she asked several people if they thought that Joan was having a lesbian relationship with a red-headed female fan who had helped her pack up her belongings when she moved from the penthouse (she wasn't). "I just know she wants to use it all for a book or something worse," Joan cried. Quirk assured her this was unlikely—"It's probably just simple curiosity on her part," he said—and asked her why she thought Christina would do such a thing. "Surely she knows, whatever your faults, that you love her and have done all that you could for her?" Quirk asked. Joan replied, "You don't know Tina. She can be very vindictive. She throws things in my face. She says she's seen things I wouldn't want my fans to know about. She's threatened me. To get money out of me. To get me to talk to people when I know it won't do any good. You don't know what that girl is capable of. She's been out to get me ever since I made her stand on her own two feet." Quirk passed it off as a paranoid delusion on Joan's part, never dreaming that Joan knew exactly what she was talking about.

Christina and her brother Christopher had been difficult children. Despite Joan's efforts to keep them from turning into spoiled Hollywood brats, that is essentially what they became. They never seemed to acknowledge or appreciate the fact that Joan had rescued them from an orphanage and given them a privileged life that they could build upon. Christopher got into trouble with the law, reminding Joan of her ne'er-do-well brother Hal. Eventually Joan and Christopher mutually agreed not to have anything more to do with one another. In contrast to the twins, Christina and Christopher were never grateful for the advantages Joan gave them but concentrated only on—indeed, obsessed over—what they couldn't achieve, or rather (as they saw it) what Joan hadn't done for them, which for Christina included making her a star. Christina was not a real-life Veda; she did not necessarily think she was better than her mother, but she did want to be her equal, not just in her own eyes or in her mother's eyes, but in the eyes of the world—which was impossible. No one who ever saw Christina Crawford act on *The Secret Storm*—or anything else—would ever think she was the equal of her mother as an actor.

One can sympathize with Christina, up to a point. It wasn't her fault she hadn't been born with those special qualities that distinguished Joan from the rest of the pack. (Obviously, this might have been the case even had she been Joan's biological child.) She hungered for recognition from the powerful, glittering people who knew her only as Joan's little girl. She wanted to move in the same exalted circles as her mother did, but even if Christina had had that star quality, it was simply too late. Joan herself didn't really move in those circles any more. She was no longer a box-office winner, no longer a top-drawer movie queen. Because she was still recognized everywhere she went, still an international icon, Christina may have overestimated her mother's clout. There wasn't all that much Joan could have done for Christina, even if she had had the requisite ability, beauty, and so on. Without it, the situation was hopeless, a fact Joan recognized all too well. She was happy every time her daughter made a small gain in the business, indeed overjoyed when she got the part on *Secret Storm* (which Christina might not have gotten in the first place had she not been Joan's daughter), but she knew it was ultimately futile. Everyone did. Christina Crawford just didn't have what it took to become a star.

And she would make her mother pay for it dearly.

Far from being the mostly unloving monster portrayed by Christina, Joan did her best for Christina and Christopher, who were, as Joan related to several of her friends, verbally abusive, flagrantly rude, entirely ungrateful, and eternally disrespectful. When her career didn't blossom as quickly or as grandly as she had hoped, Christina blamed her mother and heaped torrents of abuse upon her. She was furious that Joan wouldn't demand that she be cast in some of her later movies, but Joan knew Christina would only betray her inexperience and lack of talent. Christina would make fun of the movies Joan made (even as she desperately wanted to be in them), laugh at her appearance, call her a has-been, anything to make her feel the pain that she was feeling, the pain and disappointment at failing at what she desperately needed to do—become of *somebody*.

"For reasons that are well known to them." Christina feigned ignorance, but she knew perfectly well why she and her brother were cut out of Joan's will. But this provided her with the impetus to continue on her driven path to become *somebody*. She would literally do it over her mother's dead body.

One person who wasn't taken in by Christina and her stories was Joan's long-time friend Myrna Loy, who had had the misfortune of working with Christina in a Chicago production of *Barefoot in the Park* in which Loy was starring. "We didn't have any problems in *Barefoot* until . . . Christina Crawford appeared," Loy wrote in her autobiography *Myrna Loy: Being and Becoming*, co-written with James Kotsilibas-Davis. Christina played Loy's daughter in the play, and Loy was initially happy to welcome the daughter of her dear friend Joan to the cast. That changed quite rapidly: "I've never known anybody else like her—ever," Loy remembered. "Her stubbornness was really unbelievable. She would not do a single thing that anyone told her to do. You'd go out there on the stage and you couldn't find her. One thing an actor needs to know is exactly where people are on the stage; Christina completely disregarded her blocking, throwing the rest of us off." The stage manager was Harvey Medlinksi, whom Christina later married. Loy was at first unaware of the romance between the two and couldn't figure out why Medlinksi was letting Christina get away with behavior that would normally have gotten a cast member fired. "I don't blame Harvey," wrote Loy. "He was a victim." Things got so bad with Christina that Loy called for Richard Benjamin, director of the London production of *Barefoot in the Park,* to come to Chicago and intervene. "He couldn't do anything with her," Loy recalled. "Absolutely nothing! She was going to do it her way." Loy charitably added, "It was self-defeating and sad, because the girl had potential." Christina managed to get a good review, even though she wasn't playing the part as written. Christina was finally put in her place when the play's author, Neil Simon, came to a performance and was appalled by what he saw. Christina was playing Loy's daughter as if she were the main character. Christina was promptly fired and afterward blamed Loy instead of her own lack of professionalism. Loy did everything possible to help Christina in her role, but not even three directors and all of her determination—and everyone else's patience—could make her something she was not. "She wanted to be Joan Crawford," wrote Loy. "I think that's the basis of the book she wrote afterward and everything else. I saw what her mind created, the fantasy world she lived in. . . . She envied her mother, grew to hate her, and wanted to destroy her."

Loy told Lawrence Quirk at the D.W. Griffith awards circa 1981 that

Joan and I approached being movie stars in a different way. She liked to take limos everywhere, she was much 'grander,' for lack of a better word, and maybe I was more down to earth, but so what? Joan certainly wasn't the only movie star who liked the champagne and limousine treatment. I can tell you that when you made a friend in Joan you had a friend for life. She never forgot your birthday, and you'd get a congratulatory note from her when good things happened in your life. She cared about people and her friends, no matter what anybody says. I liked her, and I miss her, and I think her daughter's stories are pure bunk. Even if they were true, if ever there was a girl who needed a good whack it was spoiled, horrible Christina. Believe me, there were many times I wanted to smack her myself.

Joan's first husband, Doug Fairbanks Jr., who remained friends with Joan all her life, couldn't bring himself to read *Mommie Dearest*. "From what I have read and heard about it," he told interviewer Steve Randisi, "it's like a book about someone I never knew, only someone with the same name. But I don't recognize this person as anybody I ever knew. And either they are making it up, or it's a complete Jekyll and Hyde. I'd much rather keep my memories of the person I knew and was very, very fond of, respected and admired, and everything else."

Fairbanks Jr. told William Schoell: "Joan was a career-oriented woman, yes, but she wasn't a monster who ran around torturing little children. The whole idea of it is absurd. I don't believe any amount of stress or alcohol could have turned her into some cruel kind of raving creature. When we were married she drank at parties—we all did—it might have made her silly—me, too—but never outright vicious. That was simply not the woman I knew." Years before *Mommie Dearest* came out, George Cukor once gave James Kotsilibas-Davis this double-edged compliment about her: "Joan may have been preposterous, but she was never cruel."

Other Hollywood names who registered their objections to *Mommie Dearest* included Van Johnson and Joan's *Mildred Pierce* daughter, Ann Blyth. It seems that "Veda" had nothing on Christina Crawford when it came to monstrous offspring.

Joan's friend, the interior designer Carleton Varney, put it as well as anyone. "Nearly everybody admits to a few nightmarish memories of parents out of control; and nearly all parents (saints excluded) regret a shameful episode or two when they lashed out at their children." Were there "shameful episodes" in Joan's dealings with her children, or at least with Christina? And how many were there? For much of their lives, Joan and Christina did not get along, so undoubtedly there were times when Joan lost her temper and yelled at her daughter—and vice versa. This is not only normal; if a mother and father *never* argued with a child, that would be incredibly unnatural. Joan may have employed corporal punishment when Christina was a child, a practice that was common for parents of the period, as previously noted. Joan liked to drink now and then and may have gotten good and sloshed on occasion. However, drinking generally made Joan mellow and happy, not angry or vicious. In fact, all of the insane, mostly alcohol-fueled incidents in *Mommie Dearest* seem illogical to the point of fabrication, entirely fanciful—at the very least, wildly exaggerated. Christina may also have exaggerated the sheer number of bizarre, abusive incidents in order to cast her mother in the worst possible light and herself as sympathetically as possible. If nothing else, *Mommie Dearest* had no sense of balance; it lacked perspective. Christina was smart enough to know that a less sensational memoir of her relationship with her mother would not garner as much attention nor sell as many copies. If Christina learned nothing else from her mother, she knew how to promote herself.

The film version of *Mommie Dearest* came out in 1981, and it turned out to be the campy travesty that everyone expected. Because the twins disapproved of the movie, their characters were completely eliminated—and, with them, even a token attempt to balance the scales. Anne Bancroft was originally signed to play Joan but apparently thought better of it when she read the script. She wisely bowed out, leaving the field clear for Faye Dunaway, on the lookout for a meaty part. Years before, Joan had admired Faye Dunaway and thought she was among the stronger of the young actresses of the day. She had never worked with her and therefore did not share Bette Davis's contempt for Dunaway (Davis found her completely unprofessional when they worked together on the TV movie *The Disappearance of Aimee*). Dunaway, who had always been rather affected both in her on- and offscreen manner, was seen as being perfect to play Joan, whom the producers of *Mommie Dearest* presumably also saw as affected. As an actress, Dunaway was never in the league of Bancroft, who would probably have portrayed Joan as much more natural and human, at least in the scenes that didn't paint her as an out-and-out monster. If Christina had been hoping to play herself or even her mother—because her ego was every bit as large as her mother's—she was sadly disappointed; the part of Christina went to the up-and-coming starlet of the moment, Diana Scarwid, who did not even know who Joan was when she was cast.

The tone of the film is unmistakable from the very first shot, as under the credits we see "Joan" preparing herself for the day by washing her face in hot water and then rubbing it with ice cubes. Right away Henry Mancini's grim, forgettable music suggests that there's something peculiar about this daily procedure (actually an intelligent habit for a movie star whose career depends on her appearance; it promotes good circulation). Like the picture itself, Dunaway as Joan is generally over-wrought and hysterical. She doesn't play Joan at all; even those who admire the performance concede that she actually created a grotesque caricature of Joan. Dunaway confuses the on-screen Joan in some of her more intense portrayals (for instance, *Queen Bee*) with Joan herself—but Joan was never that manic, even at her worst. To be fair to Dunaway, there are moments in which she exhibits both warmth and humor and even times when she is outright sympathetic, such as after Joan is let go by Warner Brothers—but such moments are rare. There are actually only four scenes in which Joan Crawford is shown to have been a wacko, but they are so horrendous that they completely overpower everything else in the movie, preventing the audience from ever taking the character, and the real woman behind it, seriously.

The first "wacko" scene has her cutting off Christina's golden locks when she discovers the little girl innocently preening in front of the mir-ror, pretending to be her mother amidst her adoring fans. The real Joan would have been delighted and overjoyed by such a scene. What makes the scene even more ludicrous is that it happens right after Joan has gotten wonderful news about a part over the telephone (it's implied that the part is *Mildred Pierce*), and therefore has no reason to be mad at anyone, much less her daughter. The second "wacko" scene has Joan inexplicably hacking at the rose bushes in her garden. "Tina! Bring me the ax!" she screams in a scene that was clearly suggested not by any real incident but by her role in *Strait-Jacket*; this is followed by shots of Joan maniacally chopping down a tree with the implement. The third "wacko" scene, by far the most notorious and more damaging than the first two put together, is the infamous "No wire hangers—ever!!" scene. Joan forces Christina out of bed in the middle of the night for the infraction of put-ting one of her outfits on a wire clothes hanger. She then orders the girl to scrub the bathroom floor until it glistens. (A child in this situation, especially if she had already been exposed to her parent's drinking and such ludicrous behavior on so many occasions—as Christina suggested she had been—might find the whole business, and the parent, beneath contempt and simply make a show of scrubbing until the parent passed out and forgot about it.)

"Wacko" scene number four features Faye Dunaway practically salivating, flaring her nostrils, and almost literally chewing the scenery in an embarrassing example of absurd overplaying that Joan would never have dared approach in even the worst of her eighty motion pictures. (In general, Dunaway overacts much more than Joan ever did.) In this scene

Joan attacks the adult Christina after an argument in Joan's study, literally throwing herself at her daughter, knocking both of them to the ground. One is again reminded of nothing so much as Joan pinning Diane Baker to the bed and pulling off her mask in the climactic scene of *Strait-Jacket*. More than *Berserk* or *Trog, Mommie Dearest* is the horror film that "Mommie" never made.

And for all the "wacko" moments in *Mommie Dearest*, you wind up admiring Joan all over again—admiring her, for instance, for her gutsiness when she takes on the Pepsi-Cola board of directors, and for demanding that her rude, ungrateful daughter finally show her some respect. It is too bad that there is little of her bawdiness and humor in the film, little of her good works and generosity, and absolutely none of the hard work and persistence, dedication and perseverance that took her to such heights. Ultimately, there is much too little of the real Joan Crawford.

On the plus side of *Mommie Dearest* is the fact that Joan is shown wanting to adopt children for sincere motives. "I could teach a kid how to get along," Dunaway says to her boyfriend, "Greg Savitt," played by Steve Forrest. (Savitt is a composite character presumably inspired by Greg Bautzer; Forrest is quite effective in the part.) And Christina does not come off as being entirely sympathetic herself. Both Diana Scarwid and Mara Hobel (who plays Christina as a child) convey quite vividly how utterly spoiled Christina is, and how desperate she is not so much for a mother's love but for excessive attention. One scene shows young Christina standing at the doorway of her mother's mansion and looking out at the crowd of her mother's fans gathered on the grounds, as delight mixed with envy and anticipation plays across her features. The movie does more than suggest that Tina wrote *Mommie Dearest* for revenge. Parts of *Mommie Dearest* work perfectly well as a study of a war between two strong-willed (albeit mostly fictional) women, but in the end *Mommie Dearest* is not so much done in by mendacity and bad acting, but by its shallowness, one-sidedness, and sheer superficiality.

Ironically, Bette Davis's daughter, B.D. Hyman (formerly Merrill) came out with her own *Mommie Dearest*-esque tome when she published *My Mother's Keeper* in 1985. While Christina at least *seemed* to have some legitimate complaints—at least as far as the uninformed were concerned—Hyman had apparently been "born again" and was using the book to let her mother know that she would have nothing to do with her—and that Bette would never see her grandchild—unless she too found God and mended her evil ways. The book is considered even more meretricious than *Mommie Dearest,* although many of the sordid incidents described in *My Mother's Keeper* were similar to ones detailed in *Mommie Dearest.* In truth, Hyman, who as mentioned earlier appeared in *What Ever Happened to Baby Jane?* as the neighbor's daughter, also never forgave her mother for not doing more for her show-business aspirations, although unlike Christina she clothed her ingratitude and hatred in moral platitudes reminiscent of Mr. Davidson in *Rain.* Privately Davis, who knew that much, if not all, of *My Mother's Keeper* was nonsense, began to wonder if her old rival Joan had also been libeled and misjudged in the same way, although it was not for her to rush to Joan's defense, then or ever.

Joan has had the last laugh, however. She is still an American icon, still a fascinating Hollywood figure decades after her death; nothing similar can be said for anyone involved in *Mommie Dearest.* After attempting to jump-start her career with a television sitcom, Faye Dunaway found important movie roles few and far between and now glides from one minor cameo to another. While making the picture, she refused to meet with Christina, who wrote two rejected screenplays; to her credit she made it clear that she thought *Mommie Dearest* the book was hogwash. In her memoirs she denounced the film as "camp that had gone way over the edge." Five years after *Mommie Dearest,* Diana Scarwid had another high-profile role in *Psycho III,* but little has been heard of her since. "It's the curse of Joan Crawford," Joan's fans may gloat, but in fact it's simply the vicissitudes of Hollywood, which Joan survived far longer than Dunaway, Scarwid, director Frank Perry, or anyone else who worked on *Mommie Dearest.*

As for Christina, it might be said that the bad karma she exhibited came back to haunt her, for she nearly died of a stroke the same year the film was released; her entire left side was left paralyzed for a time. The rock group Blue Öyster Cult even wrote a song, "Joan Crawford," that implied that Joan was getting revenge from beyond the grave. Christina's show-business career is essentially over, and she now runs a bed and breakfast in Sanders, Idaho. Christina has been married and divorced nearly as often as her mother; her second husband was film producer C. David Koontz, and her third was Michael Brazzel, who works for the federal government. In the 1980s, Christina advertised in the *New York Times* for backers for a film adaptation of her second book, the novel *Black Widow,* which recycled "Mommie Dearest" stories and sold poorly; the film was never made.

As desperate for attention as ever, she came out with a twentieth anniversary edition of *Mommie Dearest* in 1998. The new edition included new pages devoted to her final years with her mother, which is strange because she had little to do with Joan during this period and indeed never reconciled with Joan, as she claimed in the first edition of *Mommie Dearest*. Although Christina asserted that she self-published the book because she wanted to have more control over it, the unsurprising truth is that no publisher was interested in Christina's rantings, as they had been discredited in too many quarters. Christina appeared at Town Hall in New York (and venues in other cities) along with publicity-hungry drag "entertainer" Lypsinka (dressed, of course, as Joan), where Christina—in a gesture of dubious taste—presented Lypsinka with a sequined wire hanger. Christina answered questions from the audience, and then went out into the lobby to sell copies of her book while inside the film version of *Mommie Dearest* was shown. Christina has disassociated herself from the film, mostly because her screenplays for it were rejected and she didn't make enough money from it, but this didn't stop her from using it to sell copies of her book (otherwise available only through the Internet). As one observer put it, "Christina will whore herself in any way imaginable to make money off her mother's name and to keep herself in the public eye." Judging from the poor attendance at Town Hall, the public was not very interested. In a pathetic and obvious attempt at one-upmanship, Christina had chosen to speak at the same venue where her mother had appeared as part of the "Legendary Ladies" series in 1973.

In July of 1998, her sister Cathy, now married and with the last name of Lalonde, had had enough of Christina and her remarks. Certain of Christina's comments to the press, such as the assertion that Cathy and her sister Cynthia (now Mrs. Joel Jordan) weren't really twins but were unrelated, so inflamed Cathy that in July 1998 she filed suit against Christina for defamation of character; there was reportedly a settlement. Cathy charged that she "was held up to public ridicule" and still maintains that the events described in *Mommie Dearest* were "fake and fictional."

Cathy and Cynthia live quiet lives away from the spotlight, in small towns (in Pennsylvania and Iowa, respectively) and with unlisted phone numbers, and this is just how they want it. They are tired of unkind people bothering them with idiotic jokes about the mother who, however imperfect she may have been, took them out of an orphanage and gave them a home and love. They are sick to death of Christina and what they call her "lies."

But Christina had still more venom in her. In August 2001, she told talk show host Larry King that she believed her mother had *murdered* fourth husband Alfred Steele. "I believe she killed him for the money because she profited greatly from his death." This is a ludicrous assertion, since Alfred left Joan mostly with debts. Christina claims it was suspicious for Alfred to die of heart failure when—according to her—his doctor had recently given him a clean bill of health, and he was only fifty-four years old. Yet many men in their fifties die of heart attacks, especially overweight and out-of-shape men like Alfred. Christina implied that her mother pushed Steele down a staircase in their penthouse and then instigated a cover-up. It is extremely unlikely that experienced New York City detectives would have let it slide if they even *suspected* Joan had murdered her husband. It appears that Christina will literally say anything to help sell her book and keep her mother's memory in tatters.

Christina is sixty-two years of age as of this writing. "I have no regrets," she says, "no guilt and no remorse." She claims that in the past she has worked tirelessly for adoptees' rights; for several years she served as president of an organization known as the Inter-Agency Council on Abuse and Neglect (ICAN) in Los Angeles. It would be comforting to think that something good may have come out of *Mommie Dearest,* if children have been helped by Christina's efforts, but many people who know her well insist that most of her energy goes to promoting herself as a victim—and, of course, to promoting *Mommie Dearest.* Aside from a stepson from her second marriage, Christina has no children: friends of her mother's agree that this is for the best. The general consensus is that given the way she treated her mother, both in print and in life, Christina might have made a far worse parent than she depicted Joan Crawford— who was not alive to defend herself—as being.

Lawrence Quirk with Joan Crawford and friend, snapped by a Columbia Pictures photographer at Penn Station, 1956. Lawrence J. Quirk Collection.

AFTERWORD

In October 1981, the month that the film *Mommie Dearest* was released, an item in the "Page Six" column by Richard Johnson of the *New York Post* quoted Lawrence J. Quirk on some of the good things Joan had done for people down on their luck: the hospital beds she had endowed; the checks she sent her former co-worker, the down-and-out Marie Prevost, among many others; her fight (in a much less tolerant era) to get pal William Haines established as an interior decorator after his homosexuality effectively ended his acting career; and so on. Way back in 1934, Joan made a deal with Dr. William Branch, who had once treated her for a minor complaint and become friends with her: If he would donate his services, Joan would pay the hospital bills for indigent patients—including many needy people in the film business—at the Hollywood Presbyterian Hospital. Joan did this for many, many years. Two rooms were set aside for literally hundreds of patients, many of whom received necessary surgery that they would otherwise have gone without; most never knew that they had Joan Crawford to thank for their treatment. Joan never sought publicity for this special "clinic," and she was highly annoyed when news of it leaked to the press.

The same month, at the James R. Quirk Memorial Film Symposium at Greenwich House in New York City, Lawrence Quirk held an evening entitled *Joan Crawford's Friends Defend Her.* Quite a number of Joan's admirers showed up that evening. Some came out of love for her, some out of remembrance for her many unsung kindnesses and generosities; some, belatedly, to get on the bandwagon. So many had stood by in silence while a campaign of vilification and brutal caricature followed in the wake of the book *Mommie Dearest* by Christina Crawford and the grotesque film adaptation. Addressing the audience, Quirk said that he was making no attempt to whitewash Joan, who was a human being like everyone else, with good points and bad points, both strengths and weaknesses. Then others in the audience got up and spoke about Joan, their memories of her and of the good things she had done. Of course there was one character who completely missed the point of the evening and showed up brandishing a wire hanger. Perhaps the nadir of the evening was the late appearance of a press-agent "friend" of Joan's, who arrived inebriated, took to the stage, and proceeded to tell an extremely lengthy and tedious anecdote that turned out to be about another movie star entirely. (Joan probably would have been both amused and horrified at the display.)

On May 10, 1984—nearly three years later, on the seventh anniversary of Joan's death—a full-page memorial entitled "Our Beloved Friend" appeared on page five of *Daily Variety*. Surrounding a handsome portrait of Joan was a list of about 125 names. It was hard not to notice that many of the people who had gotten their names on the page had done absolutely nothing about Joan's posthumous plight in 1978 and 1981 when the book and the movie, respectively, had been released; in fact 1984 was rather late for them to jump on the pro-Joan bandwagon. Some surely thought it politic to stay silent while Christina, and then Frank Perry and Faye Dunaway, were perpetrating what many of Joan's fans and friends saw as an abomination. These people had in no way honored Joan's memory but had only turned on her after she was dead.

However, many of the names in the memorial sincerely loved and admired Joan and certainly deserved to be listed there. This group included her daughters Cathy and Cindy and their families, who had stood up for their mother in print back in 1981; author, film commentator and designer Lou Valentino; Myrna Loy, who spoke up loud and clear against both book and movie; Dore Freeman of MGM, who had always loved Joan; Joan Evans Weatherly, Joan's god-daughter, and her husband Kirby Weatherly, who loved her for the way she had sacrificed her friendship with Evans's mother, writer Katherine Albert, to get them married in their own home; Alexander Walker, a great Crawford booster and author of a book about her; Cesar Romero, Joan's dear friend of many years; Betty Barker; Florence Walsh; Maria Romero; and many others. There were also quite a lot of Joan's true friends who for one reason or another had not made it onto the list because of politics and other factors. The memorial was the right idea, but it was perhaps put together for the wrong reasons by the wrong people.

But it doesn't matter.

Joan always knew who her friends were.

FILMOGRAPHY

NOTE: The films *Lady of the Night* and *Proud Flesh* sometimes appear on Joan's filmography in other sources, but she only worked as a stand-in in the former and her appearance in the latter—and in a few other silent films that are occasionally mentioned—has not been substantiated. Crawford's most "important" films (based on her performance or the film's effect on her career, etc.) appear in bold.

Pretty Ladies. (MGM) 1925. Director: Monta Bell
The Only Thing. (MGM) 1925. Director: Jack Conway
The Circle. 1925. (MGM) Director: Frank Borzage
Old Clothes. 1925. (MGM) Director: Eddie Cline
Sally, Irene and Mary. (MGM) 1925. Director: Edmund Goulding
The Boob. (MGM) 1926. Director: William A. Wellman
Tramp Tramp Tramp. (First National) 1926. Director: Harry Edwards
Paris. (MGM) 1926. Director: Edmund Goulding
The Taxi Dancer. (MGM) 1927. Director: Harry Millarde
Winners of the Wilderness. (MGM) 1927. Director: W.S. Van Dyke
The Understanding Heart. (MGM) 1927. Director: Jack Conway
The Unknown. (MGM) 1927. Director: Tod Browning
Twelve Miles Out. (MGM) 1927. Director: Jack Conway
Spring Fever. (MGM) 1927. Director: Edward Sedgwick
West Point. (MGM) 1928. Director: Edward Sedgwick
Rose-Marie. (MGM) 1928. Director: Lucien Hubbard
Across to Singapore. (MGM) 1928. Director: William Nigh
The Law of the Range. (MGM) 1928. Director: William Nigh
Four Walls. (MGM) 1928. Director: William Nigh
Our Dancing Daughters. (MGM) 1928. Director: Harry Beaumont.
Dream of Love. (MGM) 1928. Director: Fred Niblo
The Duke Steps Out. (MGM) 1929. Director: James Cruze
Our Modern Maidens. (MGM) 1929. Director: Jack Conway
Hollywood Revue of 1929. (MGM) 1929. Director: Charles F. Reisner.
Untamed. (MGM) 1929. Director: Jack Conway

Montana Moon. (MGM) 1930. Director: Malcolm St. Clair
Our Blushing Brides. (MGM) 1930. Director: Harry Beaumont
Paid. (MGM) 1930. Director: Sam Wood
Dance, Fools, Dance. (MGM) 1931. Director: Harry Beaumont
Laughing Sinners (MGM) 1931. Director: Harry Beaumont
This Modern Age. (MGM) 1931. Director: Nicholas Grinde
Possessed. (MGM) 1931. Director: Clarence Brown
Grand Hotel. (MGM) 1932. Director: Edmund Goulding
Letty Lynton. (MGM) 1932. Director: Clarence Brown
Rain. (United Artists) 1932. Director: Lewis Milestone
Today We Live. (MGM) 1933. Director: Howard Hawks
Dancing Lady. (MGM) 1933. Director: Robert Z. Leonard
Sadie McKee. (MGM) 1934. Director: Clarence Brown
Chained. (MGM) 1934. Director: Clarence Brown
Forsaking All Others. (MGM) 1934. Director: W. S. Van Dyke
No More Ladies. (MGM) 1935. Directors: Edward H. Griffith; George Cukor
I Live My Life. (MGM) 1935. Director: W. S. Van Dyke
The Gorgeous Hussy. (MGM) 1936. Director: Clarence Brown
Love on the Run. (MGM) 1936. Director: W. S. Van Dyke
The Last of Mrs. Cheyney. (MGM) 1937. Director: Richard Boleslawski
The Bride Wore Red. (MGM) 1937. Director: Dorothy Arzner
Mannequin. (MGM) 1937. Director: Frank Borzage
The Shining Hour. (MGM) 1938. Director: Frank Borzage
Ice Follies of 1939. (MGM) 1939. Director: Reinhold Schunzel
The Women. (MGM) 1939. Director: George Cukor
Strange Cargo. (MGM) 1940. Director: Frank Borzage
Susan and God. (MGM) 1940. Director: George Cukor
A Woman's Face. (MGM) 1941. Director: George Cukor
When Ladies Meet. (MGM) 1941. Director: Robert Z. Leonard
They All Kissed the Bride. (Columbia) 1942. Director: Alexander Hall
Reunion in France. (MGM) 1942. Director: Jules Dassin
Above Suspicion. (MGM) 1943. Director: Richard Thorpe
Hollywood Canteen (Warner Brothers) 1944. Director: Delmer Daves
Mildred Pierce. (Warner Brothers) 1945. Director: Michael Curtiz. ACADEMY
    AWARD: *Best Actress.*
Humoresque. (Warner Brothers) 1946. Director: Jean Negulesco
Possessed. (Warner Brothers) 1947. Director: Curtis Bernhardt. *Academy Award
    nomination for best actress.*
Daisy Kenyon. (20th Century Fox) 1947. Director: Otto Preminger
Flamingo Road. (Warner Brothers) 1949. Director: Michael Curtiz
It's a Great Feeling. (Warner Brothers) 1949. Director: David Butler
The Damned Don't Cry. (Warner Brothers) 1950. Director: Vincent Sherman
Harriet Craig. (Columbia) 1950. Director: Vincent Sherman

Goodbye, My Fancy. (Warner Brothers) 1951. Director: Vincent Sherman
This Woman is Dangerous. (Warner Brothers). 1952. Director: Felix Feist
Sudden Fear. (RKO) 1952. Director: David Miller. *Academy Award nomination*
for best actress.
Torch Song. (MGM) 1953. Director: Charles Walters
Johnny Guitar. (Republic) 1954. Director: Nicholas Ray
Female on the Beach. (Universal-International) 1955. Director: Joseph Pevney
Queen Bee. (Columbia) 1955. Director: Ranald MacDougall
Autumn Leaves. (Columbia) 1956. Director: Robert Aldrich
The Story of Esther Costello. (Columbia) 1957. Director: David Miller
The Best of Everything. (20th Century-Fox) 1959. Director: Jean Negulesco
What Ever Happened to Baby Jane? (Warner Brothers) 1962. Director: Robert
Aldrich
The Caretakers. (United Artists) 1963. Director: Hall Bartlett
Strait-Jacket. (Columbia) 1964. Director: William Castle
I Saw What You Did. (Universal) 1965. Director: William Castle
Berserk. (Columbia) 1968. Director: Jim O'Connolly
Trog. (Warner Brothers) 1970. Director: Freddie Francis

NOTE: Two other "movies" Joan appeared in and which are available on videocassette are *Night Gallery* and *Fatal Confinement*, both of which were made for
television.

NOTES

Chapter One

p 3 "It wasn't incest ..." Joan Crawford (JC) to Lawrence Quirk (LQ).

p 5 "I was a workhorse ..." ibid.

p 5 "They'll never get one single dollar from me ..." ibid.

p 6 "She was afraid that I'd seduce ..." ibid.

XX "The life was Kansas-style Bohemian ..." Adela Rogers St. Johns to LQ.

XX "rich bitches" JC to LQ.

XX "first love" JC to LQ.

p 8 "It made me feel close to Ray ..." ibid.

p 9 "It broke Ray's heart ..." ibid.

p 10 "It sounded more glamorous ..." ibid.

p 10 "My mother wasn't going ..." ibid.

XX "casting-couch cougar" JC to LQ.

p 11 "jumped on Ernie's couch ..." ibid.

p 12 "extra nice to Mr. Shubert ..." ibid.

p 12 "It depended on my mood ..." ibid.

p 13 "New York was the most exciting place ..." JC to William Schoell (WS).

p 15 "Paul Bern and Billy [Haines] ..." JC to LQ.

Chapter Two

p 3 Information on Joan's appearance in *The Circle* from *Joan Crawford: the Ultimate Star*, Alexander Walker.

p 4 "They had us in a big line up ..." JC to LQ.

p 5 "He was a dirty pig ..." JC to LQ.

p 5 "You know, I wouldn't have recognized ..." ibid.

p 8 "I was just an MGM contract player ..." JC to LQ.

p 8 "This was, of course ..." ibid.

p 9 "She used to get so affronted ..." William Wellman to LQ.

p 9 "*The Boob* strengthened my ambitions ..." JC to LQ.

p 10 "He liked to economize ..." Frank Capra to LQ.

p 12 "When I got back to MGM ..." JC to LQ.

p 15 "He was a handsome lug ..." ibid.

p 15 "He was slipping badly ..." ibid.

p 15 "I was overacting all over the place ..." ibid.

p 16 "I was free to go to Mayer ..." ibid.

Chapter Three

p 2 "Hal wanted to live it up ..." JC to LQ.

p 2 "No matter what I gave ..." ibid.

p 3 Hal's attempts to sell unsavory stories about his sister to journalists was confirmed by, besides Joan herself, Jerry Asher, Ruth Waterbury, Adela Rogers St. Johns and others.

p 4 "Everyone thought I was better ..." JC to LQ.

p 5 "At the end of the day ..." ibid.

p 6 "It was more his thing than mine ..." ibid.

p 6 "I galloped through it, dreaming of Douglas." *Portrait of Joan.* JC with J.K. Ardmore, p 61.

p 7 "Just another handsome rascal ..." JC to LQ.

p 8 "I became aware for the first time ..." and JC's other comments on Lon Chaney: JC to LQ and *Portrait of Joan*, p 30.

p 9 "an era went with him ..." JC to LQ.

p 9 "the scariest of experiences ..." ibid.

p 10 *The Unknown* was my first horror film ..." JC to William Schoell.

p 11 "He was so in love with Garbo ..." JC to LQ.

p 11 "Our chemistry on-screen ..." ibid.

p 13 "I learned from him to always maintain ..." ibid.

p 14 Some information on *West Point* from *Wisecracker*, by William Mann.

p 15 "had great naturalness and charm ..." *Portrait of Joan*, p 31.

p 15 "Still, it was rather sweet ..." JC to LQ.

Chapter Four

p 1 "I thought his performance ..." JC to LQ.

p 2 "For all his good looks ..." ibid.

p 5 "A load of romantic slush." *Portrait of Joan*, p 64.

p 5 "a sensitive, self-destructive type ..." JC to LQ.

p 5 "He was much too nice a man ..." ibid.

p 5 "He was nothing like ..." ibid.

p 7 "I think it helped ..." ibid.

p 8–9 Joan's bisexuality was also confirmed by Adela Rogers St. Johns, Ruth Waterbury, Hedda Hopper, and others.

p 11 "He was as handsome ..." JC to LQ.

p 15 "We all bounced ..." *Portrait of Joan*, p 65.

p 16 "I saved up some 'tricks' ..." JC to LQ.

p 19 "He was a big bitch!" ibid.

Chapter Five

p 1 "I was so desperate to go ..." JC to LQ.

p 4 "a dud. Poor Bob ..." *Conversations with Joan Crawford*, Roy Newquist, p 71.

p 7 "I have never known ..." Neil Hamilton to LQ.

p 8 "Neil's still a handsome guy ..." JC to LQ.

p 9 "Hopelessly artificial." *Portrait of Joan*, p 89.

p 11 "Lovemaking never felt ..." JC to LQ.

p 14 "He was so appealing ..." *Portrait of Joan*, p 94.

p 17 "She's let herself go ..." JC to LQ.

p 22 "Every actress is entitled ..." ibid.

Chapter Six

p 1 "Looking back ..." JC to LQ.

p 2 "I didn't need another child ..." ibid.

p 3 "remained very good friends ..." *Filmfax*, Nov. 2000.

p 4 "was extremely uncomfortable ..." Newquist.

p 7 "I was jealous, of course ..." *This 'n' That*, Bette Davis.

p 10 "That one just worked ..." JC to LQ.

p 10 "Crawford-Gable sex magnetism..." ibid.

p 10 "It wasn't easy ..." Otto Kruger to LQ.

p 11 "The man was a complete stranger ..." JC to LQ.

p 12 "We all did our best ..." Robert Montgomery to LQ.

p 13 "That one wasn't very good ..." JC to LQ.

p 13 "Later I really loved ..." ibid.

p 13 "It was illuminating ..." *Portrait of Joan*, p 108.

p 14 "He took me over ..." ibid.

p 14 "another formula film" JC to LQ.

p 16 "I was really in love with him ..." *People Will Talk*, Kenneth L. Geist.

p 17 "I would never have married ..." JC to LQ.

p 17 "the consummate movie star..." Geist.

p 17 "she is not demonstrably a proficient ..." ibid.

p 21 "Franchot did it for my sake ..." *Portrait of Joan*, p 113.

p 21 "There was no good reason ..." JC to LQ.

p 22 "I think that's where the term ..." Newquist, p 80.

Chapter Seven

p 4 "My mind wasn't on it ..." JC to LQ.

p 4 "I barely remember the thing ..." Robert Montgomery to LQ.

p 5 "We knew he was ill ..." JC to LQ.

p 7 "I knew she found me ..." ibid.

p 8 "a waste of time ..." Newquist, p 81.

p 8 "what no male director could ..." *Joan Crawford: The Last Word*, Fred Lawrence Guiles.

p 11 "He would show up for romantic scenes ..." JC to LQ.

p 11 "His drinking really was the problem ..." ibid.

p 18 "He was so contemptuous ..." ibid.

Chapter Eight

p 1 "Talk about going from ..." JC to LQ.

p 2 "Everyone was out of their ..." Newquist, p 84.

p 7 "Norma knew that she and Joan ..." Anita Loos to LQ.

p 8 "At the time it probably wasn't ..." *On Cukor*, Gavin Lambert.

p 9 "Cukor did a great job ..." JC to LQ.

p 10 "Norma and Joan could never have been ..." Anita Loos to LQ.

p 13 "It was almost a good film ..." *People Will Talk*, Kenneth L. Geist.

p 15 "That certain chemistry ..." JC to LQ.

p 15 "You've become an actress ..." Newquist, p 85.

p 16 "Peter had a tremendous sense ..." JC to LQ.

p 16 "We had enough trouble ... ibid.

p 18 "She should have remained a foolish woman..." Lambert.

Chapter Nine

p 5 "I think that was the picture ..."JC to LQ.

p 6 "When she becomes pretty ..." Lambert.

p 6 "I may have reservations about ..."George Cukor to LQ.

p 8 "I got to wear some ..." JC to LQ.

p 10 "Joan sat herself at the center ..." *A Rose for Mrs. Miniver: The Life of Greer Garson*, Michael Troyen.

p 16 "If there is an afterlife ..." Newquist, p 89.

p 17 "I think Joan was just about ..." Natalie Schafer to LQ.

p 18 "That lousy movie ..." JC to LQ.

p 19 "I think she knew ..." Richard Thorpe to LQ.

Chapter Ten

p 1   "If you think I made ..." JC to LQ.
p 5   "Jerry always had faith ..." ibid.
p 10   "Crawford gave *Mildred Pierce* a reality ..." Henry Hart to LQ.
p 11   "This is Joan Crawford!" *Three Phases of Eve*. Eve Arden.
p 13   "Frankly I thought it was ..." JC to LQ.
p 13   James M. Cain's inscribed copy of *Mildred Pierce* is described in *Joan Crawford,* by Bob Thomas.
p 16   "I realized I had never ..." *Portrait of Joan*, p 140.
p 17   "she had her uses ..." JC to LQ.
p 20   "What do you think ..." ibid.
p 20   "There are some scenes ..." ibid.

Chapter Eleven

p 1   "*Possessed* contained the best performance ..." JC to LQ.
p 5   "Damn, I knew Joan ..." Van Heflin to LQ.
p 5   "It was my first real part ..." Geraldine Brooks to LQ.
p 6   "Actresses like Bette Davis ..." JC to LQ.
p 6   "Even when she was lying prone ..." Don Maquire to LQ.
p 7   "Wouldn't you know ..." JC to LQ.
p 12   "a jockstrap of rhinestones ..." *Fonda: My Life*, Henry Fonda, H. Teichmann.
p 16   "Sidney was a really fine ..." JC to LQ.
p 16   "Movie stars and pretty ..." Sidney Greenstreet to LQ.

Chapter Twelve

p 2   "I suppose it's too much to ask ..." *Studio Affairs: My Life as a Film Director*, Vincent Sherman.
p 2   "she's gracious and considerate ..." ibid.
p 8   "They watered it down so much ..." JC to LQ.
p 9   "You can have all the talent ..." ibid.
p 10   "Sherman was a user ..." ibid.
p 17   Jack Palance's habit of listening to Richard Stauss was noted in *James Dean,* by Val Holley.
p 18   Some details on Gloria Grahame's participation in *Sudden Fear* were gleaned from *Suicide Blonde*, Vincent Curcio.
p 18   "There were days Joan looked so angry ..." Mike Connors to LQ.
p 19   "One of my better efforts ..." JC to LQ.
p 23   "The girl had talent ..." ibid.

Chapter Thirteen

p 1   "I didn't want to admit it ..." JC to LQ.

p 2   "I didn't know if he felt ..." ibid.

p 3   Some details of Gig Young's participation in *Torch Song* from *Final Gig*, George Eels.

p 5   "If that boy doesn't ..." JC to LQ.

p 5   "I really would have killed ..." ibid.

p 10 "I wasn't that crazy ..." ibid.

p 16 "I took no crap ..." Mercedes McCambridge to LQ.

p 18 "It really heightened ..." Nicholas Ray to LQ.

p 20 "At least I exposed ..." JC to LQ.

p 22 "He was a damn good actor ..." ibid.

p 24 "I don't doubt it ..." Natalie Schafer to LQ.

p 24 "I love him ..." JC to LQ.

p 25 "... a thoroughly selfish bitch ..." *Portrait of Joan*, p 174.

p 27 "(I) had the opportunity ..." *On the Other Hand*, Fay Wray.

p 27 "...in my death scene ..." Newquist, p 103.

p 28 "No, it's not Eugene ..." JC to LQ.

p 28 "I think you have to ..." ibid.

Chapter Fourteen

p 1   "felt more cozy ..." *Vanity Will Get You Somewhere*, Joseph Cotten.

p 5   "I can't tell you how much ..." JC to LQ.

p 8   "There's something flat and dead ..." ibid.

p 9   "Everything clicked on *Autumn Leaves* ..." ibid.

p 10 "If that bitch thinks ..." ibid.

p 10 "These things get dirty ..." ibid.

p 12 "Crawford may get angry ..." Henry Hart to LQ.

p 12 "To hell with what she thinks ..." ibid.

p 14 "A middle-aged, regal ..." *Second Act*, Joan Collins.

p 15 "I get so sick of these young ..." JC to LQ.

p 15 "It's ridiculous ..." ibid.

p 17 "in my own pitch ..." Newquist, p 104.

p 19 "what made (the film) a delight ..." *Portrait of Joan*, p 191.

p 19 "Absolutely one of the most gorgeous ..." JC to LQ.

p 20 "I think I cried more ..." ibid.

p 21 "It was the most solid ..." ibid.

p 23 "all those young bitches ..." ibid.

Chapter Fifteen

p 1   "We were polite to each other ..." *I'd Love to Kiss You... Conversations with Bette Davis*, Whitney Stine.
p 6   "In the scene when I discover ..." Victor Buono to LQ.
p 9   "Weights! And have Bette ..." JC to LQ.
p 14   "Delectable. In the old studio ..." ibid.
p 15   "My brother died for me a long ..." ibid.
p 19   "Yes, and such sexy lips ..." ibid.

Chapter Sixteen

p 2   Some details of the filming of *Hush ... Hush, Sweet Charlotte* from *The Divine Feud*, Shaun Considine.
p 4   "There is just no dealing ..." JC to LQ.
p 6   "She's practically directing ..." ibid.
p 6   "Bette is determined ..." Joseph Cotten to LQ.
p 7   "It was not a 'dignified' exhibition ..." ibid.
p 7   "I think we all wanted ..." ibid.
p 12   "I can't think of a picture ..." Robert Aldrich to LQ.
p 12   "There! That ought to ..." *There's No Place Like Home*, Carleton Varney.
p 19   "Paul Burke is my idea ..." JC to LQ.

Chapter Seventeen

p 9   "This kind of picture ..." JC to LQ.
p 10   "pretty, but she doesn't have ..." ibid.
p 10   "a cow , absolutely disgusting ..." ibid.
p 11   "it must have been a man ..." ibid.
p 11   "it's highly unlikely ..." *Come by Sunday: The Fabulous, Ruined Life of Diana Dors*, Damon Wise.
p 12   " He just wouldn't listen ..." JC to LQ.
p 15   "was sort of past it ..." *Filmfax* interview.
p 16   Some details of Joan's participation in *Night Gallery* from *Magic Man: The Life and Films of Steven Spielberg*, William Schoell.
p 17   "I do whatever I can for her ..." JC to LQ.
p 18   "I think she could be very happy ..." ibid.

Chapter Eighteen

p 2   "How do they expect to get along ..." JC to LQ.

p 3 "She could be very nice, sweet, and charming ..." Don Koll to WS.
p 8 "she was no psychopath ..." Varney.
p 9 "God, even my interior decorator ..." JC to LQ.
p 10 "The only thing better is horse pee ..." *Being and Becoming*, Myrna Loy with James Kotsilibas-Davis.

Chapter Nineteen

p 4 "I think Christina was jealous ..." *Us*, Nov. 1998
p 6 "I wrote the book as a personal journal ..." "Mommie Must Advertise," *Next* Magazine, May 8, 1998.
p 7 "It takes two to feud ..." *Portrait of Joan*, p 153.
p 8 "I worry about what's going to happen ..." JC to LQ.
p 9 "It's stardom for Christina ..." ibid.
p 15 "From what I have read ..." *Filmfax*, Nov. 2000.
P 15 "Joan may have been preposterous..." George Cukor to James Kotsilibas-Davis, who related it to LQ.
p 15 "Nearly everybody admits to a few ..." Varney.
p 21 Details of Christina Crawford's bed and breakfast and her life after "Mommie Dearest" from assorted press reports, including *People*, Aug. 8, 1994.
p 23 Details of the twins' attack on "Mommie Dearest" and Cathy Lalonde's lawsuit from press reports and *Us*, Nov. 1998, as well as confidential sources.
p 24 "I have no regrets." *Next*, May 8, 1998.

BIBLIOGRAPHY

Arden, Eve. *The Three Phases of Eve*. New York: St. Martin's, 1985.

Collins, Joan. *Second Act*. New York: St. Martin's, 1996.

Considine, Shaun. *Bette & Joan: The Divine Feud*. New York: E.P. Dutton, 1989.

Cotten, Joseph. *Vanity Will Get You Somewhere*. San Francisco: Mercury House, 1987.

Crawford, Christina. *Mommie Dearest*. New York: William Morrow, 1978.

Crawford, Joan and Jane Kesner Ardmore. *A Portrait of Joan*. Garden City: Doubleday, 1962.

Curcio, Vincent. *Suicide Blonde: The Life of Gloria Grahame*. New York: William Morrow, 1989.

Davis, Bette with Michael Herskowitz. *This 'n That*. New York: Putnam's, 1987.

Dewey, Donald. *James Stewart: A Biography*. Atlanta: Turner, 1996.

Douglas, Melvyn and Tom Arthur. *See You at the Movies*. Lanham, MD.: University Press of America, 1986.

Eells, George. *Final Gig*. New York: Harcourt, Brace and Jovanovich, 1991.

Fonda, Henry with Howard Teichmann. *Fonda: My Life*. New York: NAL, 1981.

Geist, Kenneth L. *Pictures Will Talk*. New York: Scribner's, 1978.

Guiles, Fred Lawrence. *Joan Crawford: The Last Word*. New York: Birch Lane, 1995.

Holley, Val. *James Dean*. New York: St. Martin's, 1995.

Hopper, Hedda. *From Under My Hat*. New York: Macfadden, 1963.

Kotsilibas-Davis, James and Myrna Loy. *Myrna Loy: Being and Becoming*. New York: Alfred A. Knopf, 1987.

Lambert, Gavin. *On Cukor*. New York: Capricorn, 1973.

Mann, William J. *Wisecracker*. New York: Viking, 1997.

Newquist, Roy. *Conversations with Joan Crawford*. Secaucus: Citadel Press, 1980.

Preminger, Otto. *Preminger: An Autobiography*. Garden City, N.Y.: Doubleday, 1977.

Quirk, Lawrence J. *The Complete Films of Joan Crawford*. New York: Citadel Press, 1968 (revised 1988).

———. *The Films of Fredric March*. Secaucus, N.J.: Citadel Press, 1971.

———. *The Complete Films of William Powell*. New York: Citadel Press, 1986.

————. *Margaret Sullavan: Child of Fate*. New York: St. Martin's Press, 1986.

————. *Norma: The Story of Norma Shearer*. New York: St. Martin's Press, 1988.

————. *Fasten Your Seat Belts: The Passionate Life of Bette Davis*. New York: William Morrow, 1990.

————. *James Stewart: Behind the Scenes of a Wonderful Life*. New York: Applause, 1997.

St. Johns, Adela Rogers. *The Honeycomb*. Garden City, N.Y.: Doubleday, 1969.

Sherman, Vincent. *Studio Affairs: My Life as a Film Director*. Lexington: University Press of Kentucky, 1996.

Schoell, William. *Stay Out of the Shower: 25 Years of Shocker Films Beginning with "Psycho."* New York: Dembner, 1985.

Stine, Whitney. *I'd Love to Kiss You... Conversations with Bette Davis*. New York: Pocket, 1990.

Thomas, Bob. *Joan Crawford*. New York: Simon and Schuster, 1978.

Troyan, Michael. *A Rose for Mrs. Miniver: The Life of Greer Garson*. Lexington: University Press of Kentucky, 1999.

Warrick, Ruth with Don Preston. *The Confessions of Phoebe Tyler*. Englewood Cliffs, NJ: Prentice-Hall, 1980.

Walker, Alexander. *Joan Crawford: The Ultimate Star*. New York: Harper and Row, 1983.

Williams, Esther, with Digby Diehl. *The Million Dollar Mermaid*. New York: Simon and Schuster, 1999.

Wise, Damon. *Come by Sunday: The Fabulous, Ruined Life of Diana Dors*. London: Macmillan, 1998.

Varney, Carleton. *There's No Place Like Home*. New York: Bobbs-Merrill; 1980.

Wray, Fay. *On the Other Hand*. New York: St. Martin's, 1989.

INDEX

Above Suspicion (film), 117-20
Across to Singapore (film), 39-40
Adams, India, 170, 174
Addams Family, The (TV series), 15
Adonis, Joe, 153
Adrian, 61, 72, 113, 134
Agee, James, 140-41
Ahern, Brian, 75
Albert, Katherine, x, 165, 270
Aldritch, Robert, 192-94, 206, 209,
   219, 223-26
All That Glitters (Tryon), 248-49
American Women's Voluntary Services,
   124
Anderson, Maxwell, 63
Andrews, Dana, 144-46
Andrews sisters, the, 123
Anthony, Mike, 83
Architectural Digest, 245
Arden, Eve, 71, 124, 127, 129, 149,
   157
Armstrong, Robert, 53
Arnold, Edward, 72
Arnold, Johnny, 9, 16, 21
Arthur, George K., 16
Arthur, Jean, 247
Arzner, Dorothy, 85-87, 155
Asher, Jerry, ix; JC's attitude about sex,
   41-43; JC on Garbo, 60; on
   Franchot Tone, 80, 93; JC's desire
   for children, 92; on Jimmy Stewart,
   99; JC on Greer Garson, 114; on

Phillip Terry, 131; on Jeff Chan-
   dler, 182; on Alfred Steele, 190; on
   JC's child-rearing methods, 191
Astaire, Fred, 71, 246
Asther, Nils, 39, 61
Astor, Mary, 222
Ayres, Lew, 97, 99
Autumn Leaves (film), ix, x, 192-94,
   250

Bainter, Fay, 90, 92
Baker, Diane, 215-16, 229, 264
Bakewell, William, 53
Ballard, Lucien, 212
Bara, Theda, 180
Barker, Betty, 270
Barrie, Barbara, 212
Barrymore, John, 58-61
Barrymore, Lionel, 58-61, 79-80
Bartlett, Hall, 211, 213
Batman (TV series), 55, 206
Bautzer, Greg, 133, 264
Baum, Vicki, 58
Beaumont, Harry, 40-41, 52
Beery, Wallace, 58
Benjamin, Richard, 260
Bennett, Bruce, 126, 129
Bennett, Constance, 15
Benny, Jack, 123
Bergan, Polly, 212-13
Bern, Paul, 9, 37
Bernhardt, Curtis, 140, 142-43

Berserk (film), 31, 237-40
Besserer, Eugenie, 14
Best of Everything, The (film), 201-2, 216
Bickford, Charles, 229
Big Tree, Chief John, 27
Billy Smart Circus, 237
Biroc, Joseph, 227
Blake, Robert (Bobby), 135
Block, Robert, 214
Blondell, Joan, 214
Blyth, Ann, 126, 129-30, 261
Boardman, Eleanor, 14
Boland, Mary, 101
Boleslawski, Richard, 85, 86
Bondi, Beulah, 62, 79
Boob, The (film), 16, 18
Borgnine, Ernest, 177
Borzage, Frank, 14, 88-90, 92, 105
Bow, Clara, 26, 41
Bride Wore Red, The (film), 86-87
Brady, Scott, 175, 177, 179
Branch, Dr. William, 269
Brandeis University, 228
Brando, Marlon, 193
Brazzi, Rossano, 197, 200
Brazzel, Michael, 265
Brian, David, 147, 149, 154, 159
Brooks, Geraldine, 139, 142
Brown, Clarence, 57, 61, 72, 79
Brown, Harry Joe, 70
Brown, Johnny Mack, 40, 43, 49, 53, 54
Browning, Tod, 28-29
Brush, Katherine, 88
Buono, Victor, 206-8, 210
Burke, Paul, 229-30
Bushman, Francis X., Jr., 27

Cain, James M., 125, 128
Cameron, Kate, 123
Capra, Frank, 18-19, 20
Caretakers, The (film), 211-14, 240
Carlson, Richard, 229
Carradine, John, 177, 179
Carroll, Madeline, 157
Carson, Jack, 126, 128, 150
Cassin, Billie. *See* Joan Crawford

Cassin, Harry, 1, 7; sex with JC, 2, 214
Castle, William, xiii, 214, 226-27
Catholic Legion of Decency, 104
Chained (film), 72-73
Chandler, Jeff, 73, 180-83
Chandler, Joan, 135
Chaney, Lon, xiii, 28-30
Chaney, Lon, Jr., 30
Circle, The (film), 13
Cirone, Bettina, 245
Clark, Dane, 123
Clarke, Mae, 41
Cline, Eddie, 15
Coca-Cola, 189, 195
Cochran, Steve, 154-55
Cohen, Harry, 115
Cohen, Herman, 237-41
Cohn, Harry, x, 169
Colbert, Claudette, 83
Columbia Pictures, x, 183, 192, 215, 245
Connolly, Mike, 132, 180, 208
Connors, Mike, 163
Conway, Jack, 14, 32, 46, 48
Coogan, Jackie, Jr., 14-15
Coogan, Jackie, Sr., 15
Cooper, Ben, 177
Cooper, Gary, 69
Corey, Wendell, 156
Cortez, Ricardo, 49
Costello, Frank, 153
Cotten, Joseph, 189, 221-23
Cowan, Jerome, 48
Coward, Noël, 196
Cox, Mitchell, 189, 216, 246
Crawford, Cathy (daughter), 147, 191, 201, 250, 253-67, 270
Crawford, Christina (daughter), 26, 117, 130, 133, 173, 190-91, 253-67; *Mommie Dearest*, xi, xiv, xv, 80, 133, 191, 199, 208, 227-28, 230, 233-34, 238, 243, 249, 250-51
Crawford, Christopher (son), x, 129, 190-91, 250-51, 253-67
Crawford, Cindy (daughter), 147, 191, 201, 250-51, 253-67, 270

Crawford, Joan: Academy Awards, 112, 114, 128, 129-30, 132, 140, 165, 210-11, 220, 248; bisexuality, 5, 7, 38, 41-43, 86, 173, 235, 258; children, adoption of, 92, 116-17, 129, 253-54, 264; Christian Science, 250-51; as dancer, 1, 5, 6, 7, 9, 16, 41, 45, 47, 53-55, 71, 91, 124, 169; drinking, x, 89, 167, 173, 174, 179, 183, 200, 212, 216, 221, 227, 234, 237, 239, 241, 249, 250; as "escort," ix, 8, 21-22; friendship with homosexual men, 9, 33, 39, 173, 235; generosity, x, 114, 146, 186, 196, 249, 269; *Mommie Dearest*, damage to JC from, xv, 173, 230, 253-67; professionalism, 73, 78, 92, 102, 118-19, 120, 148, 156, 162, 165, 166, 172, 176, 213, 219, 238, 241; sex, attitude toward, 2, 3, 4, 7, 43, 52, 56, 70, 86, 99, 119, 164, 166; sex with stepfather, 2, 214; as singer, 47-49, 53-55, 57, 72, 75, 98, 124, 149, 169, 170, 171, 174; style, sense of, 5, 6, 7, 16, 46, 52, 235; tuition, work in exchange for, 3-4
—films: *Above Suspicion*, 117-20; *Across to Singapore*, 39-40; *Autumn Leaves*, ix, x, 192-94, 250; *Berserk*, 31, 237-40; *Best of Everything, The*, 201-2, 216; *Boob, The*, 16, 18; *Bride Wore Red, The*, 86-87; *Caretakers, The*, 211-14, 240; *Chained*, 72-73 *Circle, The*, 13; *Daisy Kenyon*, xi, 143-47; *Damned Don't Cry, The*, 32, 153-55, 159, 198; *Dance, Fools, Dance*, 54, 56; *Dancing Lady*, 54, 71, 129, 246; *Dream of Love*, 38-39, 44; *Duke Steps out, The*, 34, 44; *Female on the Beach*, 173, 180-83; *Flamingo Road*, xii, 51, 147-49, 159; *Forsaking All Others*, 73, 76; *Four Walls*, 32, 39; *Goodbye, My Fancy*, 157; *Gor-geous Hussy, The*, 76-78, 92, 97, 111; *Grand Hotel*, 40, 58-61, 195; *Harriet Craig*, 155-57, 183; *Hollywood Canteen*, 123; *Hollywood Revue of 1929*, 47, 172; *Humoresque*, xv, 133-36, 139, 142, 153, 201; *I Live My Life*, 74-75, 76; *I Saw What You Did*, 226-27; *Ice Follies of 1939*, 54, 97, 113; *It's a Great Feeling*, 149-50, 160; *Johnny Guitar*, 165, 175-80, 195, 220; *Lady of the Night*, 13; *Last of Mrs. Cheyney, The*, 85-86; *Laughing Sinners*, 54-55; *Law of the Range, The*, 28, 39, 175; *Letty Lynton*, 39, 61; *Love on the Run*, 83; *Mannequin*, 87-89, 246; *Mildred Pierce*, xii, 71, 101, 112, 125-32, 139-40, 149, 183, 195, 198, 216, 223, 263; *Montana Moon*, 49; *No More Ladies*, 74; *Old Clothes*, 14-15; *Only Thing, The*, 14; *Our Blushing Brides*, 52; *Our Dancing Daughters*, 34, 40-41, 44, 52; *Our Modern Maidens*, 44-45; *Paid*, 41, 53; *Paris*, 20-21; *Possessed* (1931), 56-57, 61; *Possessed* (1947), 98, 112, 139-43, 193, 195, 212; *Pretty Ladies*, 13; *Proud Flesh*, 14; *Queen Bee*, 51, 183-86, 199, 242, 263; *Rain*, 61-64, 98, 101, 134, 140, 195, 265; *Reunion in France*, 117-19; *Rose-Marie*, 37, 38-39; *Sadie McKee*, 72, 207; *Sally, Irene and Mary*, 15, 16; *Shining Hour, The*, 90; *Spring Fever*, 33; *Story of Esther Costello, The*, 196-200; *Strait-Jacket*, xii, xiii, xiv, 206, 214-16, 221, 237, 246, 263; *Strange Cargo*, 103-6, 209; *Sudden Fear*, ix, 106, 159, 161-65, 198, 247; *Susan and God*, 111-12, 114, 130; *Taxi Dancer, The*, 26; *They All Kissed the Bride*, 115-16; *This Modern Age*, 55-56; *This Woman Is Dangerous*, 32, 155, 159-64, 198; *Today We Live*,

69; *Torch Song*, 169-73, 208; *Tramp Tramp Tramp*, 18, 20; *Trog*, xiii, 159, 240-41; *Twelve Miles Out*, 31-32, 40; *Understanding Heart, The*, 27; *Unknown, The*, xii, 28-29; *Untamed*, 41, 48; *West Point*, 33; *What Ever Happened to Baby Jane?*, xii, 42, 78, 132, 159, 166, 193, 205-11, 265; *When Ladies Meet*, 113-15; *Winners of the Wilderness*, 27-28, 175; *Woman's Face, A*, xii, xiii, 109-13, 123, 130, 140, 159, 195, 216; *Women, The*, xii, 99-103, 106, 112, 129, 195, 209

Crothers, Rachel, 106
Crowther, Bosley, 154, 158, 160-61, 195, 198, 201
Cudahy, Michael, 9, 166
Cukor, George, 74, 86, 100-102, 106, 109-14, 226, 201
Curtis, Alan, 88
Curtis, Tony, 183
Curtiz, Michael, 125, 127-28, 130

Daisy Kenyon (film), xi, 143-47
Damned Don't Cry, The (film), 32, 153-55, 159, 198
Dance, Fools, Dance (film), 54, 56
Dancing Lady (film), 54, 71, 129, 246
Dano, Royal, 177
Davidson, Max, 14
Davis, Bette, 86, 123, 132, 194; JC's attraction to, 42; crush on Franchot Tone, 70; JC on, 142-43; and Vincent Sherman, 153; *The Star*, 165-66; in *Whatever Happened to Baby Jane?* 205-11; in *Hush...Hush, Sweet Charlotte*, 219-26; on Faye Dunaway, 262
Davis, Edwards, 18, 20
Dawson, Richard, 239
Day, Doris, 150
Dekker, Albert, 103, 105
de Havilland, Olivia, 141, 225
Delmar, Viña, 72
de Mille, William, 155

Dern, Bruce, 221
de Ruiz, Nick, 28
DeVol, Frank, 206
Dietrich, Marlene, 196
Dillon, Josephine, 56
Dixon, Jean, 72
Dorn, Philip, 118-19
Dors, Diana, 237-39
Douglas, Melvyn, 78, 80, 90, 92, 109, 111
Dozier, William, 156
Dream of Love (film), 38-39, 44
Dressler, Marie, 47
Duke Steps out, The (film), 34, 44
Dunaway, Faye, 262-65, 270

Edwards, Harry, 18
Egan, Richard, 154-55
El Jodo, 47, 49, 51, 67
Emerine, Katherine, 6
Ericson, Leif, 215
Eunson, Dale, 165
Evelyn, Judith, 181

Female on the Beach (film), 173, 180-83
Fairbanks, Douglas, Jr., 28, 32, 37-38, 40, 44, 49, 51-52, 56, 64, 67-69, 70, 81, 131, 190, 264; *Salad Days, The*, 47
Fairbanks, Douglas, Sr., 38, 46, 51, 68, 70
Farnham, Joseph, 20
Farrell, Henry, 205, 219
Fashion Institute of Technology, 228
Fatal Confinement (Royal Bay, Della, TV series), 216, 229-31
Faulkner, William, 69
Fay, Frank, 41
Feist, Felix, 160
Fellowes, Rockliffe, 27
Ferguson, Helen, 41, 46
film noir, 127, 159
Fitzgerald, F. Scott, 100
Fitzmaurice, George, 85
Five Daughters Affair, The (The Karate Killers, TV episode), 228-29

Fix, Paul, 176
Flamingo Road (film), xii, 51, 147-49, 159
Flamingo Road (TV series), 149
Fleming, Victor, 101
Fogelson, Buddy, 115
Folsey, George, 73
Fonda, Henry, 144-46
Fontaine, Joan, 99, 101
Fontanne, Lynn, 40
Ford, Glenn, 116
Forrest, Allan, 15
Forrest, Steve, 264
Forsaking All Others (film), 73, 76
Four Walls (film), 32, 39
Francis, Alec B., 18
Francis, Freddy, 241
Frederick, Pauline, 55
Freeman, Dore, 270
Frey, Leonard, 234-35
Furness, Betty, 114

Gable, Clark, 42-44, 54, 56-57, 64, 67-69, 70, 71, 75, 83, 103-4, 131, 136, 161, 171, 201, 254
Garbo, Greta, 31, 32, 59-61, 113
Garfield, John, 123, 133-34, 136
Gargan, William, 62-64
Garrett, Andi, 227
Garson, Greer, 106, 113-15, 169
Geeson, Judy, 238
George, John, 28
Gilbert, John, 31-32
Gilchrist, Connie, 110
Gillespie, Gina, 207
Gilmore, Douglas, 20-21, 26
Gish, Lillian, 45
Glyn, Elinor, 14
Goddard, Paulette, 99, 101
Gold, Zachary, 135
Goldwyn, Samuel, 8
Goodbye, My Fancy (film), 157
Gorgeous Hussy, The (film), 76-78, 92, 97, 111
Gough, Michael, 237
Goulding, Edmund, 16, 20, 21, 27, 125
Grady, Billy, 99

Grahame, Gloria, 161-63, 165
Grand Hotel (film), 40, 58-61, 195
Grauman's Chinese Theatre, 46
Green, Lorne, 192-93
Green Hornet, The (TV series), 213
Greenstreet, Sydney, 147-48
Greenwich Village, 145-46
Griffith, D.W., 55
Griffith, E.H., 74
Guiles, Fred Lawrence, 87

Haines, William, xi, 9, 15, 33-34, 38, 43, 46, 47, 56, 132, 136, 171, 194, 235-37
Haller, Ernest, 127
Hamilton, Neil, 54-55
Hardin, Ty, 238
Harding, Ann, 113
Harlow, Jean, 9
Harriet Craig (film), 155-57, 183
Harryhausen, Ray, 112
Hart, Henry, 128, 195-96
Hawkes, Howard, 69
Hayden, Sterling, 166, 176-79
Hayes, John Anthony, 216
Hayworth, Rita, 196
Hazard, Lawrence, 88
Head, Edith, 240
Heflin, Van, 139, 142
Heller, Lukas, 207, 219-20, 223
Hertz, David, 145
Hepburn, Katharine, 158, 172, 225
Higginbotham, Ann, 180
Hill, Virginia, 153
Hill, Robert, 180
Hitchcock, Alfred, 111, 119, 127, 164-65
Hobel, Mara, 264
Hollywood Canteen, 124
Hollywood Canteen (film), 123
Hollywood Revue of 1929 (film), 47, 172
Hopper, Hedda, 101-3, 132-33, 223
Hovey, Tim, 184-85
Howard, Ray, 16
Hudson, Rochelle, 215
Hudson, Rock, 180
Humoresque (film), xv, 133-36, 139, 142, 153, 201

Hunter, Ian, 103
Hush...Hush, Sweet Charlotte (film), 219-26
Huston, Walter, 62
Hutton, Robert, 123
Hyman, B.D. Merrill, 208-9, 264-65; My Mother's Keeper, 209-10
Hyman, Bernard, 76
Hyman, Jeremy, 208

I Live My Life (film), 74-75, 76
I Saw What You Did (film), 226-27
Ice Follies of 1939 (film), 54, 97, 113
Ireland, John, 184, 226
It's a Great Feeling (film), 149-50, 160

Jaffe, Rona, 201
Janeway, Elizabeth, 145
Jenkins, Allen, 116
Jimmy Fund, 186
Joan Crawford School of Dance, 228
Johnny Guitar (film), 165, 175-80, 195, 220
Johnson, Richard, 269
Johnson, Van, 130, 264
Jones, Jennifer, 254
Jourdan, Louis, 201

Kansas City, Kansas, 3, 5, 6, 8, 28
Kellaway, Cecil, 181
Kelly, George, 155
Kendall, Donald, 246
Kennedy, George, 215
Kennedy, Joe, 9
Kerr, Deborah, 169
Kerry, Norman, 30
Kilgallen, Dorothy, 216
King, Larry, 267
Kolker, Henry, 15
Koll, Don, 246-47
Koontz, C. David, 265
Kotsilibas-Davis, James, 259
Krasna, Norman, 174
Kruger, Otto, 72-73

Lady of the Night (film), 13
Lake, Alan, 239

Lamarr, Hedy, 253
Lancaster, Burt, 169
Lane, Burton, 72
Langdon, Harry, 18-20, 246
Lange, Hope, 201-2
Langham, Ria, 56
La Rocque, Rod, 44
Last of Mrs. Cheyney, The (film), 85-86
Laughing Sinners (film), 54-55
Laurel and Hardy, 47
Law of the Range, The (film), 28, 39, 175
Lawrence, Gertrude, 106
Lawton, Oklahoma, 1, 251
Lease, Rex, 28
Lee, Anna, 208
Lee, Edna, 183
Lee, Gwen, 41, 48, 53
Leigh, Janet, 183
Leigh, Vivien, 94, 196, 225
Leonard, Robert Z., 71
Lessley, Elgin, 19
Lester, Bruce, 120
LeSueur, Anna Bell Johnson (mother), 1, 22, 26, 165, 200; divorce from LeSueur, 1, 2
LeSueur, Hal (brother), 1, 2, 4, 22, 25-26, 165, 190, 213-14, 258
LeSueur, Lucille Fay. See Joan Crawford
LeSueur, Thomas (father), 1, 2, 73
Letty Lynton (film), 39, 61
Levant, Oscar, 133, 135
Logan, Joshua, 174
Lom, Herbert, 229
Lombard, Carole, 56, 104, 115
Long, Ray, 9
Lonsdale, Frederick, 85
Loos, Anita, 100, 102, 106
Lorre, Peter, 10
Louis, Jean, 198
Love, Bessie, 199
Love on the Run (film), 83
Lovejoy, Frank, 158
Loy, Myrna, 13, 85, 113, 115, 247, 250, 259-61, 270
Lubitsch, Ernst, 101
Luce, Clare Boothe, 100

Lukas, Paul, 103
Lunt, Alfred, 40
Lyons, Leonard, 145

MacDonald, Jeanette, 98
MacDougall, Ranald, 126, 140, 183-85
MacInnes, Helen, 119
MacMurray, Fred, 119-20
Main, Marjorie, 110
Man from U.N.C.L.E., The (TV series), 228-29
Mancini, Henry, 262
Manheimer, Irving, 180
Mankiewicz, Joseph L., 76-78, 83, 87, 89, 93-94, 103-4, 117
Mann, Hank, 17
Mann, William, 41
Mannequin (film), 87-89, 246
Mansfield, Jayne, 166
March, Fredric, 106-7, 111
Markle, Fletcher, 178
Marlow, Lucy, 184
Marlowe, Jo Ann, 126
Marshall, Herbert, 113, 213
Massen, Ona, 109-10
Massey, Raymond, 139, 142
Maugham, W. Somerset, 14
Mayer, Louis B., xi, 8, 13, 21-22, 31, 59, 67, 76, 77, 79, 87, 94, 99
McBain, Diane, 212-13
McCallum, David, 229
McCambridge, Mercedes, 175-79
McCoy, Tim, 27, 28, 175
McDaniel, Hattie, 91
McGivern, William, 226
McGuire, Don, 142
McGuire, Dorothy, 113
McKay, James, 39
McPhail, Douglas, 98
McQueen, Butterfly, 101, 129
Medlinsky, Harvey, 228, 260
Meehan, John, 72
Meek, Donald, 84, 110
Merrill, B.D. *See* Hyman, B.D.
Merrill, Gary, 208
Merv Griffin Show, The (TV talk show), 233-34

Metro Company, 8
MGM studio, 8, 14, 17, 19, 42, 45, 46, 53, 67, 76-78, 83, 94, 98, 99-100, 102, 111, 114, 116, 118, 134
Mildred Pierce (film), xii, 71, 101, 112, 125-32, 139-40, 149, 183, 195, 198, 216, 223, 263
Miles, Vera, 192-94
Milestone, Lewis, 63
Millarde, Harry, 26
Miller, David, 161-63, 196-97, 198
Mona Lisa, 53
Monroe, Marilyn, 166, 180, 197, 238
Monsarrat, Nicholas, 200
Montana Moon (film), 49
Montgomery, Douglass (Kent Douglass), 53
Montgomery, Robert, 48-49, 52, 61, 73, 74, 75, 85
Moore, Owen, 26
Moorehead, Agnes, 222, 225
Moran, Polly, 47
Moreno, Antonio, 28
Morgan, Dennis, 150, 159-60
Morgan, Frank, 74
Murray, Charlie, 17
Murray, James, 39
My Mother's Keeper (Hyman), 209-10
My Way of Life (J. Crawford), 228
Myers, Carmel, 32

Nader, George, 180
Nagel, Conrad, 47
Naish, J. Carrol, 135
Negulesco, Jean, 135, 201-2
Nelson, Ham, 70
Nelson, Ruth, 135
New York City, xiii, 7, 8
Newman, Paul, 254
Niblo, Fred, 39
Nichols, Richard, 111
Nigh, William, 39
Night Gallery (TV series), 241-42
No More Ladies (film), 74
Norman, Maidie, 205, 208
Novarro, Ramon, 39

O'Brien, Sheila, 169
O'Connolly, Jim, 238
Odets, Clifford, 134-35
Old Clothes (film), 14-15
Oliver, Edna May, 74
Olivier, Laurence, 196
Olmstead, Gertrude, 16, 17
O'Neil, Sally, 15
Only Thing, The (film), 14
Our Blushing Brides (film), 52
Our Dancing Daughters (film), 34, 40-41, 44, 52
Our Modern Maidens (film), 44-45

Paid (film), 41, 53
Paige, Janis, 212-13
Page, Anita, 40, 43, 44, 52
Palance, Jack, 161-65, 180
Palmer, Betsy, 183-84
Papich, Darinka, 251
Paris (film), 20-21
Parker, Suzy, 201
Parrish, Helen, 116
Parsons, Louella, 132
Patrick, Gail, 114
Patrick, Lee, 126
Patterson, Lee, 197, 200
Pell, Barnabus, 83
Pepsi-Cola, 189, 190, 194-95, 196, 201-2, 213, 216, 246
Perry, Frank, 265, 270
Phillips, Mary, 88
Photoplay, xi, 3, 9, 16, 21, 26, 46, 52, 59, 166, 180
Pickfair, 46, 48, 51, 213
Pickford, Mary, 38, 46, 51, 68, 70, 213, 248
Pitts, Zasu, 13
Ponselle, Rosa, 75
Portrait of Joan, A (J. Crawford), 256
Possessed (1931 film), 56-57, 61
Possessed (1947 film), 98, 112, 139-43, 193, 195, 212
Powell, William, 75, 85
Pratt, Purnell, 53
Preminger, Otto, 144-46
Pretty Ladies (film), 13

Prevost, Marie, 53
Price, Vincent, 214
Proud Flesh (film), 14

Queen Bee (film), 51, 183-86, 199, 242, 263
Quigley, Rita, 106
Quirk, James R., x, 9, 16, 21, 59, 234; James R. Quirk Memorial Film Symposium, 269
Quirk, Lawrence J., ix, x, 103, 139, 142, 146, 161, 178, 195-96, 221, 224-25, 233-37, 247, 257, 260, 269; Films of Joan Crawford, The, x, xi, xii, 112, 233-35, 242, 247

Rackmil, Milton, 180, 183
Rain (film), 61-64, 98, 101, 134, 140, 195, 265
Rainer, Luise, 87
Raines, Cristina, 149
Rambeau, Marjorie, 55
Randall, Ron, 197, 200
Randisi, Steve, 68, 264
Rapf, Harry, 8, 13, 98
Rathbone, Basil, 120
Ray, Charles, 20-21
Ray, Martha, 42
Ray, Nicholas, 165, 175-79
Raymond, Gene, 72
Republic Studios, 175
Reunion in France (film), 117-19
Richards, Silvia, 140
Ritzer, Mike, 250
Robertson, Cliff, x, 192-94, 250
Rockingham Academy (boarding school), 3, 4
Rogers, Buddy, 51
Rogers, Ginger, 247
Rogers, Roy, 123
Romani, Romano, 75, 98
Romero, Cesar, 116, 270
Romero, Marie, 270
Romulus Films, 196
Rose-Marie (film), 37, 38-39
Rule, Janice, 157

Rush, Barbara, 180
Russell, Rosalind, 73, 99-101, 155-56, 158

Sadie McKee (film), 72, 207
Salamunich, Yucca, 216
Sally, Irene and Mary (film), 15, 16
Scarwid, Diana, 262, 264-65
Schafer, Natalie, 118, 181-82
Schary, Dore, 146, 173
Schoell, William, xii, 264
Scott, Zachary, 126, 128, 147-49
Sears, Heather, 197, 199
Sebastion, Dorothy, 41, 52
Secret Storm, The (TV soap opera), 234, 243, 258-59
Serling, Rod, 242
Selznick, David O., 80
Shearer, Norma, 13, 30, 47, 53, 85, 99-103, 105-6, 113, 149
Sheinberg, Sid, 242
Shepperton Studios, 239
Sherman, Hedda, 153-54, 158
Sherman, Vincent, 153-58
Shields, Jimmy, 235
Shining Hour, The (film), 90
Shubert, J.J., 7
Sidney, Sylvia, 247
Siegel, Bugsy, 153
Simon, Neil, 260
Smith, Kent, 154
Spear, George, 19
Spielberg, Steven, 241-43
Spring Fever (film), 33
Stack, Robert, 212-13
St. Agnes (parochial school), 3, 4
Stanwyck, Barbara, 41, 123, 125, 126, 175, 197, 225, 226, 253
Steele, Alfred (husband), 57, 132, 189-92, 210, 213, 227, 253, 267
Steele, Lillian, 189
Stephens College (Columbia, Mo.), 4, 5
Sterling, Jan, 181
Sterling, Ray, 5, 6, 130
Stewart, James, 79, 94, 99
St. John, Adela Rogers, 4; Honeycomb, The, 57

Story of Esther Costello, The (film), 196-200
Strait-Jacket (film), xii, xiii, xiv, 206, 214-16, 221, 237, 246, 263
Strange Cargo (film), 103-6, 209
Strickling, Howard, 42, 102-3
Sudden Fear (film), ix, 106, 159, 161-65, 198, 247
Sullavan, Margaret, 89-92, 113, 155-56
Sullivan, Barry, 183, 242
Susan and God (film), 111-12, 114, 130
Swanson, Gloria, 62

Taylor, Elizabeth, 171
Taylor, Robert, 78, 79-80, 113
Taxi Dancer, The (film), 26
Technicolor, 97, 169, 171, 176
Terry, Phillip (husband), 116-17, 124, 129, 130-33, 165, 190
Terry, Phillip, Jr. See Crawford, Christopher
Thalberg, Irving, 94, 102
Thau, Benny, 114, 169
They All Kissed the Bride (film), 115-16
This Modern Age (film), 55-56
This Woman Is Dangerous (film), 32, 155, 159-64, 198
Thomas, Bob, 166
Thorpe, Richard, 120
Three Stooges, The, 71
Today We Live (film), 69
Todd, James, 171
Tone, Franchot (husband), 69-78, 83-84, 89, 93-94, 116, 131; Bette Davis's crush on, 42; 208; physical abuse of JC, 80-81, 94, 132-33, 190
Torch Song (film), 169-73, 208
Torrence, Ernest, 32, 40
Tracy, Spencer, 87-89, 93, 246
Tramp Tramp Tramp (film), 18, 20
Trevor, Claire, 175
Trog (film), xiii, 159, 240-41
Tryon, Tom, 247-49
Twelve Miles Out (film), 31-32, 40
Twentieth Century-Fox, 144

Understanding Heart, The (film), 27
Universal Studios, 180, 183, 242
Unknown, The (film), xii, 28-29
Untamed (film), 41, 48
USO, 42

Valentino, Lou, 270
Valentino, Rudolph, 39
Van Doren, Mamie, 166
Van Dyke, Woody, 27, 39, 73
Variety, 19, 20
Varney, Carleton, 228, 249, 261
Veidt, Conrad, 109-13

Wald, Jerry, 125, 130, 135, 201
Walker, Alexander, 270
Walsh, Florence, 270
Walters, Charles, 171, 173-74
Warner, Jack, 125, 160
Warner Brothers, 70, 123, 124, 126,
    131, 134, 139, 143, 144, 159, 263
Warrick, Ruth, 144, 146-47
Waterbury, Ruth, 3
Wayne, John, 117-20
Waxman, Franz, 86, 91, 143
Weatherly, Joan Evans, x, 165, 208,
    270
Weatherly, Kirby, x, 165, 270
Wellman, William A., 17
West Point (film), 33
What Ever Happened to Baby Jane?
    (film), xii, 42, 78, 132, 159, 166,
    193, 205-11, 265

Westman, Nydia, 116
When Ladies Meet (film), 113-15
White, Gordon, 196
Widmark, Richard, 161
Wilder, Robert, 147-48
Wilding, Michael, 170-71
Williams, Esther, 173
Williams, Van, 212-13
Winchell, Walter, 145
Winners of the Wilderness (film), 27-
    28, 175
Winter, Keith, 90
Woman's Face, A (film), xii, xiii, 109-
    13, 123, 130, 140, 159, 195, 216
Women, The (film), xii, 99-103, 106,
    112, 129, 195, 209
Wood, Dr. James, 4
Woodward, Joanne, 167
Woolf, James, 196-97
Woolf, John, 196
Wyman, Jane, 180
Wray, Fay, 184, 199

Young, Elizabeth, 77
Young, Ernie, 6
Young, Gig, 170-71
Young, Loretta, 76, 77, 140, 225, 254
Young, Robert, 69, 86, 90-91, 158
Young, Roland, 116
Young, Waldemar, 28

Zimmerman, Fred, 169
Zucco, George, 86